American Enterprise Institute
Studies in Political and Social Processes

At the Polls

THE FRENCH NATIONAL ASSEMBLY ELECTIONS OF 1978

Edited by Howard R. Penniman

THE FRENCH NATIONAL ASSEMBLY ELECTIONS OF 1978

THE FRENCH NATIONAL ASSEMBLY ELECTIONS OF 1978

Edited by Howard R. Penniman

American Enterprise Institute for Public Policy Research
Washington, D.C.

Library of Congress Cataloging in Publication Data

Main entry under title:

The French National Assembly elections of 1978.

(Studies in political and social processes)
(AEI studies ; 269)
   Includes index.
   1. France. Parlement (1946–   ). Assemblée
nationale—Elections.   2. Elections—France.
3. France—Politics and government—1969–
I. Penniman, Howard Rae, 1916–   II. Series.
III. Series: American Enterprise Institute for Public
Policy Research. AEI studies ; 269.
JN2959.F76   324.944'0837   79-28590
ISBN 0-8447-3372-5

AEI Studies 269

Printed in the United States of America

AEI's AT THE POLLS STUDIES

The American Enterprise Institute
has initiated this series in order to promote
an understanding of the electoral process as it functions in
democracies around the world. The series will include studies
of at least two national elections in each of nineteen countries
on five continents, by scholars from the United States and
abroad who are recognized as experts in their field.
More information on the titles in this series can
be found at the back of this book.

CONTENTS

PREFACE

The French National Assembly Elections of 1978 is the second study of a French election published by the American Enterprise Institute (AEI). Both this and the earlier volume, analyzing the 1974 presidential election, are in the *At the Polls* series, which now includes publications describing elections in thirteen democratic countries and will eventually cover at least two elections in each of nineteen countries.[1]

These democracies have very different political and historical backgrounds and employ a variety of electoral systems. Great Britain and Switzerland have conducted elections continuously for centuries. A number of the other countries have either returned to democracy or held free elections for the first time since World War II. In 1977 India demonstrated a continuing commitment to the free choice of its rulers in the face of an authoritarian threat, and Spain and Greece elected national legislatures after periods of authoritarian rule. Roughly half of the countries studied employ some form of proportional representation. A half dozen use one of several forms of the single-member-district system. The Irish Dáil and Australian Senate use versions of the single transferable vote. The unique Japanese system restricts each voter to the choice of one candidate in districts from which three to five legislators are elected.

In addition to the individual country studies, the series includes a description of the first direct election of representatives from nine countries to the European Parliament, scheduled for publication in 1980. Also expected in 1980 is *Democracy at the Polls*, a volume written by a dozen American and foreign experts who have examined

---

[1] The table of contents of *France at the Polls: The Presidential Election of 1974*, edited by Howard R. Penniman and published by AEI in 1975, is printed at the back of this book.

comparatively the theory and practice of democratic elections, drawing on the experience of more than two dozen countries.

The French election analyzed in this volume was the ninth held in the twenty years since the creation of the Fifth Republic in 1958. Coalitions of the center-right that included the followers of Charles de Gaulle have always won, but the last two elections have been very close. Valéry Giscard d'Estaing won the presidency in 1974 over François Mitterrand by 50.8 to 49.2 percent, and in 1978 the widely favored left, though it was decisively defeated in National Assembly seats, lost by a narrow margin in the popular vote. While results in recent years have been close, it should not be assumed that a trend has developed that will lead to an electoral triumph of the left in the near future. Indeed, authors in this volume argue that conflicts within the left coalition—the Union of the Left—undermine the chances of the Communist party (PCF) and the Socialist party (PS); that the present Government, by following a century-old French practice of writing election laws to significantly improve its chances of victory, has created new problems for the left; and that the expectations of a left victory in 1978 were themselves unwarranted.

Georges Lavau and Janine Mossuz-Lavau confront the most basic question about the Union of the Left when they ask whether its defeat was the result of "Suicide or Congenital Weakness." They note the bitter rivalry between the "partners" vying for predominance on the left and lay most of the blame for the division at the feet of the Communist party, which has not welcomed the Socialist gains at the polls that in recent years have made the PCF the minority member of the coalition.

The PCF is not pleased at the prospect of being the junior partner in a left Government either. Examining the PCF, Jeane J. Kirkpatrick stresses that it *"still seeks a radical transformation of French society and politics,"* a commitment the Communists made clear in "their polemics against the Socialists" in 1977 and 1978. She also points out that the PCF showed itself to be "still capable of *sharp and unexpected shifts in policy*" when it assumed the mantle of Eurocommunism. Perhaps for these reasons—and because the memories of older Socialists and centrists are long—the PCF has *"remained unacceptable to a substantial number of voters who were willing to support other candidates of the left."*

The Gaullists have long sought to polarize the choices offered the voters. Charles de Gaulle himself always believed that if French voters were forced to choose between a legislative majority that included a strong Communist party and one controlled by the center-right they would consistently support the latter. Changes in the electoral laws over the past decade and a half have been designed to ensure this polarization. Initially a candidate was required to win 5 percent of the first round vote in his district to be eligible for the runoff. Since most of the candidates other than those of the left or center-right coalitions who met this minimum were centrists or rightists, their presence in the second round benefited the left by cutting into the support for the Gaullists and their allies. The Government therefore has twice raised the requirements for second round eligibility, first to 10 and then to 12.5 percent—not merely of the votes cast but of the total number of names on the register. The decline in the average number of candidates competing in the second round reflects the impact of these changes: in 1958 the average was 3.1 per district; in 1962, 2.4; in 1973, 2.12; and in 1978 no district had more than two candidates. Another way of gauging the impact of the rule changes is to see what difference they made in 1978: under the rule requiring 5 percent of the votes cast, the average candidate would have needed 3,023 votes to compete in the second round; the requirement of 12.5 percent of registered voters raised the figure to 9,070 votes, or slightly more than three times as many.

Curiously, while the left coalition has been unable to win a national election in France, it has often done well in the preelection opinion poll forecasts—a fact that has led to considerable criticism of the polls by the media and the politicians. The case can be made that much of the criticism has been overstated. French law now prohibits the publication of any poll results for two weeks before the elections. (In 1974 Acting President Alain Poher used the prestige of his office to prevent publication of a poll the day before the election, arguing that the prohibition on campaigning during the thirty-six hours before the polls open would prevent a response from the party predicted to lose.) The last polls published just before the ban went into effect in 1978 showed the left with more than 50 percent of the public's support. It was a shock to many Frenchmen, then, when in the first round the Union of the Left received only 45.56 percent of the popular vote and the center-right coalition won 46.49 percent. The reported poll estimates were misleading on two counts. They often included in the left's total not only backers of the Union of the Left but also supporters of the extreme-left, which openly opposed the coalition. And second, to expect poll results that were at least two weeks out of date to accurately predict the election results was to assume that the voters' intentions would not change during the official campaign. But evidence from many elections in many countries suggests that campaigns have an impact on outcomes and that sometimes a great many people change their minds during the weeks or days immediately before voting. In France in 1978 the Socialist vote dropped by nearly six percentage points in the fortnight after the last polls were published. This development agrees with other evidence that some Socialist party members and sympathizers simply could not bring themselves to vote for a coalition that included an aggressive PCF, persistent in its attacks on its allies and in its demand for policies that went beyond those upon which there had long been agreement.

There remains the interesting question whether polarization is a requirement of French politics. There is some evidence, as various contributors to this volume have suggested, that the answer is no. One alternative would be the development of a coalition between the centrist Union for French Democracy (UDF), the right wing of the Socialist party, and other center-left groups. Such a coalition would isolate the Gaullists on the right and the Communists on the left, perhaps creating a legislative majority of the center-left. Many commentators have speculated that Giscard might make such a turn to the left. Certainly it could happen. In early 1980, however, with a new presidential election just over a year away, clear evidence of an opening to the left to replace the successful center-right coalition is not yet visible.

In this volume Roy Pierce describes the background of the electoral system. Jérôme Jaffré discusses the political attitudes of the French electorate. Georges Lavau and Janine Mossuz-Lavau analyze the left and its peculiar internal difficulties, while Jean Charlot discusses the campaign and the prospects for the center-right coalition. Roland Cayrol examines the role of the media in the campaign. And Monica Charlot initiates what will become a regular feature of *At the Polls* studies with a chapter on the role of women in politics. Finally, Jeane J. Kirkpatrick has summarized some of the findings of earlier chapters, adding her own analysis of the current state of French political life and looking briefly toward the future. The ballots used in the sixth district in Paris are reproduced in Appendix A, and in Appendix B Richard M. Scammon provides a detailed breakdown of the electoral returns.

HOWARD R. PENNIMAN

THE FRENCH NATIONAL ASSEMBLY ELECTIONS OF 1978

1
French Legislative Elections: The Historical Background

Roy Pierce

France has a tradition of national legislative elections that dates back more than a century. Except during the short-lived Vichy regime (1940–1944), there have been regular legislative elections in France since 1871. The longest hiatus between elections since that date was the ten years between 1936, the year of the last legislative election of the Third Republic, and 1945, the year of the first post–World War II election. Not counting the election of 1871, which took place in abnormal circumstances, there were sixteen legislative elections during the Third Republic (1875–1940), five elections preparatory to and during the Fourth Republic (1945–1958), and five elections during the Fifth Republic (inaugurated in 1958), including that of March 1978.[1]

Legislative Elections during the Third Republic
(1876–1936)

During the Third Republic, the franchise was restricted to males over twenty-one years of age excluding the military on active duty. There was no provision for voting by proxy; mail ballots were permitted beginning in 1919, in very limited circumstances. Registration was

---

[1] During the Third Republic, the popularly elected legislative chamber was called the Chamber of Deputies; since World War II it has been called the National Assembly. The French legislature has always been bicameral, but the second chamber, called the Senate during the Third and Fifth Republics and the Council of the Republic during the Fourth Republic, has never been directly elected. The legislative powers of the Senate have varied, depending on the period. During the Third Republic it was equal with the Chamber of Deputies, during the Fourth Republic it was subordinate to the National Assembly, and under the Fifth Republic it can block a measure adopted by the National Assembly only with the cooperation of the Government.

simple and permanent. Turnout was slightly higher during the twentieth century than turnout at contemporaneous British legislative elections. The mean turnout in Great Britain for the ten elections held between 1900 and the outbreak of World War II (excluding the hastily called "khaki election" of 1918, at which the turnout was less than 60 percent) was 76.7 percent. In France, for the nine elections during the same time span, the mean turnout was 80.0 percent. In addition, there was somewhat less variation in turnout in France than in Britain (again excluding the khaki election). Turnout in France was highest during the later part of the period: at the four French legislative elections from 1924 to 1936, turnout averaged 83.7 percent.

The ballot was secret, in principle, but legal provisions to ensure privacy in voting were not enacted until just before World War I, when polling places were required to contain voting booths; uniform, opaque envelopes were supplied to the voters for enclosing their ballots; and election officials were prohibited from handling the voters' envelopes, which had to be placed in the ballot boxes by the voters themselves.[2]

The Party System. The electoral record of the Third Republic is fraught with confusion for the general historian, and the elections themselves were in all probability confusing to many French voters as well. During the nineteenth century there were no parties to facilitate the selection of like-minded candidates and to help standardize electoral labels in the hundreds of electoral districts. Parties began to be constituted after the turn of the century, and they contributed somewhat toward clarifying electoral choices, but there was little coherence to the structure of electoral conflict in France before World War II. Prior to World War I, when parties either did not exist or were in their incipient stages and most candidates ran for office with ambiguous electoral labels and purely local support, the only clear evidence of what the voters decided at the ballot box lies in the activities of the victorious candidates. It is just not possible, without detailed historical studies at the level of the individual districts, to tell what the political coloration of the losing candidates actually was. François Goguel, the distinguished authority on the history of French electoral geography, more often bases his maps

---

[2] Joseph Barthélemy, *Traité de Droit Constitutionnel* [Treatise on constitutional law] (Paris: Librairie Dalloz, 1933), pp. 418-419. Also see Stein Rokkan, "The Comparative Study of Political Participation," in Stein Rokkan, *Citizens, Elections, Parties* (New York: David McKay, 1970), pp. 31-36.

illustrating French electoral behavior between 1875 and 1914 on the way the deputies from the various departments voted on major issues in the Chamber of Deputies than on the distribution of votes cast by the electorate for the competing candidates.[8]

The principal parties of the Third Republic were constituted during the first decade of the twentieth century. The Radical party (officially the Parti républicain radical et radical-socialiste), formed in 1901, was the dominant party of the republic. Its continuity of nomenclature and symbolism probably enabled it to become an object of more or less enduring voter loyalties, but it was locally oriented, ill-disciplined in Parliament, and plagued by leadership rivalries. The conservative parties that were formed at about the same time were no less individualistic than the Radicals and even less well organized in the country.

The main problems were the lack of direct correspondence between the electoral parties and the parliamentary groups, on the one hand, and the lack of discipline within the parliamentary groups, on the other. There were numerous parliamentary groups and they seldom matched electoral parties directly. There were electoral parties without parliamentary groups and groups without parties. Successful candidates from the same party would divide into two or more groups, and some groups normally contained members from two or more parties.

No single group ever held a majority of the seats in the Chamber, so coalitions were always necessary for parliamentary majorities. Most groups were poorly disciplined in parliamentary voting, and the combination of the need for coalitions and the lack of group discipline contributed to the pattern of ministerial instability that was one of the hallmarks of the French Third Republic.

Among the parties of the Third Republic, only the Socialists (who formed a united party in 1905) and, later, the Communists (constituted as a party in 1920) were able regularly to maintain electoral cohesion and parliamentary discipline, although even they suffered schisms.

The Left-Right Axis. For some thirty years, therefore, there were no parties at all to give coherence to the relationship between voting and legislative decision making, and for the remaining thirty-five years, most of the parties that did exist tended to reflect, rather than counteract, the individualism that characterized French electoral and

---

[8] François Goguel, *Géographie des élections françaises sous la Troisième et la Quatrième République* [The geography of French elections under the Third and Fourth Republics] (Paris: Armand Colin, 1970), Cahiers de la fondation nationale des sciences politiques, p. 159.

3

parliamentary politics. In circumstances such as these, it is not particularly surprising that observers and even participants should have resorted to terminological shortcuts in order to impose some order on a fluid and often obscure reality. The notions of left and right, relating to seating arrangements in the Chamber that harked back to France's postrevolutionary assemblies, were commonly employed to describe the main contending forces, with the left designating the forces desiring change and the right those of conservatism.

The center was, of course, the intermediate position and for more refined types of analysis could be divided into a center-left (or moderate left) and a center-right (or moderate right). Groups pressing for the most radical policies constituted the extreme-left, and the more blatant reactionaries the extreme-right. In this framework, the salient, fixed points of reference for France's multiple and unstable party system were not the parties or parliamentary groups but rather locations on a hypothetical left-right dimension: it was the left-right categories themselves that were primary. The way to make the system intelligible was to relate the parties or the groups active at any given moment to those categories.[4]

---

[4] André Siegfried employed this method in order to highlight the persistence of stable tendencies across a multitude of changing political labels in his *Tableau politique de la France de l'Ouest* [Political panorama of Western France] (Paris: Armand Colin, 1913) and in his *Tableau des partis en France* (Paris: Bernard Grasset, 1930), translated as *France: A Study in Nationality* (New Haven, Connecticut: Yale University Press, 1930). François Goguel preferred to employ only two basic tendencies, order and movement, in his *La Politique des partis sous la IIIe République* [Party politics under the Third Republic] (Paris: Editions du Seuil, 1946), but he employed left-right terminology in his *Géographie des élections françaises*.

More recent empirical work on the left-right dimension includes Eméric Deutsch, Denis Lindon, and Pierre Weill, *Les Familles Politiques, Aujourd'hui en France* [Political families in France today] (Paris: Les Editions de Minuit, 1966); J. A. Laponce, "Note on the Use of the Left-Right Dimension," *Comparative Political Studies*, vol. 2 (January 1970), pp. 481-502; Philip E. Converse and Roy Pierce, "Basic Cleavages in French Politics and the Disorders of May and June, 1968," a paper prepared for presentation at the Seventh World Congress of Sociology, Varna, Bulgaria, September 1970; J. A. Laponce, "Dieu—à droite ou à gauche?" [Is God on the right or the left?], *Canadian Journal of Political Science*, vol. 3 (June 1970), pp. 257-274; J. A. Laponce, "In Search of Stable Elements of the Left-Right Landscape," *Comparative Politics*, vol. 4 (July 1972), pp. 455-475; Philip E. Converse, "Some Mass-Elite Contrasts in the Perception of Political Space," International Social Science Council, *Social Science Information*, vol. 14, no. 3/4 (1975), pp. 49-83; and Ronald Inglehart and Hans Klingemann, "Party Identification, Ideological Preference and the Left-Right Dimension among Western Mass Publics," in Ian Budge, Ivor Crewe, and Dennis Farlie, *Party Identification and Beyond, Representations of Voting and Party Competition* (New York: John Wiley & Sons, 1976), chap. 13. See also Jeane Kirkpatrick's discussion of the left-right dimension in this volume, p. 195.

Accordingly, the numerous groups that have populated the electoral and parliamentary scenes of French republics have always been placed in the mental containers supplied by the left-right nomenclature. The Radical party staked a claim to the leftist label early in the Third Republic. The Socialists, appearing on the scene as the extreme-left, later found themselves pushed toward the mere left when a new extreme-left emerged in the form of the Communist party. Those three parties, which all claim to be the heirs of the revolutionaries of 1789 and which are the only parties formed during the Third Republic that still exist under the Fifth, cling jealously to the symbols of the left.[5] The other parties of the Third Republic, including certain factions of the Radicals, have been placed by most analysts near the center or on the right.

Locating the parties on the left-right dimension has always been a delicate task, because of the indiscipline of the parliamentary groups and the variety of issues on which they have had to take positions. While it is always a matter of subjective judgment, recent research has shown that there is a considerable amount of consensus among both the political leadership and the public at large with respect to the left-right locations of the parties today, if not with regard to the meaning of the left-right dimension itself.[6]

The Religious Factor. The great issues that divided left from right during the formative years of the Third Republic were the establishment and consolidation of the republic[7] and the separation of Church and state, in particular the secularization of the public elementary school system. Indeed, those two issues, separable analytically, were for all practical purposes one and the same politically. For the first twenty years of its existence, the Third Republic was formally opposed by the Catholic Church, and many French Catholics opposed it for longer than that. The republicans were anticlerical, and the antirepublicans were proclerical. The republicans were so hostile to the

---

[5] The Radicals ceased to be a major electoral force during the Fourth Republic although they continued to furnish many of the regime's leaders. In 1978, they were divided between a Movement of Leftist Radicals or MRG (Mouvement des Radicaux de Gauche) and a more conservative Radical party that criticized but supported President Giscard d'Estaing and his Government.

[6] See Converse, "Mass-Elite Contrasts."

[7] In the French political vocabulary, the word *republic* is equivalent to the word *democracy*. Monarchy is not incompatible with democracy logically, but it turned out to be incompatible with democracy in France historically, and what is always termed the republican movement in France could also be termed the democratic movement without any distortion in meaning.

5

clerical forces that when, acting on an encyclical by Pope Leo XIII in 1892, certain Catholics (called the *ralliés*) accepted the republic, they were met with deep mistrust on the part of the republicans. After the Dreyfus affair at the turn of the century, the Radical party launched a vindictive attack on the Church, and the old cleavage between the people attached to the Church and those who considered themselves republican fundamentalists was revived with renewed vigor.

The distinction between left and right in terms of a simultaneous cleavage involving attitudes toward the republic and attitudes toward the Church did not, of course, emerge full-blown with the launching of the Third Republic. Its intellectual roots were embedded in the Enlightenment, which exalted the authority of reason over that of faith, and its first explosive expression occurred with the Revolution of 1789. Church and state were so closely entwined during the Old Regime that the revolutionary onslaught against that regime was inevitably an attack on the Church as well as the state. In the political conflicts of the nineteenth century, which saw a succession of different regimes precede the Third Republic, the Church always aligned itself against the republican movement. The republicans who founded the Third Republic regarded their efforts to weaken and even humiliate the Church as part of a task that had been begun a century earlier.[8]

The fact that attitudes toward the Church were fundamental to the political cleavages of the time almost surely explains how the voters were able to orient themselves to the electoral competition when there were no parties to clarify the issues at stake. With the Church engaged in the political struggle, a whole network of institutional agents could be mobilized on the clerical side to try to counteract the anticlerical thrusts of the republicans. On the other side, the Radical party in particular drew organizational support from the Freemasons and the teaching corps of the developing public school system. The parish priest and the primary school teacher were not merely symbols of political conflict during the Third Republic; they were agents from whom the mass of voters could receive cues concerning which candidate they should vote for. The historical distinction between left and right on the basis of attitudes toward the Church, which antedates the Third Republic but which became engrained in electoral politics during that regime, endures to the present day. No social or demographic factor correlates with mass electoral preferences as closely as the degree of religious practice does.

---

[8] The main lines of this analysis follow François Goguel, *France under the Fourth Republic* (Ithaca, New York: Cornell University Press, 1952), chap. 5.

The Electoral System. In thirteen of the sixteen elections held during the Third Republic, the electoral system used was essentially the same as the electoral system that has been used during the Fifth Republic. France was divided into single-member districts. An election was held among the competing candidates in each district, and any candidate receiving a majority of the valid ballots cast, including at least one-fourth of the number of registered voters in the district, was elected. If no candidate was elected, a runoff ballot was held two weeks later (one week later after 1927). At the second ballot, the candidate with a plurality of the votes was elected.

A first-ballot candidate with a poor chance of election on the second ballot would drop out of the race in an effort to throw his support to another candidate who was better placed to defeat a common opponent. When this kind of electoral cooperation was practiced among republican candidates, it was known as "republican discipline." The same kind of second-ballot cooperation, of course, could also be displayed by the republicans' antirepublican opponents.

In fact, prior to World War I, the need for this kind of second-ballot discipline, while sometimes crucial for the survival of the republic, was comparatively infrequent. Republican discipline was decisive at the election of 1885 (although the single-member district system was not used at that election)[9] and at the election of 1889, when the republicans overwhelmed both their traditional antirepublican and their Boulangist opponents. But at the elections held under the single-member district, two-ballot system before World War I, almost three-fourths of the seats on the average were won at the first ballot. The proportion of seats won at the first ballot tended to be largest at the earliest elections: it was 80 percent in 1876, 98 percent in 1877, and 86 percent in 1881. It trended downward in the twentieth century and reached a pre–World War I low of 57 percent in 1914.[10] No summary statistics on the number of candidates who

---

[9] In 1885, the department was the electoral district, and each department had at least three seats. Candidates could run individually or on party lists, and to be elected a candidate had to have either a majority of the votes at the first ballot or a plurality at the second. Only 53 percent of the seats were won at the first ballot, and superior discipline at the second ballot enabled the republicans to turn the election into a rout of the conservatives. See Peter Campbell, *French Electoral Systems and Elections since 1789* (London: Faber and Faber, 1958), pp. 75-79.

[10] For 1876, see Jacques Chastenet, *Histoire de la Troisième République* [History of the Third Republic], vol. 1, *L'Enfance de la Troisième, 1870-1879* [Infancy of the Third Republic, 1870-1879] (Paris: Librairie Hachette, 1952), p. 215. For all other single-member district, two-ballot elections under the Third Republic, see Mattei Dogan, "Changement de régime et changement de per-

ran at each election have been published, but there are indications that there were comparatively few candidates early in the Third Republic.[11]

France departed from the single-member district, two-ballot system for the first two elections after World War I. The elections of 1919 and 1924 were conducted according to electoral laws that provided for multimember districts; these were the departments or, in the case of a few large departments, fractions of departments. Candidates could run as individuals or on party lists, and the voters could cast as many votes as there were seats for the district. They could split their votes among candidates on different lists, but they could not vote for the same candidate more than once. Candidates who received a majority of the votes were elected, and any remaining seats for the district were distributed among the competing lists by a form of proportional representation.[12]

The remaining three elections of the Third Republic were conducted under the traditional single-member district, two-ballot system. At these elections, however, the comparative simplicity of pre–World War I electoral operations disappeared. The average number of candidates who competed for each seat was more than six in 1928 and 1932, and it rose to more than eight for the last election of the Third Republic in 1936. At the same time (and probably also partly as a consequence), the proportion of seats decided at the first ballot declined sharply from pre–World War I levels. Almost 60 percent of the seats were decided at the second ballot in 1932, and some 70 percent of them were decided at the second ballot in 1928 and 1936. The increased proportion of seats allocated at the second ballot made the candidates' second-ballot strategies, and the voters' response to them, more important than ever for the political composition of the Chamber. Moreover, it did so in circumstances where the distinc-

---

sonnel" [System change and elite change], in Jean Touchard et al., *L'Etablissement de la Cinquième République, le référendum de septembre et les élections de novembre 1958* [The establishment of the Fifth Republic, the referendum of September and the elections of November 1958] (Paris: Librairie Armand Colin, 1960), Cahiers de la fondation nationale des sciences politiques, 109, p. 243.

11 Campbell notes that in 1877 there were only two candidates in "most" districts and that in 1898 there were three candidates per district on the average. Campbell, *French Electoral Systems*, pp. 34 and 35. Frédéric Bon reports that in 1902 there were only two candidates in "many" districts. Frédéric Bon, *Les Elections en France, Histoire et Sociologie* [History and sociology of elections in France] (Paris: Editions du Seuil, 1978), p. 51.

12 A second ballot was technically possible, in districts where turnout was unusually light or no list received a certain minimum share of the vote, but a second ballot was held only in one district, in 1919. See Campbell, *French Electoral Systems*, pp. 90-96.

tion between left and right had lost its earlier clarity and the once vital practice of republican discipline had greatly diminished relevance for the conduct of public affairs.

Electoral and Parliamentary Alignments. As long as the major issues confronting Parliament were the consolidation of the republic and the separation of Church and state, the division of the electorate on a left-right basis that expressed gradations in attachment to the Catholic Church was tolerably congruent with the divisions among the elites and parties. Indeed, even when economic and social matters were added to the agenda, the distinction between left and right tended to be both clear and equivalent for both the elites and the mass electorate. Some early French republicans (and their successors within the young Radical party) were quite radical in social and economic matters by the standards of the time, and the antirepublicans tended to be conservative in those same domains. There were, of course, factional differences among the republicans, but these were generally subordinated to their overriding commonality of purpose with respect to the consolidation of republican institutions and the separation of Church and state.[13] In the comparatively rare cases when a second ballot was necessary, and either republican discipline or antirepublican discipline or both were displayed by candidates, at least the logic of the situation was such that the voters from each camp who could no longer vote for their first-ballot preference could switch their vote to the remaining candidate from their bloc without violating their basic sympathies.

During the interwar period, both the relations between the parties and their voters and the relations among the parties themselves became more complicated. Once the republic appeared secure, the separation of Church and state was an accomplished fact, and economic and social problems became more pressing, the divisions among the republicans over economic and social matters could not so easily be contained.

The main difficulty in this regard lay in the relations between the Radicals and the growing Socialist party. Radicals and Socialists got along very well together as long as the issues were defending the republic or attacking the Church. But the two groups could not

---

[13] There were factional divisions among the early antirepublicans as well, for these included supporters of each claimant to head a nonrepublican regime: the Legitimists (who supported the Bourbon pretender), the Orleanists, and the Bonapartists. The inability of these groups to suppress their differences made possible the establishment of the republic, by a parliamentary margin of a single vote.

always agree on economic and social policy. The Radicals were hostile to hereditary social privilege and sympathetic to the little man, but most Radicals defended private property and financial orthodoxy, while the Socialists were Marxists, in the rhetorical style characteristic of continental Socialist parties prior to the Russian Revolution. Moreover, the two leftist parties had different kinds of constituency. The Radicals found their support among farmers, small businessmen, and professionals in the small towns and rural areas, while the Socialists recruited their supporters among industrial workers in and around the urban areas. Dissension on the left increased still further after the formation of the Communist party, which adopted all the symbols of French republicanism but whose economic and political objectives could not easily be reconciled with those of either the Radicals or the Socialists.

At the same time, the right-wing forces, once both antirepublican and proclerical, evolved with the passage of time. Former antirepublicans became resigned or attracted to the republic. Catholic voters supported moderate republicans, politicians who were attached to the republic, respectful of the Church but indifferent to its political claims, and conservative in economic and social outlook. The French right was always divided during the Third Republic, and it contained elements that were bitterly opposed to the secular republic. During the 1930s in particular, rightists were often attracted to authoritarian solutions to France's problems. The thinness of their attachment to the republic was demonstrated by the enthusiasm with which they welcomed its dismantling during the first years of the Vichy regime. The leftists' ingrained suspicion of the right as antirepublican always had some grounding in reality. But right-wing extremism was much stronger outside Parliament than within it, and the parliamentary right contained moderates who could get along quite well on economic and social matters even with doctrinaire anticlerical Radicals.

During the interwar period, there was recurring tension between the left-wing parties' electoral strategies and their capacity to govern together in situations where economic policy was crucial. Radicals and Socialists normally allied with one another for electoral purposes, because they had a common cause in the emotive themes of republicanism and anticlericalism. But when they won, they could not govern together for more than half the interval before the next scheduled election. They would govern together for two years; then the coalition would break up, the Socialists would go into the opposition, and the new governing formula would be a coalition of Radicals and conservatives.

At the election of 1919, the Radicals, who had been supporting Clemenceau in a coalition with conservatives and who had been shaken by the Russian Revolution, did not ally with the Socialists, but at the remaining elections of the Third Republic Radicals and Socialists maintained their traditional electoral alliance. In 1924, the Radicals formed joint lists with the Socialists under the label Cartel des Gauches.[14] In 1928 and 1932, Radicals and Socialists practiced republican discipline at the second ballot, mutually withdrawing in favor of whichever leftist candidate was best placed to defeat the right. In 1936, the left-wing electoral alliance was enlarged to include the Communist party. At earlier elections, the Communist party had remained isolated, and at the elections of 1928 and 1932 it did not withdraw its candidates at the second ballot, thereby contributing to a division of the leftist vote. After the Nazi seizure of power in Germany, however, the Soviet Union and the Third International began to promote antifascist Popular Fronts including Communist and other left-wing parties. Against a background of international danger, economic crisis, and internal disorder provoked by right-wing groups outside of Parliament, French Communists, Socialists, and Radicals agreed to form a Popular Front alliance for the election of 1936, involving mutual withdrawals at the second ballot and even a common program.[15]

The allied leftist parties won parliamentary majorities on three occasions, in 1924, 1932, and 1936. Each time they were able to convert their electoral alliance into a governing coalition for about two years.[16] At the end of two years, the coalitions broke up; the Socialists moved into the opposition with the Communists while the Radicals joined the conservatives in a new governing coalition.[17] This sequence of electoral competition between left and right, defined in historic terms relating to attitudes toward the republic and the Church, the formation of governing and opposing coalitions based on the same cleavage, and the breakdown of the two opposing blocs into a coalition

[14] In 1919 and 1924, it will be recalled, the single-member district, two-ballot electoral system was replaced with a multi-member district system that combined majority rule with proportional representation.

[15] See Georges Dupeux, Le Front Populaire et les élections de 1936 [The Popular Front and the 1936 elections] (Paris: Librairie Armand Colin, 1959), Cahiers de la fondation nationale des sciences politiques, 99.

[16] The Communists did not participate in the Popular Front Governments between 1936 and 1938, but they supported them.

[17] For an excellent study of the Radicals' defection from the Popular Front governing coalition and an analysis of the reasons for their defection, see Paul Warwick, The French Popular Front, A Legislative Analysis (Chicago: University of Chicago Press, 1977).

of the most moderate elements of each bloc and an opposing coalition of the extreme elements of each bloc, was not new for France. Prost and Rosenzveig find that same pattern between 1881 and 1885.[18] Between the wars, however, the pattern occurred with considerable regularity.[19]

There are indications that during the interwar period some Radical voters were not happy with the Radical party's electoral alliances with the Socialists and, in 1936, with the Communists, and it is likely that some Socialist voters were not happy with the Popular Front alliance either. The left-wing parties could not always muster as many votes for their single candidate at the second ballot as they had won in the same district at the first ballot, when they ran several candidates. Electors who could not vote at the second ballot for the same candidate they had supported at the first ballot, because that candidate had withdrawn in favor of another, did not always vote for that other candidate. In other words, the first-ballot supporters of the various leftist parties did not always display the same kind of discipline at the second ballot that the candidates did. François Goguel has estimated that more than 400,000 votes cast for Radical candidates at the first ballot of the 1928 election went to moderate conservatives at the second ballot, even though the Radicals had withdrawn in favor of Socialist candidates.[20] Georges Dupeux has pointed out that at the 1936 election, in districts where there was a single left-wing candidate and a serious contest at the second ballot, the leftist candidates lost votes by comparison with the total leftist vote at the first ballot in the same districts and that the proportionate loss of votes was least where the single leftist candidate was a Radical, more than twice as large where the single leftist candidate was a Socialist, and still larger where the single leftist candidate was a Communist.[21] In the absence of survey data it is not possible to make reliable estimates of the vote transfers that took place from the first to the second ballot, but it is evident that the solidarity of the Popular Front alliance was far from complete at the level of the voters. Some fraction of first-ballot Communist and/or Socialist voters refused to vote for Radical candidates

---

18 Antoine Prost and Christian Rosenzveig, "La Chambre des députés (1881-1885): Analyse factorielle des scrutins" [The Chamber of Deputies (1881-1885): Factor analysis of roll-call votes], *Revue française de science politique*, vol. 21 (February 1971), pp. 5-50.

19 It may have occurred regularly during earlier periods as well. We do not know whether it did or not, however, because there are not enough detailed studies of French legislative behavior during the Third Republic.

20 Goguel, *La Politique des partis*, p. 247.

21 Dupeux, *Le Front Populaire*, p. 136.

at the second ballot; a larger proportion of Radical and/or Communist voters refused to vote for Socialist candidates; and an even larger proportion of Radical and/or Socialist voters refused to vote for Communist candidates.

At the end of the Third Republic, therefore, French electoral coalitions at the elite level were still shaped by the division between left and right that had expressed the substance of political conflict at its founding. At the level of the electorate, however, this stark division was not wholly accepted, at least by leftist voters, some fraction of whom do not appear to have regarded the left-wing parties as essentially interchangeable. Perhaps because of this, the divisions at the elite level within the leftist bloc, between Radicals and Socialists, and between Radicals and Communists, prevented the left-wing parties from translating parliamentary majorities into durable left-wing governing coalitions.

Legislative Elections during the Fourth Republic
(1945–1956)

In August 1944, the Vichy regime collapsed, Paris was liberated, and Charles de Gaulle returned to France to head a provisional government that was committed to restoring democratic institutions to France. The first postwar legislative elections were held on October 21, 1945. At the same time, the voters were asked whether they wanted the assembly they were electing to be a constituent assembly. Only the Radicals among France's parties wanted to return to the constitution of the Third Republic, and some 96 percent of the voters repudiated the Third Republic by responding "yes." The Constituent Assembly drafted a constitution, but the text was rejected by 53 percent of the voters at a referendum on May 5, 1946, probably because it was supported only by the Socialists and the Communists and only the Communists campaigned for it with enthusiasm. On June 2, a Second Constituent Assembly was elected, and on October 13, 1946, the constitution it drafted was adopted by some 54 percent of the voters at a referendum at which more than a third of the electorate abstained. On November 10, 1946, France's voters elected the first National Assembly of the Fourth Republic. There were to be two more legislative elections during the Fourth Republic, on June 17, 1951, and January 2, 1956.

The electorate was more than doubled in size after World War II when the franchise was extended to women over twenty-one years of age, as well as to the armed forces. Voting by proxy was permitted in certain circumstances, and opportunities for mail ballots were enlarged. The average turnout at the five elections associated with the Fourth Republic was just about the same as the average turnout under the Third Republic after 1900.

The traditional electoral system providing for single-member districts and a second ballot was abandoned during the Fourth Republic.[22] Instead, the election of 1945 and the two elections of 1946 were organized under proportional representation based on the highest average, a system that produces parliamentary representation roughly proportional to the number of votes cast for each party but that tends to favor the larger parties over the smaller ones. In most cases the department was the electoral district; some of the larger departments were divided into more than one district. Candidates could not run individually; they had to run on lists, which had to contain as many names as there were seats to be filled for the district. Voters were required to cast their ballots for an entire list; they could not split their votes among lists. No provision was made for expressing preferences among the names on a single list for the elections of 1945 and June 1946; at the election of November 1946, the voters were permitted to alter the order of the names on a list, but the changes could be taken into account only if half of the voters for a list exercised their right to express their preferences, a condition that was nowhere fulfilled. At all three elections, therefore, seats were allocated to each list in the order in which the candidates' names appeared on the lists.

The Postwar Partisan Configuration: 1945 and 1946. The first three elections after the war, held within a span of little more than a year, produced a large turnover in parliamentary personnel relative to the prewar period, as well as large changes in the electoral fortunes of the various parties. Prewar members of Parliament who had voted to give full powers to Marshal Pétain in 1940 were (until 1953) ineligible for public office unless they could demonstrate that they had participated in the Resistance. In fact, France's postwar parliamentary elite came out of the Resistance. The parties that did best electorally right after the war were those that were associated with the Resistance: the Communists, the Socialists, and the Popular Republican Movement or MRP (Mouvement Républicain Populaire), which had been formed by liberal Catholics during the war. The parties that suffered most were those associated with the Third

---

[22] Except, after 1951, for by-elections when there was only one seat to be filled in a district.

Republic (the Radical party) or with the Vichy regime (the conservatives). Women constituted between 10 and 14 percent of the candidates at the first three postwar elections and held between 5 and 6 percent of the seats. Their numbers dwindled thereafter, from a high of thirty-two women elected in November 1946 to nineteen elected in January 1956. The number of women deputies declined further with the advent of the Fifth Republic, during which women never held even 2 percent of the seats. In the discussion of electoral results that follows in this chapter, the reader may find it useful to consult Table 1–1, which shows the electoral results in terms of proportions of the votes cast, and Table 1–2, which shows the results in terms of seats in the Assembly for the entire period from 1945 through 1978.

The Communist party, which had achieved its prewar electoral high in 1936 with slightly more than 15 percent of the votes, almost doubled its vote and emerged at the first postwar election as the largest party in the Assembly. The Socialists did slightly better in October 1945 than their norm of about 20 percent of the votes during the interwar period, although they later trended downward and lost almost a fourth of their votes in barely over a year. The most spectacular success of the early postwar period was the MRP, which averaged more than 25 percent of the votes in 1945 and 1946, to a large extent because it had displaced the discredited right. Together, the Communists, Socialists, and MRP won more than 70 percent of the votes at these early postwar elections and an even larger proportion of the seats in the Assembly. Moreover, they governed together until the middle of 1947 through a coalition formula that was known as tripartism. Some people regarded this formula as marking a new era of political stability for France, to be characterized by a small number of large, disciplined parties, which would negotiate policy agreements at the upper echelons and see them carried out faithfully by loyal supporters in Parliament. In fact, there was to be more instability in the French party system during the Fourth Republic than at any other time since the growth of parties during the early twentieth century.

Instability in the Party System: 1951 and 1956. Within six months of the election of November 1946, tripartism came to an end. The coming of the cold war hardened the attitude of the Communist party, and in the spring of 1947 the Communist ministers were dropped from the Government and the party moved into the opposition. At about the same time, Charles de Gaulle, who had resigned as head of

TABLE 1-1

RESULTS OF ELECTIONS FOR THE NATIONAL ASSEMBLY, 1945–1978, METROPOLITAN FRANCE[a]

(in percentages of valid ballots)

Party	Oct. 1945	June 1946	Nov. 1946	June 1951	Jan. 1956	Nov. 1958	Nov. 1962	Mar. 1967	June 1968	Mar. 1973	Mar. 1978
Communists (PCF)	26.0	26.2	28.6	25.8	25.7	18.6	21.8	22.5	20.0	21.4	20.6
Extreme-left and PSU	—	—	—	0.8	0.4	1.2	2.3	2.2	3.9	3.3	3.3
Socialists[b]	23.8	21.1	17.9	14.5	14.9	15.2	12.5	—	—	—	25.0
Radicals and similar groups	11.1	11.5	12.4	10.2	15.6	7.2	7.7	—	—	—	—
Federation[c]	—	—	—	—	—	—	—	18.9	16.5	20.6	—
MRP	24.9	28.1	26.4	12.5	11.1	10.8	8.0	—	—	—	—
Conservatives	13.3	12.8	12.8	12.8	14.5	21.4	10.9	—	4.0	—	—
Centrists[d]	—	—	—	—	—	—	—	13.1	10.4	12.6	—
Gaullist Centrists[e]	—	—	—	—	—	—	—	—	—	7.0	—
Independent Republicans	—	—	—	—	—	—	—	5.4	6.3	7.0	—
Union for French Democracy (UDF)	—	—	—	—	—	—	—	—	—	—	20.4
Gaullists[f]	—	—	1.6	21.8	4.4	19.8	35.9	32.3	37.3	23.9	22.4
Extreme-right and Poujadists	—	—	—	—	13.2	2.5	0.9	0.7	—	—	—
Miscellaneous[g]	0.9	0.3	0.3	1.6	0.2	3.3	—	4.9	1.6	4.2	8.3
Total	100.0	100.0	100.0	100.0	100.0	100.0	100.0	100.0	100.0	100.0	100.0

[a] For the elections from 1958 on, first-ballot results are given. [b] Includes 2.2 percent for left-wing Radicals (MRG) in 1978. [c] UGSD in 1973. [d] Democratic Center in 1967, PDM in 1968, Reformists in 1973. [e] CDP. [f] Gaullist Union in 1946, RPF in 1951, Social Republi-

cans in 1956, UNR in 1958, UNR-UDT in 1962, UD-Ve in 1967, UDR in 1968 and 1973, RPR in 1978. g Includes 2.2 percent for Ecologists in 1978.

SOURCES: For 1945 and 1946, Raoul Husson, *Elections et référendums des 21 octobre 1945, 5 mai et 2 juin 1946* [Elections and referendums of October 21, 1945, and May 5 and June 2, 1946] (Paris: Le Monde, 1946), p. 261; and Husson, *Elections et référendums des 13 oct., 10 et 24 nov., et 8 déc. 1946* [Elections and referendums of October 13, November 10 and 24, and December 8, 1946] (Paris: Le Monde, 1947). p. 253. For 1951, République Française, Ministère de l'Intérieur, *Les Elections législatives du 17 Juin 1951* [The legislative elections of June 17, 1951] (Paris: La Documentation Française, 1953), p. 42. For 1956, République Française, Ministère de l'Intérieur, *Les Elections législatives du 2 Janvier 1956* [The legislative elections of January 2, 1956] (Paris: La Documentation Française, 1957), p. 72. For 1958, François Goguel, Alain Lancelot and Jean Ranger, "Analyse des résultats" [Analysis of the results] in Jean Touchard et al., *L'Etablissement de la Cinquième République, le référendum de septembre et les élections de novembre 1958* [The establishment of the Fifth Republic, the referendum of September and the elections of November 1958] (Paris: Librairie Armand Colin, 1960), Cahiers de la fondation nationale des sciences politiques, 109, p. 298. For 1962, François Goguel, "Analyse des résultats" [Analysis of the results] in François Goguel et al., *Le Référendum d'octobre et les élections de novembre 1962* [The referendum of October and the elections of November 1962] (Paris: Libraire Armand Colin, 1965), Cahiers de la fondation nationale des sciences politiques, 142, pp. 306–308 (with slight adjustments). For 1967 and 1968, République Française, Ministère de l'Intérieur, *Les Elections législatives de 1967* [The legislative elections of 1967] (Paris: Imprimerie Nationale, 1967), p. 114, and *Les Elections législatives de 1968* [The legislative elections of 1968] (Paris: Imprimerie Nationale, 1969), p. 114. For 1973, *L'Année Politique 1973* [The political year 1973] (Paris: Presses Universitaires de France, 1974), p. 402, and République Française, Ministère de l'Intérieur, *Les Elections législatives de 1973* [The legislative elections of 1973] (Paris: Imprimerie Nationale, 1973), p. 105. For 1978, République Française, Ministère de l'Intérieur, *Les Elections législatives de 1978* [The legislative elections of 1978] (Paris: Imprimerie Nationale, 1978), p. 101.

TABLE 1-2

Distribution of Metropolitan Seats in the National Assembly, 1945–1978

Party	Oct. 1945	June 1946	Nov. 1946	June 1951	Jan. 1956	Nov. 1958	Nov. 1962	Mar. 1967	June 1968	Mar. 1973	Mar. 1978
Communists (PCF)	148	146	166	97	145	10	41	72	33	73	86
PSU	—	—	—	—	—	—	2	4	—	1	—
Socialists[a]	134	115	90	94	92	44	65	—	—	—	112
Radicals and similar groups	23	39	55	77	77	23	42	—	—	—	—
Federation[b]	—	—	—	—	—	57	—	116	57	102	—
MRP	141	160	158	82	72	133	36	—	—	—	—
Conservatives	62	62	70	80	96	—	28	—	—	—	—
Centrists[c]	—	—	—	—	—	—	—	40	31	32	—
Gaullist Centrists (CDP)	—	—	—	—	—	—	—	—	—	28	—
Independent Republicans	—	—	—	—	—	—	20	40	60	54	—
Union for French Democracy (UDF)	—	—	—	—	—	—	—	—	—	—	119
Gaullists[d]	—	—	5	107	16	198	229	190	282	173	145
Poujadists	—	—	—	—	42	—	—	—	—	—	—
Miscellaneous	14	—	—	7	4	—	2	8	7	10	12
Total	522	522	544	544	544	465	465	470	470	473	474

a Includes 10 left-wing Radicals (MRG) in 1978. b UGSD in 1973. c Democratic Center in 1967, PDM in 1968, Reformists in 1973. d Gaullist Union in 1946, RPF in 1951, Social Republicans in 1956, UNR in 1958, UNR-UDT in 1962, UD-Ve in 1967, UDR in 1968 and 1973, RPR in 1978.

SOURCES: For 1945 through 1968, Roy Pierce, *French Politics and Political Institutions* (New York: Harper & Row, 1973), 2nd edition, p. 160. For 1973, *L'Année Politique 1973* [The political year 1973] Paris: Presses Universitaires de France, 1974), pp. 378-380. For 1978, République Française, Ministère de L'Intérieur, *Les Elections législatives de 1978* [The legislative elections of 1978] (Paris: Imprimerie Nationale, 1978), pp. 95-97.

the provisional government in January 1946 because he disapproved of the constitution that was being drafted by the First Constituent Assembly, and who had outlined the kind of constitution that he preferred in his famous Bayeux speech in June 1946, formed what was to be the first of a succession of Gaullist parties, the Rally of the French People or RPF (Rassemblement du Peuple Français). A number of deputies elected from other parties formed a Gaullist intergroup in the Assembly. With the Communists in the opposition, as well as (until 1953) the Gaullists, the parliamentary center of gravity was pushed to the right. Radicals and conservatives were now indispensable for the formation of parliamentary majorities, and they brought their characteristic individualism back onto the parliamentary scene. Unstable coalitions including Socialists, the MRP, Radicals, and conservatives governed in what was called a third force formula until the elections of 1951.

Faced with the combined opposition of the Communists and the Gaullists, the third force parties feared that they would lose their parliamentary majority at the 1951 election, so they altered the electoral system to their advantage. The departments (or, for the larger departments, subdivisions of them) remained the electoral districts, and competing candidates were required to run on lists containing as many names as there were seats to fill for the district, but parties that ran candidates under the same label in at least thirty departments were permitted to ally with one another in any district other than the eight districts of Paris and its suburbs. If any single list or group of allied lists won a majority of the votes in a district, that list or group of allied lists was awarded all the seats for the district. When a group of allied parties won a majority in a district, the seats were awarded to the various allied parties on the basis of the number of votes each party had contributed to the total won by the group, according to proportional representation based on the highest average. If no single list or group of allied lists won a majority, the seats for the district were allocated by proportional representation based on the highest average among all the competing lists, counting groups of allied parties as single lists. After all the seats for the district were allocated, the seats won by the group of allied parties were distributed to those parties by proportional representation of their contributions to the total vote won by the alliance, again based on the highest average.

The rationale for this complicated system was the desire of the third force parties to profit from their willingness to ally with one another, in various combinations and in various districts, as they had been doing in governing coalitions in Parliament. In a loose sense, they were converting their governing coalition into electoral coalitions at the district level and awarding themselves a premium in seats wherever their coalitions were successful. On the other hand, the Communists could not ally with any other party and the Gaullists would not (except in about a dozen districts), and both were to suffer for their isolation.

At the same time, there was one aspect of the new electoral system that was an unalloyed power play. No alliances were permitted in the eight districts of the Paris region, where the election was held under a straight system of proportional representation based on the largest remainder. While proportional representation based on the highest average favors the larger parties, proportional representation based on the largest remainder favors the smaller parties. The third force parties expected the Gaullists to do particularly well electorally in the city of Paris, and the Communists regularly did well in the working-class suburbs surrounding the city (and known as the Red Belt), so the proportional representation system employed there could be expected to work to the advantage of the smaller, third force parties. On the other hand, the third force parties expected to do well, especially when allied with one another, in the provinces, and the different proportional representation system used there would again work to their advantage.

At the 1951 election, the Gaullists made a good showing, as expected. They won some 20 percent of the votes, cutting the electoral strength of the MRP by more than 50 percent in the process and probably also contributing toward reducing the electoral support of the Socialists to its lowest level since World War I. Communists, Radicals, and conservatives each won about as many votes proportionately as they had in 1946. But the electoral law accomplished what it was designed to do with respect to the distribution of parliamentary seats. The Gaullists emerged as the largest single group, but the Communists lost more than 40 percent of their seats. All the third force parties except the MRP gained seats, and together the third force parties retained an arithmetical parliamentary majority.

The third force parties, however, could not convert their parliamentary majority into a stable governing coalition. Between 1951 and 1956, there was a succession of unstable governments, sometimes oriented toward the Socialists, sometimes oriented toward the conservatives. Prior to 1953, France's governing parties had been preoccupied mainly with domestic issues; after that date overseas problems came to the fore: decolonization in North Africa, the Indochina War, the European Defense Community Treaty, and German rearmament. These issues deeply divided the third force parties, internally as well as one from another. The Socialists became estranged from the MRP. The Radicals were badly divided between one group, led by Pierre Mendès-France, who sought a coalition with the Socialists, and another group, headed by Edgar Faure, who favored a coalition with the MRP and the conservatives. With the third force parties so divided and unable to form extensive electoral alliances, the 1951 electoral law was no longer appropriate, but there was no majority in favor of any alternative, so the system was retained by default. Still, the Socialists, the MRP, the Radicals, and the conservatives all had some ground for electoral optimism as the 1956 election approached. The Gaullists had split since the previous legislative elections, and de Gaulle dissolved the RPF in 1953. It could be expected that without de Gaulle's participation in the campaign, the Gaullists seeking office would do poorly and the large Gaullist vote of 1951 would flow back to the other non-Communist parties.

The hope was frustrated. The Gaullists did run poorly, polling only some 5 percent of the votes and losing some ninety seats. The conservatives made gains, as did the Radicals, but the latter's gains were divided between their two warring factions. The Socialists, however, barely did better than they had done in 1951, and the MRP did even less well than it had at the previous election. The Communists won the same share of the vote that they had won in 1951, but because they were seldom confronted by a victorious alliance of non-Communist parties, they gained some fifty seats. The big winners in 1956 were the Poujadists, the spokesmen for a tax revolt in the small towns and rural areas that were the chief victims of postwar French economic modernization. Marginal farmers who were hard pressed by more efficient competitors, and the small businessmen in the commercial centers for the marginal farm areas, responded to the Poujadists' extensive and sometimes spectacular campaign. The Poujadists and other extremists won some 13 percent of the vote and ended up with more than forty seats. France's governing parties had been exhausting themselves with overseas questions only to discover that the biggest transfer of votes took place as a result of the deleterious effects of economic growth upon people living off marginal sectors of the economy.

The Assembly elected in 1956 was the least governable, and the last, of the Fourth Republic. France was at war with the Algerian nationalist movement, and successive Governments failed to find an acceptable formula for making peace. Despite undeniable successes in other domains, the political leadership of the Fourth Republic lost its authority with the French citizenry. When, in the wake of an uprising in Algeria by French colonists in May 1958, the French army there seized power, there were no reserves of loyalty on which the Government in Paris could rely. The army called for Charles de Gaulle's return to power, and the Assembly acquiesced by a vote of 329 to 224—by the standards of the Fourth Republic, a rousing majority.

Legislative Elections during the Fifth Republic (1958–1973)

The Electoral System. A new constitution was drafted during the summer of 1958 and ratified at a popular referendum in September. It gave the Government temporary authority to enact the electoral law by ordinance. Under this power, the Government restored the single-member district, two-ballot system that had been used during most of the Third Republic, with, however, some modifications. Under the new system, no candidate could run at the second ballot who had not also run at the first ballot. During the Third Republic, new candidates had been able to enter the race at the second ballot.[23] Moreover, no candidate might run at the second ballot who had not received at least 5 percent of the valid votes cast at the first ballot. Prior to the election of 1967, this threshold was raised to 10 percent of the *registered voters*, and in 1976 it was raised further to 12.5 percent of the registered voters. The voting age continued to be set at twenty-one until 1974, when it was lowered to eighteen. Provisions continued to be made for voting by proxy, but mail ballots were abolished in December 1975.[24]

In July 1977, a new provision for voting by proxy was adopted whose implementation at the 1978 election provoked outraged opposition. French citizens residing outside of France were allowed to register in any town of at least 30,000 inhabitants they wanted to, and qualified voters were entitled to cast up to five proxies. Suspici-

---

[23] In 1936, more than 500 candidates ran at the second ballot who had not run at the first. See Campbell, *French Electoral Systems*, pp. 101-102.

[24] Figures for proxy voting and mail ballots were not published prior to 1951. While voting by proxy shows no particular trend and never amounted to as much as 0.5 percent of the registered voters at any legislative election between 1951 and 1973, mail ballots were more numerous and showed an almost steady increase. The figures for mail ballots, in proportions of registered voters, are as follows: 1951, 0.25 percent; 1956, 0.48 percent; 1958, 0.73 percent; 1962, 0.82 percent; 1967, 1.28 percent; 1968, 1.20 percent; 1973, 1.31 percent. Almost 400,000 persons voted by mail in 1973, and another 75,000 voted by proxy.

ously large numbers of overseas French proceeded to register in certain marginal districts. Government supporters had made efforts to concentrate the registration of overseas voters in districts where Government candidates were expected to have difficulty holding their seats. Irregularities were committed by French authorities abroad, and some requests for registration in particular towns were rejected by the courts. But some concentrations of overseas registrants were permitted to stand, and the opposition parties suspected connivance at the ministerial level to turn the newly permitted proxies to the Government's advantage by the improper use of foreign service personnel and facilities.

During the Third and Fourth Republics, complaints about improper electoral conduct were heard by the legislative assembly itself when it decided on the credentials of its members. Decisions on contested elections therefore were often politically motivated, and on at least one occasion during the Fourth Republic the Assembly decided identical cases in contrary ways. In 1956, eleven Poujadist deputies were unseated for technical violations of the electoral law. Under the Fifth Republic, the validation of electoral returns is the responsibility of the Constitutional Council, a quasi-judicial body of nine persons who are appointed for nine-year terms, three by the president of the republic and three by the presidents of each of the two legislative chambers, plus any living former president of the republic. Complaints of electoral irregularities may be made either by candidates or by voters, and the Constitutional Council has a legal staff and full power to investigate the complaints. When the Constitutional Council determines that irregularities may have been decisive in the election of a deputy, the deputy is unseated and a new election is held. Between the beginning of the Fifth Republic and 1975, the Constitutional Council investigated almost 700 complaints of electoral irregularities during regular legislative elections and invalidated the election of twenty deputies. After the elections of 1978, the Constitutional Council invalidated the election of five more deputies, one of them on the ground that the decisive votes in his favor were proxies for voters in overseas France who had not personally selected the district in which their votes were cast.[25] At the subsequent by-elections in 1978, three of the deputies whose election had been invalidated regained their seats, but two of them failed to do so, including the one who had earlier benefited from irregular proxies for voters overseas.

---

[25] *Le Monde*, July 15, 1978.

Each candidate for the National Assembly has an alternate (*remplaçant éventuel* or, more colloquially, *suppléant*) whose name appears on the ballot along with that of the candidate. If a deputy dies in office or accepts appointment to the Government (or certain other posts), he must resign his seat in the Assembly and is replaced by his alternate. A by-election is held only if a deputy resigns in other circumstances or if an alternate who has already replaced a deputy dies while serving in the Assembly, and by-elections may not be held during the last twelve months of the Assembly's maximum legal term. The average number of alternates to replace deputies during a legislative term since 1958 is larger than fifty.

The Polarization of the Party System. Between 1958 and 1967, the structure of French political conflict became increasingly polarized between Gaullist and leftist electoral coalitions. The multiparty system produced multiple candidates at the first ballot of legislative elections, but comparatively few seats were won at the first ballot. Even in 1968, when the Gaullists won a landslide victory following the upheaval of May and June, only a third of the seats for metropolitan France were decided at the first ballot, while at the elections of 1962, 1967, and 1973, an average of only 15 percent of the seats were won at the first ballot. The great majority of seats were decided at the second ballot, and second-ballot competition became increasingly a matter of straight fights between a Gaullist and a "single candidate of the left." Between 1958 and 1973, the average number of candidates per seat at the first ballot averaged more than five and never dropped below 4.7 for any election. The average number of candidates per seat at the second ballot, however, dropped from 3.1 in 1958 to 2.4 in 1962, and then to 2.2 for the elections of 1967, 1968, and 1973. In most districts, at the second ballot, France had an approximation of a two-party system.

The main reason for the reduction in the number of candidates at the second round of balloting was the growth of two large coalitions: a Gaullist bloc and a Popular Front type of alliance among Communists, Socialists, and left-wing Radicals. Between 1958 and 1968, the proportion of second-ballot contests that were straight fights between a Gaullist and a leftist increased regularly. In 1958, only 10 percent of the second-ballot contests were limited to a Gaullist and a leftist. In 1962, the proportion of such straight fights rose to 50 percent; in 1967 it was 66 percent; and in 1968 and 1973 it rose further to 73 percent. In the growth of this polarization, which gave a degree of clarity to second-ballot electoral choices that they had never had before with such regularity, the election of 1962 was the turning point. By 1967 the configuration had crystallized, and it reappeared in 1968 as well as in 1973.

The Growth of the Gaullist Bloc. Throughout the entire period from 1958 to 1978, the Gaullist party was the largest single party in the National Assembly.[26] Beginning in 1962, it became the largest single party in terms of votes as well. The Gaullists made a respectable electoral showing in 1958, when they won some 20 percent of the votes at the first ballot, but they did less well than the Gaullist party had done at the single-ballot election of 1951; they were outdistanced by the conservatives, and they barely did better than the Communist party. But the Gaullists gained impressively at the second ballot and were very efficient in converting votes into seats. The first-ballot strength displayed by the conservatives had the effect of presenting the Gaullists as centrists, and they profited greatly from this position. Leftist voters preferred them to conservatives in districts where the left-wing parties had no possibility of winning, and conservative voters preferred them to leftist candidates in districts where the conservatives could not win, with the result that the UNR won more than 40 percent of the seats for metropolitan France.

In the fall of 1962, President de Gaulle announced his intention of holding a referendum in order to amend the Constitution to provide for the direct popular election of the president.[27] Angered by what

---

[26] I say Gaullist party because the name of the Gaullist party has changed frequently. Early in the postwar period, some of de Gaulle's followers formed a Gaullist Union, but it was not endorsed by de Gaulle. The party formed by de Gaulle in 1947 was called the Rally of the French People or RPF (Rassemblement du Peuple Français). De Gaulle dissolved the RPF in 1953, but some of the general's followers tried to keep the Gaullist movement alive with a group called the Social Republicans (Républicains Sociaux). The main Gaullist party in 1958 was called the Union for the New Republic or UNR (Union pour la Nouvelle République). In 1962, the UNR absorbed a group of Gaullist leftists called the Democratic Union of Labor or UDT (Union Démocratique du Travail) and became the UNR-UDT. In 1967 the party's name was changed to Union of Democrats for the Fifth Republic or UD-Ve (Union des Démocrates pour la Ve République). The party fought the 1968 election under the label Union for the Defense of the Republic or UDR (Union pour la Défense de la République) and, later in the same year, became the Union of Democrats for the Republic, still the UDR but now standing for Union des Démocrates pour la République. The party and its allies fought the 1973 election under the label Union of Republicans for Progress or URP (Union des Républicains du Progrès), but the party did not actually change its name again until the end of 1976, when it became the Rally for the Republic or RPR (Rassemblement pour la République).

[27] See Roy Pierce, "Presidential Selection in France: The Historical Background," in Howard R. Penniman, ed., *France at the Polls* (Washington, D.C.: American Enterprise Institute, 1975), pp. 15-21.

many of them took to be an unconstitutional effort to establish a method of presidential election that lay outside the French republican tradition, a majority of the deputies voted to censure the Government that was cooperating with de Gaulle, and de Gaulle promptly dissolved the Assembly. De Gaulle's constitutional amendment passed handily at a referendum in October 1962, and new elections were held in November. At the 1962 election, the Gaullists' first-ballot electoral strength rose to some 34 percent of the votes, and the Gaullist party now won a shade less than half of the seats for metropolitan France.

The Gaullist party not only gained votes and seats in 1962, compared with 1958. It also displaced the right in doing so. While the Gaullists had appeared as a center party in 1958, they now occupied most of the right side of the political spectrum. There were two reasons for this. The first is that the Gaullists' gains in votes came mainly at the expense of the conservatives, who made their poorest electoral showing since the end of World War II. Right-wing voters deserted the conservatives and threw their support to the Gaullists. The second reason is that the second-ballot competition took on a left-right character that it had not had in 1958. The first, informal steps toward the creation of a left-wing electoral alliance, which will be discussed more fully below, appeared in 1962. Leftist parties cooperated with one another at the second ballot of the 1962 election as they had not done in 1958. Half of the second-ballot contests were straight fights between a Gaullist and a candidate from one of the leftist parties, and this inevitably gave a left-right cast to the competition in those districts.

Moreover, some of the conservative candidates at the 1962 election decided to cast their lot with the Gaullists. A number of conservatives who had supported de Gaulle's campaign to amend the Constitution were endorsed by the Gaullists, who refrained from running candidates of their own in their districts. Those conservatives, led by Valéry Giscard d'Estaing, formed a new party called the Independent Republicans. Whenever their parliamentary numbers permitted, the Independent Republicans maintained a separate parliamentary group, and their relations with the orthodox Gaullists were sometimes strained, but the two parties constituted a governing coalition that remained united on all major issues. Although the Independent Republicans were not, strictly speaking, Gaullists, they cooperated sufficiently with the orthodox Gaullists in Parliament and at election time to warrant speaking of the two parties between 1962 and 1973 as constituting a Gaullist bloc.

Indeed, at the election of 1967 the Gaullist bloc displayed an astonishing degree of tactical unity. Under the two-ballot system, electoral cooperation between parties allied on a national scale normally takes the form of mutual withdrawals in support of whichever candidate of the allied parties in each district is most likely to win the seat at the second ballot. At the first ballot, however, candidates from parties that plan to ally at the second ballot compete with one another. The first ballot becomes, for allied parties, a kind of primary election to determine which candidate the allied parties will support in each district at the second ballot. In 1967, however, the Gaullist bloc presented only one candidate in each district at the first ballot. There were, in effect, no withdrawals among the Gaullists at the second ballot because there was only one Gaullist candidate in each district in the first place. Giscard d'Estaing's Independent Republicans would have preferred primaries, in order to allow them to compete with orthodox Gaullists for the chance to represent the bloc at the second ballot. But even though the lion's share of the candidacies went to orthodox Gaullists, Independent Republican interests were protected in the allocation of candidacies, and the Gaullist bloc (which also included some prominent ex-Radicals and ex-MRP members) fielded a single candidate in every district.

The complete electoral unity achieved by the Gaullist bloc in 1967 was not repeated in 1968 or 1973, but at those elections the parties within the Gaullist bloc still maintained a rare electoral discipline. In 1968, forty-five Independent Republicans competed against orthodox Gaullists at the first ballot, but only in districts held by their common opponents.[28] At the 1973 election, the Gaullist bloc was enlarged to include certain centrists as well as orthodox Gaullists and Independent Republicans, so there were more competing interests to try to fit under the Gaullist umbrella (now referred to as "the Majority") than there had been before. The bloc eased the pressure by nominating more than one candidate in some thirty-five districts, thereby permitting official primaries. There were unofficial primaries among candidates from the Gaullist bloc (contests that had not been approved of by its leaders) only in thirty-six additional districts.[29] These departures from electoral discipline were modest indeed and occurred only at the first ballot. At the second ballot, discipline

---

[28] David Goldey, "The Election of June 1968," in Philip M. Williams, *French Politicians and Elections, 1951-1969* (Cambridge: Cambridge University Press, 1970), p. 265.

[29] D. G. Goldey and R. W. Johnson, "The French General Election of March 1973," *Political Studies*, vol. 21 (September 1973), pp. 325 and 334-335.

prevailed without exception. Between 1967 and 1973, the Gaullist bloc displayed a degree of electoral unity that the French right had never been able to achieve before.[30] During the same period, the forces on the left came close to matching the achievement of the Gaullist bloc.

The Unification of the Left. The left-wing parties did very poorly at the election of 1958, in terms of both first-ballot votes and parliamentary seats. Communists, Socialists, and Radicals together had always won a majority of the votes during the Fourth Republic, but that situation was dramatically reversed in 1958, when their total dropped to slightly more than 40 percent of the votes at the first ballot. The Socialists actually gained slightly in popular support, but the Communist party's vote dropped by a fourth in 1958, bringing it to less than 20 percent for the first time since World War II, while the Radicals' vote was cut by more than 50 percent.

The left parties' share of the seats was nowhere near proportionate even to their reduced share of the first-ballot votes. The main reason for this was that the Communist party and the non-Communist left parties did little to help one another at the second ballot in 1958. The Communists were still isolated in the political ghetto they had occupied since the middle of 1947. None of the other parties, including the leftists, wanted to be responsible for helping Communists to be elected by withdrawing in districts where that might tip the balance in their favor. Socialists tried to help Radicals, and vice versa, but there were comparatively few districts where the combined non-Communist left vote was large enough to produce electoral victory. Gaullists and conservatives therefore profited enormously at the second ballot from the divisions among their left-wing opponents.

That situation began to change at the 1962 election. There was no formal alliance between the Communists and the non-Communist left parties in 1962, but they helped one another at the second ballot in many districts. Communists withdrew in favor of Socialists, and vice versa, and both parties also withdrew to help Radicals defeat Gaullists. In some districts, the Communists even withdrew in favor of another leftist candidate who had received fewer votes at the first ballot than the Communist candidate had received, an unprecedented

---

[30] At the election of 1936, the conservative opponents of the Popular Front fielded a single candidate at the first ballot in only 40 percent of the districts. If one discounts districts where there was more than one conservative candidate but one of them won at least nine times as many votes as his nearest conservative competitor, the conservatives managed to present a united or quasi-united front in only half of the districts. Dupeux, *Le Front Populaire*, p. 125.

form of electoral generosity. This cooperation on the left, combined with the emergence at the same time of a strong and united Gaullist bloc, gave the second ballot of the 1962 election the quality of a left-right conflict that later elections were to display even more markedly.

The informal unification of the left produced gains in seats for the left-wing parties even though their combined share of the vote in 1962 was little different from what it had been four years earlier. The Communists quadrupled their representation in the Assembly (although they started from an extremely low base), the Radicals almost doubled their parliamentary representation, and the Socialists increased the number of their seats by half. Together, the leftist parties almost doubled the size of their 1958 representation in the National Assembly.

The cooperation among the left-wing parties at the legislative elections of 1962 was followed by another major step toward unification of their electoral efforts three years later when they adopted a common candidate to oppose President de Gaulle at the presidential election of 1965.[31] Communists, Socialists, most of the Radicals, and the small Unified Socialist party or PSU (Parti Socialiste Unifié) supported François Mitterrand as the sole left-wing presidential candidate. Mitterrand won only 32 percent of the vote at the first ballot of the presidential election, considerably less than the combined left-wing parties had won at the first ballot of the legislative elections of 1958 or 1962, but in a straight fight with de Gaulle at the second ballot he won some 46 percent of the votes.

Shortly before the presidential election of 1965, the Socialists and the Radicals had joined together with some other small leftist groups in an organization called the Federation of the Democratic and Socialist Left. After the election, Mitterrand became president of the Federation, and under his leadership it began preparing the way for an electoral alliance with the Communists at the next legislative elections. The electoral cooperation between Communists and non-Communist leftists at the legislative elections of 1962 had been tacit and informal, and, strictly speaking, the decision by all the leftist parties to support Mitterrand at the presidential election of 1965 had not required any negotiations at all among the left-wing parties; each of them had simply made its own separate decision to support Mitterrand. But between 1964 and 1966, popular attitudes toward the Communist party, particularly among Socialist and Radical voters, changed dramatically in a way that facilitated the formal creation of

---

[31] See Pierce, "Presidential Selection," pp. 21-29.

a new Popular Front-type alliance embracing the Communist party and the Federation of the Democratic and Socialist Left. In 1964, non-Communist leftist voters had been suspicious of and hostile to the Communist party. In 1966, large majorities of non-Communist leftist voters held a much more indulgent attitude towards the Communists. By 1966, the French Communist party enjoyed greater public acceptance than at any other time since the inception of the cold war.[32]

The Communists appear to have been as eager to exploit their new-found respectability as the non-Communist leftists were. For the election of 1967, the Communists, the Federation, and the small PSU agreed on a formal, national basis to withdraw at the second ballot in favor of the leftist candidate best placed to win the seat wherever there was a chance for a leftist to win. Moreover, just as the orthodox Gaullists and the Independent Republicans shared candidacies at the first ballot, in order not to compete with each other, the parties of the Federation also presented only one candidate in each district that they contested, so that Socialists and Radicals did not compete with each other. The first-ballot unity of the Federation was designed to prevent the Communists from outdistancing the non-Communist left at the first ballot because of a division of the non-Communist left vote, while the Communist-Federation alliance at the second ballot was designed to enhance the chances of whichever left-wing candidate was best placed to win the seat.

With the cooperation of the Socialists and Radicals within the Federation, the alliance between the Federation, the Communists, and the PSU, and the emphasis on concerted support at the second ballot for "the single candidate of the left," the elements of what was to be the basic strategy of the left-wing parties at the elections of 1967, 1968, and 1973 were in place.

The formula worked very well for the left-wing parties in 1967. Although they won fewer votes proportionately at the first ballot than they had in 1962, their efficiency at the second ballot produced a gain of more than forty seats for them. The Communists were the main beneficiaries—their parliamentary representation increased by three-fourths—but the non-Communist leftist parties gained as well. The Gaullist bloc, on the other hand, saw the size of its Assembly contingent reduced by some 10 percent, even though it made a marginal gain in votes at the first ballot. Orthodox Gaullists and Independent Republicans together did not win a majority of the seats from metropolitan France, although their domination of the seats from over-

---

[32] See Alain Duhamel, "L'Image du Parti Communiste" [The Communist Party's image], *Sondages*, no. 1 (1966), pp. 57-71.

seas districts gave them a nominal majority of the Assembly provided they could maintain complete parliamentary discipline among their troops. In fact, they were having great difficulty in doing so when the life of the legislature elected in 1967 was cut short as a result of the explosion of mass discontent that was triggered by student riots in May 1968. For much of May, France was racked with mass demonstrations and paralyzed by a near-general strike. President de Gaulle dissolved the National Assembly at the end of the month, and elections were held in June.

The left-wing parties followed the same electoral strategy in 1968 that they had employed in 1967, but this time they suffered badly. The rioting and demonstrations during May had frightened many voters, and the electorate shifted markedly to the right.[33] The left-wing parties lost votes in 1968, the Gaullist bloc gained even more, and the outcome was a landslide for the right-wing parties. The orthodox Gaullists won almost 40 percent of the votes at the first ballot and a majority of the seats in the Assembly, the first time in the history of French democratic elections that a single party had done so. The Independent Republicans won another 6 percent of the votes, and together the two branches of the Gaullist bloc held almost three-fourths of the seats for metropolitan France. The left-wing parties, on the other hand, lost half of their seats and were reduced to an ineffectual parliamentary opposition for the next four years.

For several of those years, there was an interruption in the pattern of electoral cooperation among the left-wing parties. In part this was due to mutual recriminations between the Communist party and the parties of the Federation over their tactics during the May upheaval. More important, the invasion of Czechoslovakia by Soviet and other East European troops in August 1968 convinced many non-Communist leftists that it would be damaging to them to remain aligned with the Communist party, even though it had expressed its disapproval of the Czechoslovakian invasion, thereby criticizing a Soviet foreign policy move for the first time in its history. The Socialists and Radicals abolished the Federation, and the leftist parties approached the 1969 presidential election in total disarray, while the Gaullist bloc remained united in support of Georges Pompidou. The Communists, the Socialists, and the PSU each presented a

---

[33] The strong association between demonstrations and rightward shifts in political orientation is shown in Philip E. Converse and Roy Pierce, "Basic Cleavages in French Politics and the Disorders of May and June, 1968," a paper prepared for presentation at the Seventh World Congress of Sociology held at Varna, Bulgaria, September 1970.

candidate, and the Socialist candidate did not even have the complete support of his own party. None of the left-wing candidates survived to the second ballot, which Pompidou won comfortably against a little-known centrist, Alain Poher.

The 1969 presidential election left the Socialist party in a shambles, and it was taken over by François Mitterrand and his supporters, who proceeded to point it leftward once again. Throughout the entire period between 1962 and 1968, the Communists had cooperated with the non-Communist left without posing any special conditions. After the 1968 election, however, the Communist party insisted that before there could be a renewal of the Popular Front-type electoral alliance of 1967 and 1968, the left-wing parties should adopt a common governmental program. The Communist party has always suspected the motives of the non-Communist left parties with which it has allied. Its fear is that those parties will profit from the support of Communist voters at the second ballot to win parliamentary seats, only to ally themselves with other non-Communist parties against the Communists in Parliament after the elections. The more firmly the Communists can commit the non-Communist left to a program that the remaining parties would find unacceptable, the less likely this kind of desertion becomes. Moreover, the Socialists themselves, newly organized under Mitterrand's leadership, were not reluctant to make such a commitment, and a Common Program for a Government of the left was agreed upon by the Communists and the Socialists in June 1972, and later ratified also by the leftist Radicals who constituted the Movement of Leftist Radicals or MRG (Mouvement des Radicaux de Gauche). The Common Program called for extensive nationalization of industry and financial institutions, enlarged social security measures, changes in the tax system, a curtailment of presidential powers and reduction of the president's term of office, renunciation of the nuclear striking force, and the pursuit of a foreign policy independent of military blocs. The Common Program was more circumspect about the future of European institutions, on which Communists and Socialists differed widely. Only two months before it was signed, the Socialists and the Communists had taken different positions at the referendum called by President Pompidou to ratify the admission of Great Britain, Ireland, and Denmark to the Common Market, the Communists recommending a "no" vote and the Socialists recommending abstention.

The left-right configuration at the elections of 1973 was virtually the same as it had been in 1967 and 1968. The Gaullist bloc ran under the label Union of Republicans for Progress or URP (Union des

Républicains du Progrès) and was referred to colloquially as "the Majority," as this time it included not only orthodox Gaullists and Giscard d'Estaing's Independent Republicans but also centrists and a number of independents whom the bloc endorsed. As we have noted, first-ballot discipline was not as complete among the Majority in 1973 as it had been in 1968 or 1967, but this was almost inevitable under the circumstances. The size of the Majority in the Assembly had been inflated by the exceptional swing to the right in 1968, and the temptation to compete for Gaullist seats that were perceived to be vulnerable was very strong. In the circumstances, the degree of coordination that the Majority managed to achieve was remarkable; it ran a single candidate at the first ballot in more than 90 percent of the metropolitan districts.

The leftist parties, too, were as united as they had been in 1967. The Federation no longer existed, but Socialists and left-wing Radicals shared constituencies just as they had done in 1967 and 1968 and ran under the common label of Union of the Socialist and Democratic Left or UGSD (Union de la Gauche Socialiste et Démocratique). The UGSD was allied with the Communist party and the PSU at the second ballot, although this time the Communists made no "gifts" to the non-Communist left in the form of second-ballot candidacies in districts where the Communists had placed first at the first ballot. (In 1967 they had made more than a dozen such gifts, in 1968 three.)

The outcome of the 1973 election was mildly ironical. The leftists gained in votes at the first ballot by comparison with the election of 1967; indeed, for the first time since the left-wing alliance was formed, the non-Communist left ran neck and neck with the Communist party. The Majority, however, gained seats relative to 1967. The Majority's relative success in terms of seats did not, therefore, come about because of any weakness in the electoral showing of its leftist opponents. It occurred mainly because in 1973 the Majority bloc, which had included only orthodox Gaullists and Independent Republicans in 1967 and 1968, now was enlarged to include certain centrists as well.

The Vicissitudes of the Center. The polarization of electoral competition never became complete between 1958 and 1973 because there always were centrist groups that resisted absorption into either of the two main contending blocs. The centrists include Christian Democrats descended from the MRP, anti-Gaullist conservatives, Radicals who rejected the leftward orientation of the Federation and of the Movement of Leftist Radicals, and various other middle-of-the-roaders without any fixed major-party affiliation.

Early in the development of the two main blocs, the centrists were largely opposed to the governing Gaullist bloc, even though their voters generally preferred Gaullists to leftists when forced to choose between them at the second ballot. In 1965, the centrists supported Jean Lecanuet at the first ballot of the presidential election, and Lecanuet won more than 15 percent of the votes, depriving de Gaulle of a first-ballot victory. At the 1967 legislative elections they were grouped in an organization called the Democratic Center, which won less than 15 percent of the votes. At the 1968 election, the centrists, now running under the label Center for Progress and Modern Democracy or PDM (Progrès et Démocratie Moderne), won an even smaller percentage.

At the 1969 presidential election, the centrists split; one group supported Alain Poher, the other Georges Pompidou. Poher's supporters retained their affiliation with the Democratic Center (which had continued to exist even though the centrists used a different label in 1968), while Pompidou's supporters formed a new organization called the Center for Democracy and Progress or CDP (Centre Démocratie et Progrès). Deputies from the Democratic Center and the CDP belonged to a common parliamentary group in the Assembly, but the Democratic Center deputies tended to oppose the governing Gaullist bloc while those from the CDP supported it.

At the 1973 election, the CDP joined the Majority, for which it won almost thirty seats. The Democratic Center, however, joined with moderate Radicals who had refused to join the Movement of Leftist Radicals to form what was called the Reformist Movement (Mouvement Réformateur). The Reformists won a larger proportion of the first-ballot votes in 1973 than the PDM had in 1968, but only about the same number of seats. Moreover, most of those seats were won because the Reformists mutually cooperated with the Majority at the second ballot. In 1967, the centrists were a small but autonomous electoral force that represented a real middle ground between the two large electoral blocs to their right and to their left. By 1973, one element of the centrists had been directly incorporated into the Majority while the other survived only because of the Majority's cooperation with it.

Problems of Cohesion within the Major Blocs. Electoral conflict between 1962 and 1973 was characterized by the confrontation of two large electoral blocs separated by a small centrist group that eventually became virtually incorporated into one of the two larger ones. The two main blocs, however, were not wholly symmetrical.

The Gaullist or Majority bloc always governed after 1962, while the left-wing bloc was in the opposition. The parties of the Gaullist bloc demonstrated that they could govern together. The leftist coalition was an unknown quantity in that regard, although it tried to allay doubts about its solidarity by adopting a common governmental program in 1972.

The main difference between the two blocs, however, lay in the solidarity of their electorates. The electorate of the Gaullist bloc was more politically homogeneous than that of the leftist bloc. The parties that made up the bloc never competed against one another in 1967, seldom did so in 1968 (and only at the first ballot), and still showed impressive restraint in 1973. The Majority bloc, despite its inevitable inner tensions, was for electoral purposes virtually a single party.

The left-wing bloc was not. Socialists and Radicals avoided competing with one other, but those two groups together—first within the Federation and later within the Union of the Socialist and Democratic Left—competed regularly with the Communist party. It was only at the second ballot, when Communists and non-Communist leftists mutually withdrew in favor of the best placed leftist candidate, that the leftist electoral alliance came into play. This made the pattern of vote transfers by leftist voters from the first to the second ballot of crucial importance to the success of the left-wing alliance.

Second-ballot vote transfers. Second-ballot vote transfers were of importance to the Gaullist bloc as well as to the left-wing bloc. But the Majority bloc was primarily concerned with gaining second-ballot votes from first-ballot centrist voters. Because it ran more than one candidate in so few districts, the Majority was not faced with the problem of recouping at the second ballot, with a single candidate, votes that at the first ballot had been cast for more than one candidate from the Majority.

The left-wing bloc sought second-ballot votes from first-ballot centrists also. But its primary aim was to amass in each district, at the second ballot, as many votes as the leftist parties had won together at the first ballot. More often than not, they could not achieve that objective, mainly because of the anticommunism of a significant proportion of the first-ballot voters for the non-Communist left.

The overwhelming majority of first-ballot Communist voters switch to the non-Communist leftist candidate at the second ballot when they can no longer vote for a Communist, but a substantial proportion of non-Communist leftist voters do not vote for a Communist at the second ballot. Detailed analysis of a postelection survey conducted by SOFRES in 1967 indicates that not more than about 60 percent of non-Communist left voters at the first ballot voted for the Communist candidate in districts where the second-ballot competition was a straight fight between a Communist and a candidate from the Gaullist bloc.[34]

Directly comparable data are not available for the 1973 election, but there is evidence to suggest that the proportion of non-Communist left voters who voted for Communist candidates in similar forced-choice situations was no larger in 1973 than it had been in 1967.[35] There is a large minority of non-Communist leftist voters who dislike the Communist party and who, when faced with a forced choice between a Communist and another candidate at the second ballot, either vote for the other candidate, take refuge in abstention, or express their discontent with the constraints on their choice by deliberately spoiling their ballots. This is almost surely a latter-day expression of the same phenomenon that Georges Dupeux detected by other means in connection with the differential fall-off of votes at the second ballot for the parties of the Popular Front alliance in 1936, to which we have already referred.

Conflict within the majority. Until now, we have limited our discussion to legislative elections, but it would be misleading if we did not also refer, if only briefly, to the presidential election of 1974.[36] If we limit ourselves to the legislative elections between 1962 and 1973, we must emphasize—as we have—the impressive electoral discipline displayed by the parties of the Gaullist or Majority bloc. The presidential election of 1974, however, strained that bloc as

---

[34] The survey was conducted for Philip E. Converse and the present author in connection with a study of political representation in France that is currently in preparation.

[35] There are no data from a postelection survey that would enable us to estimate the vote transfers from one ballot to the other in 1973. However, IFOP polls taken between the two ballots in 1967 and 1973 show that, in both years, virtually the same proportion of non-Communist left voters indicated their intention to vote for the Communist candidate in straight fights between Communists and Gaullists at the second ballot. Surveys conducted between the ballots register only vote intentions and are less reliable as estimates of the actual vote than postelectoral surveys, but there is no reason why the results of a postelectoral survey in 1973 would have differed any more from the results of the preelectoral survey in 1973, with regard to vote transfers, than those of our own postelectoral survey of 1967 differed from the results of IFOP's preelectoral survey in the same year. For IFOP's estimates, see *Sondages,* no. 3 (1967), p. 98, and no. 1 (1973), p. 13.

[36] For a full account, see Penniman, ed., *France at the Polls, 1974.*

nothing had before. Valéry Giscard d'Estaing, the leader of the Independent Republicans, competed successfully at the first ballot with orthodox Gaullist Jacques Chaban-Delmas, and then went on to win the presidency at the second ballot by the narrowest of margins. The split in the Majority that was expressed by its inability to field a common presidential candidate was not a simple conflict between Independent Republicans and orthodox Gaullists; the latter were themselves divided between the two candidates. But for the first time in the history of the Fifth Republic the president was not a pure Gaullist, and that fact alone carried risks of further division between the supporters of the president and the orthodox Gaullists, who could be expected to work toward regaining the high office which they regarded as rightly belonging to one of their own. And if the rivalry between the president's followers and the orthodox Gaullists were to spill over into the domain of legislative elections, the situation of the Majority would more closely resemble that of the left: divided at the first ballot, it would depend for success on favorable second-ballot vote transfers from the first-ballot supporters of competing Giscardians and Gaullists.

2
The French Electorate in March 1978

Jérôme Jaffré

On the eve of the parliamentary elections of 1978, the left seemed ready to win a majority of the seats in the National Assembly for the first time in twenty years. For three years local elections, by-elections, and opinion polls on voting intentions all had confirmed this prospect. To many observers the question was not whether the left could win but how the Fifth Republic could function with a conservative president and a leftist majority in the National Assembly. The election results surprised everyone: the left did not obtain an absolute majority in the first round, nor did the second ballot give it a majority of seats in the Assembly.

The Left's Trump Cards on the Eve of the Elections

Leftist Trends in the Electorate. Since the Second World War the economic modernization of France has been accompanied by a profound social transformation, which at present seems to be benefiting the left. One source of change has been demographic: some of the more conservative sectors of the population have conspicuously decreased in numbers, while strata whose orientation is more favorable to the left have increased.

A comparison of the makeup of the active population in the 1954 census with that of 1975 shows a striking decrease in the number of farmers and agricultural workers (see Table 2–1). In 1954 farmers and agricultural workers represented a little more than a quarter of the active population, whereas in 1975 they had fallen to one-tenth. This category strongly supports the right, so much so that in the

This chapter was translated from the French by Allen J. Grieco and Sara F. Matthews.

TABLE 2–1

OCCUPATIONAL BREAKDOWN OF THE FRENCH ELECTORATE, 1954 AND 1975

(in percentages; change in percentage points)

Occupation	1954	1975	Change, 1954–1975
Farmers	21.3	8.2	−13.1
Agricultural workers	5.1	1.6	− 3.5
Shopkeepers and craftsmen	13.3	8.2	− 5.1
Professionals, executives, businessmen	3.2	7.2	+ 4.0
Middle management and technicians	6.7	13.5	+ 6.8
White-collar workers	11.1	18.6	+ 7.5
Blue-collar workers	31.8	34.6	+ 2.8
Service workers	4.6	5.6	+ 1.0
Other	2.9	2.5	− 0.4
Total	100.0	100.0	

SOURCE: Adapted from Michel Levy, "Le corps électoral" [The electorate], in *Population et sociétés* (February 1978).

presidential election on May 19, 1974, 72 percent voted for Valéry Giscard d'Estaing.[1] The decline in the number of farmers and agricultural workers in France has been accompanied by a decline in the rural population overall (see Table 2–2). At present, 27 percent of the French live in towns with fewer than 2,000 inhabitants as compared with 41 percent in 1954. A majority of today's population, 56 percent, lives in towns of over 20,000. It is known that rural voters tend to support the right more than those living in big cities; in 1974, 54 percent of the rural population voted for the conservative candidate as compared with 50.6 percent of the entire population.

In addition there has been a rather conspicuous decrease in religious identification. In the opinion polls of ten years ago 90 percent of all adults identified themselves as Catholics. In 1974 this percentage had fallen to 84 percent, and in 1978 it was only 80 percent, a drop of 3 million people in ten years. Furthermore, mass attendance has fallen to 16 percent of the population—from 25 percent at the end of the 1960s. It is well known that religious identification correlates closely with electoral behavior. Regularly practicing Catholics overwhelmingly vote for the right (77 percent for Giscard d'Estaing

[1] The references to the presidential election of 1974 are taken from Alain Lancelot, "Opinion Polls and the Presidential Election, May 1974," in Howard R. Penniman, ed., *France at the Polls* (Washington, D.C.: American Enterprise Institute, 1975), pp. 175-206.

TABLE 2–2

URBAN CONCENTRATION OF THE FRENCH POPULATION, 1954–1975

(in percentages)

Residential Setting	1954	1962	1968	1975
Rural	41.4	36.6	30.0	27.1
Urban	58.6	63.4	70.0	72.9
Total	100.0	100.0	100.0	100.0

NOTE: Towns with fewer than 2,000 inhabitants are classified as rural, those with more than 2,000 inhabitants as urban.

SOURCE: Institut National de la Statistique et des Etudes Economiques (INSEE), *Données sociales*, 1978, p. 7.

in 1974) while nonpracticing Catholics and people who have no religious affiliation overwhelmingly vote for the left (respectively 74 percent and 86 percent for Mitterrand).

While the social and ideological groups sympathetic to the right have been declining, other segments of the population traditionally more sympathetic to the left have been gaining in strength. The ratio of salaried workers to the self-employed has increased considerably. In 1954, salaried workers represented 64 percent of the active population whereas in 1978 they represented 83 percent. Politically this category is quite clearly oriented towards the left: 61 percent voted for the left candidate in 1974. Part of the increase in the number of salaried workers can be explained by the transformation of the female work force. In 1954, 25 percent of working women were employed in the agricultural sector and 23 percent in the middle management or white-collar-worker category. By 1975 these figures had become 7 percent and 46 percent respectively. This phenomenon is related to the profound changes in female voting habits, which had generally been thought to be conservative. In 1974, 25 percent of the women working in the agricultural sector voted for the left and 51 percent in the middle management and white-collar category did so.

If we look at the electorate as a whole, the average age is decreasing. In 1976, 36 percent of the voters were under thirty-five years old as compared with 28 percent in 1962. There are two reasons for this phenomenon, one demographic and the other juridical. In the first place the increasing youth of the electoral body is due to the coming of age of the "baby boom" generation born after the Second World War. In the second place in 1974 the legal voting age was lowered from twenty-one to eighteen immediately after Giscard d'Estaing's election. This measure increased the potential electorate by 2.5 million voters overnight. It is true that not all of these potential voters registered and that the young often abstain; nevertheless, their enfranchisement favored the left. One opinion poll taken in 1974 showed that 59 percent of the eighteen to twenty year old group would have voted for François Mitterrand if they had been eligible in the presidential election, eliminating most of Giscard d'Estaing's winning margin.

To the sociological changes undergone by the French electorate must be added the consequences of the end of the Gaullist era. According to Jean Charlot one of the characteristics of electoral behavior under de Gaulle was that a large part of the lower classes (and in particular the industrial working class) supported the right, in the tradition of the plebiscitarian and Bonapartist working class of the nineteenth century.[2] Once General de Gaulle left the scene, political life resumed its traditional divisions. As the following figures show, the percentage of the working-class vote that went to leftist candidates rose significantly between the legislative elections of 1967 and 1973:[3]

Working-Class Vote	1967	1973
Left	54	68
Gaullist	35	21
Other center and right	11	11
Total	100	100

Local and By-Election Victories, 1974–1977. The parliamentary elections of March 1978 were the first general elections since the presidential poll of 1974. Nevertheless, in the four years between these two elections, some local and by-elections provided measures of public opinion, and they signaled an advance for the left. In 1974 six legislative by-elections were held, followed by seven more in November 1976 which, for the most part, were organized to permit ex-ministers to be reelected as deputies once they had left the Government. On the other hand, cantonal elections were held in March 1976 to elect half of the department councillors, while municipal elections, for local councillors and mayors, were held in March·1977.

Shortly before the 1974 presidential election a new political alignment crystallized when the Reformist Movement of Jean Lecanuet and Jean-Jacques Servan-Schreiber rallied to the Majority, making

[2] See Jean Charlot, *Le phénomène gaulliste* [The Gaullist phenomenon] (Paris: Fayard, 1970), p. 208.

[3] SOFRES opinion polls for *Le Nouvel Observateur*.

the opposition synonymous with the left. The polarization of political life became total: on the one side was the Majority, including the Gaullists, Giscard d'Estaing's followers, the centrists, and the Radicals, while on the other side there was the Union of the Left including the Socialist party, the Communist party, and the Leftist Radicals (the MRG). Thus any moderate voter who was not content with governmental policy had to choose between voting for the Socialist party, the Communists' ally, and overcoming his objections to the Majority. It was in this context that the left won all of the elections held between 1974 and 1977.

In the six parliamentary by-elections held three months after the presidential elections the left managed to advance by 8.3 percentage points over its showing in 1973. Within the left, it was the Socialist party that scored the greatest success; indeed, the Communist party actually lost ground. Eighteen months later, during the cantonal elections, the leftist parties obtained an absolute majority, 52.5 percent of the votes cast during the first ballot, of which 29 percent were cast for the Socialist party and the MRG. As a result the left won the presidency of forty-one department councils (as compared with the twenty-seven it had held before the elections) out of a total of ninety-five in metropolitan France.

One year later the municipal elections confirmed the trend: opposition candidates obtained 50.8 percent of the votes in towns with over 30,000 inhabitants, outdistancing their conservative opponents by more than five percentage points. After the municipal elections the left controlled 155 of the 221 towns of this size, as opposed to 98 before. Union of the Left lists headed by Communists won in large cities like Reims and Saint-Etienne, giving them Communist mayors, while lists headed by Socialists won in the Catholic and conservative towns of the West such as La-Roche-sur-Yon and Angers. In Paris the Majority, though divided between the RPR list (led by Jacques Chirac) and the Giscardian list, managed to defeat the left on the second ballot.

The seven parliamentary by-elections held three months earlier had already confirmed the advance of the left, though the Communist party had lost votes to the Socialists. This fact certainly worried the Communist leaders, who knew that the parliamentary elections of 1978, quite unlike the municipal elections, would pit the two parties of the left against each other on the first ballot.

The Opinion Polls. In the last few years studies carried out by opinion polling institutes have confirmed the majority position of the

FIGURE 2–1
POPULARITY OF THE POLITICAL PARTIES, FEBRUARY 1977

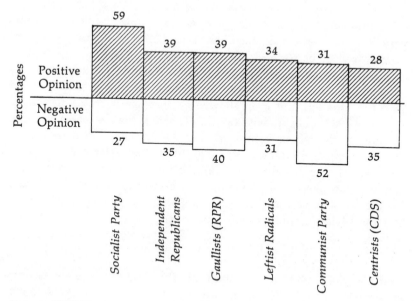

SOURCE: SOFRES opinion polls for *Le Figaro*.

left and the high esteem in which it is held by the public.[4] This may be seen in the results given by three indicators at the beginning of 1977, just before the municipal elections, namely the popularity of the Socialist party, the lack of confidence in the president of the republic, and voting intentions for the parliamentary elections. In February 1977, 59 percent of the French had a good opinion of the Socialist party whereas only 27 percent had a bad opinion of it (see Figure 2–1). The Socialists outdistanced their closest competitors, Giscard's Independent Republicans and the RPR (which had just replaced the UDR), by twenty points. On the other hand the Communist party was held in very low esteem, a fact that proves (if such proof be necessary) the extent of the French electorate's anti-Communist feelings.

According to the regular IFOP opinion polls carried out for *France-Soir*, 45 percent of the French electorate were satisfied with Giscard d'Estaing's work as president, not much more than the 38

[4] For a description of the French opinion poll institutes see Alain Lancelot, in Penniman, ed., *France at the Polls*, pp. 176-177.

percent who were dissatisfied. It is true that his position had improved since the RPR was created, when only 39 percent of the electorate had been happy with him. However, if his popularity is compared with that of Presidents de Gaulle and Pompidou after the same amount of time in office (two years and nine months) it appears very low: 65 percent of the French had approved and 25 percent disapproved of both de Gaulle and Pompidou.

A succession of surveys on voting intentions taken after the presidential elections confirmed that more than half of the voters supported the left and even showed an increase in its lead between 1974 and 1977: in February 1977, 53 percent of the electorate intended to vote for the left as compared with 51 percent immediately after the presidential elections (see Table 2–3). Just after the municipal elections but before the beginning of the long campaign for the parliamentary elections, public opinion massively predicted a victory for the left (53 percent); only a fifth of those interviewed thought that the Majority could win (20 percent).

Public Opinion during the Campaign

First Signs of a Shift toward the Majority. The first signs of a drop in the left's popularity, along with an increase in the president's, appeared in the spring and summer of 1977, just before the breakdown of the Common Program negotiations on September 22. According to opinion surveys the Socialist party and the Communist party reached their greatest popularity in April, just after the municipal elections. Five months later their rating had conspicuously worsened (see Figure 2–2): the difference between favorable opinions and unfavorable ones dropped from +39 to +33 percentage points

TABLE 2–3

VOTING INTENTIONS, JUNE 1974–FEBRUARY 1977

(in percentages)

Party	June 1974	January 1976	February 1977
Communist party	21	20	20
Extreme-left	3	3	3
Socialist party and Leftist Radicals	27	30	30
Majority	49	47	47
Total	100	100	100

SOURCE: SOFRES opinion polls for *Le Nouvel Observateur* and *Le Figaro*.

FIGURE 2–2
POPULARITY OF THE SOCIALIST AND COMMUNIST PARTIES, FEBRUARY 1977–MARCH 1978
Difference between Favorable and Unfavorable Ratings
(in percentage points)

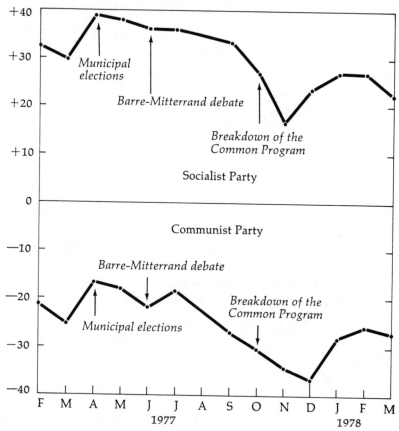

SOURCE: SOFRES opinion polls for *Le Figaro*.

in the case of the Socialist party, whereas the Communist party (whose popularity has always been negative) slipped from −17 to −26 points.

Conversely, Giscard's popularity began to climb in June. The proportion of the electorate who were satisfied with his handling of the nation's problems (49 percent) was greater than the proportion who were not satisfied (40 percent) for the first time since the municipal elections (see Figure 2–3). The Majority acted as if it had for-

45

FIGURE 2–3
POPULARITY OF VALÉRY GISCARD D'ESTAING,
FEBRUARY 1977–FEBRUARY 1978

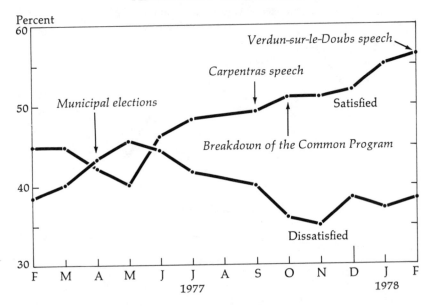

SOURCE: IFOP opinion polls for *France-Soir*.

gotten Giscard and Chirac's "battle for Paris." The signing of a "Majority pact" on July 19, 1977, united all of the conservative parties, committing them to some vague goals but also to a specific policy concerning the withdrawal of candidates before the second ballot. This show of unity corresponded to the desires of moderate voters, regardless of partisan affiliation (see Table 2–4). It was just before the breakdown of the Common Program, then, that the forecasts changed. At the end of the summer, 32 percent of the electorate still believed in a victory of the left while 36 percent thought a victory of the Majority likely.

Dissension within the Left. The breakdown of the Common Program on September 22, 1977, and the five months of incessant disputes that followed changed the relationship between the Socialist and Communist electorates. The Socialists' suspicion of the Communists increased, dealing a heavy blow to the Communists' desire for unity.

Unlike the supporters of the PCF, the Socialist electorate had never been totally convinced of the desirability of a united left.

TABLE 2–4

VOTERS' OPINIONS ON RELATIONS BETWEEN THE MAJORITY PARTIES,
JULY 1977

(in percentages)

Respondent's Party	Majority parties should be:		
	More united	More independent	No opinion
Centrists and Radicals	68	23	9
Republican party	70	18	12
RPR	77	14	9

NOTE: The survey question was: "Do you think that the different parties making up the Majority should be more closely united or should each maintain its independence?"

SOURCE: SOFRES survey carried out between June 30 and July 5, 1977. Unpublished.

Immediately after the presidential election of 1974, in which the Communist party had supported Mitterrand's candidacy on the first ballot, the popularity of the Communist party with the Socialist electorate had reached a record 64 percent and the popularity of the Socialist party with the Communist electorate a high of 92 percent. Normally barely half of the Socialist electorate had a positive opinion of the Communists and two-fifths had a negative opinion, but during the rift of late 1977 the proportions were the other way around (see Table 2–5).

TABLE 2–5

SOCIALIST VOTERS' OPINIONS OF THE COMMUNIST PARTY,
APRIL–DECEMBER 1977

(in percentages)

Opinion of the Communist Party	April	May	June	July	Sept.	Oct.	Nov.	Dec.
Favorable	53	54	43	47	44	34	34	31
Unfavorable	33	37	43	40	45	57	54	57
No opinion	14	9	14	13	11	9	12	12
Total	100	100	100	100	100	100	100	100

SOURCE: SOFRES opinion polls for Le Figaro.

TABLE 2–6

Communist Voters' Opinions of the Socialist Party,
April–December 1977
(in percentages)

Opinion of the Socialist Party	April	May	June	July	Sept.	Oct.	Nov.	Dec.
Favorable	84	81	78	82	77	67	62	65
Unfavorable	13	14	11	13	20	24	30	28
No opinion	3	5	11	5	3	9	8	7
Total	100	100	100	100	100	100	100	100

Source: SOFRES opinion polls for Le Figaro.

Within the Communist electorate, commitment to the Union of the Left, which had been very high, fell off. At the end of 1977, 65 percent of the Communist electorate still had a good opinion of the Socialist party, as compared with 84 percent just after the municipal elections (see Table 2–6).

It is surprising to note that as much as two-thirds of the Communist electorate retained its good opinion of the Socialist party despite the repeated attacks on the Socialists launched by the secretary general of the PCF, George Marchais. At the same time, a majority of the Communists approved of Marchais's actions: 66 percent felt that the Socialist party had "swerved to the right," whereas 55 percent believed that the Socialist party was "not sincerely attached to the unity of the left" (28 percent held the opposite view). The Communist electorate continued to express a favorable attitude towards the Socialists, which was the result of a wish for reconciliation and unity. In fact, in mid-February 1978, 81 percent of the Communist electorate wanted their party to come to an agreement with the Socialist party concerning withdrawals of first-ballot candidates—even as the Communist daily, L'Humanité, threatened to deny Communist votes to the Socialist candidates who had done best among the left's candidates on the first ballot.

In November, 54 percent of a survey sample forecast the victory of the Majority and only 18 percent the opposite. The disunity of the left had further damaged its popularity (see Figure 2–2). In the case of the Socialist party, the margin of favorable opinions over unfavorable ones was +16 percentage points in November as compared with +33 in September, whereas the Communist party had dropped to −34 as compared with −26 in September. Despite the difficulties

TABLE 2–7
VOTERS' OPINIONS ON RELATIONS WITHIN THE TWO PARTY BLOCS,
FEBRUARY 1978
(in percentages)

Respondent's Party	Relations between the parties of the left are improving	Relations between the Majority parties are improving
Majority	10	66
Left	25	30
Total Electorate	17	42

NOTE: The survey question was: "In your estimation, are relations between the parties constituting the left/the Majority tending to improve or to worsen at present?"

SOURCE: SOFRES survey carried out February 14-17, 1978, for Le Nouvel Observateur.

plaguing the Majority after the RPR's refusal to accept Raymond Barre as the head of its electoral campaign and its displeasure at the creation of the UDF, the left appeared to be by far the less united of the two coalitions.

The unity of the Majority and the division of the left were reflected in Giscard d'Estaing's increasing popularity (see Figure 2–3). Every month his popularity increased slightly: in September, 49 percent of respondents were satisfied with his work; by March the figure had increased to 56 percent, and the president was supported not only by all the parties of the Majority but also by part of the left, in particular the Socialists.

Four Parties, Three Electorates. The disagreements on the left were all the more dangerous in that, within the electorate, the alliance of Communists and Socialists was more fragile than the alliance of the Majority parties. In fact, there were clearly two leftist electorates, compared with only one for the Majority (despite Jacques Chirac's attempts to establish a differentiation).

The fundamental cleavage in the French electorate, of course, is between the left (the PCF and the PS) and the right (the RPR, the PR, the centrists, and the Radicals) as may be seen in Table 2–8. Any consensus between them—on the "European issue," for example—is quite the exception. Within the Majority the partisans of the RPR are less often in favor of change or of social and economic

TABLE 2–8

POLITICAL ATTITUDES OF THE FRENCH ELECTORATE, BY PARTY PREFERENCE
(in percentages)

	Party Preference				
Item	Communist party	Socialist party	Centrists, Radicals	Republican party	RPR
U.S. foreign policy is basically right.	37	48	73	58	61
France should continue to work toward a united Europe.	69	69	68	73	68
France should have a nuclear deterrent force.	37	42	49	59	72
Banks should be nationalized.	78	64	34	26	20
Raising the minimum wage to 2,400 francs a month would be one of the best ways of promoting equality.	54	42	22	27	24
Trade union decisions stem from political preoccupations.	32	51	65	72	80
Security is more important than change.	19	38	78	85	89
Morals in France are too liberal.	38	41	52	54	53

SOURCE: Louis Harris France and SOFRES surveys, September 1977 to February 1978 for different newspapers.

reform than their partners.[5] Nevertheless, the dominant impression is that, whether the subject be the liberalization of social customs or the foreign policy of the United States, there is a very strong convergence of ideas within the Majority's electorate. Jean Lecanuet's and Jean-Jacques Servan-Schreiber's supporters are those least ready to accept the ideological positions and strategy choices of the Majority; certainly they are less so than Jacques Chirac's supporters. Thus one

[5] Jérôme Jaffré and Roland Cayrol,"Les électeurs de la Majorité: unité et clivages" [The Majority electorate: united and divided], Le Monde, March 11, 1978.

can appreciate why the UDF was created: it consolidated the weakest link in the chain of Majority parties by regrouping the centrist conglomerate and stabilizing a segment of the electorate that had been drifting towards the Socialist party for the past three years.

On the left there are clear differences in outlook between the Communists and the Socialists, the only consensus being on issues connected to the liberalization of social mores. The Socialists are less committed to social and economic reform, more concerned with security even at the risk of giving up some of their freedom, and more strongly inclined to support the Atlantic alliance. The Socialist electorate is the least homogeneous of all. Questioned a month before the elections as to possible government formulas, Socialist voters were found to be of three minds: some preferred a Government combining Socialists and Communists (38 percent); some a homogeneous Socialist Government (26 percent); and, finally, some an alliance of the Socialist party with the Majority (27 percent).

The Trend toward the Socialist Party. The Socialist electorate had probably never been so divided, but at the same time public opinion had never been so strongly in its favor. Despite the disunity of the left, the Socialist party continued to benefit from the public's persistent discontent with Government policy as well as from its wish for reform.

Two-thirds of the French were dissatisfied with the Government's action against inflation and unemployment. Moreover, the prime minister was less popular than the president—in one year the percentage who approved of Giscard d'Estaing's work increased by sixteen points while Raymond Barre's popularity improved by only five points. In February 1978 those who were dissatisfied were still more numerous than those who were satisfied: 46 percent as opposed to 44 percent. Furthermore, the public's disgruntlement was accompanied by criticism of the Majority's conservative policies. Questioned in May 1977, 59 percent of a survey sample expressed the hope that the Government would push through more reforms in the coming year than it had in the past three years. This included a majority of the respondents in all sociodemographic and political categories including the agricultural sector and the partisans of the Majority. Most people said they favored the nationalization of large companies and either a tax on personal fortunes or a reduction in salary differentials.

The trend in favor of the Socialist party seemed to represent the wish for peaceful, orderly change that characterized public opinion in general. Just after the breakdown of negotiations within the left, the Socialist party was considered the "most capable" of all the

51

TABLE 2–9

VOTERS' PERCEPTIONS OF THE PARTIES' POSITIONS
ON THE LEFT-RIGHT AXIS, FEBRUARY 1978
(in percentages)

Position	Party				Respondent's Self-Placement
	Communist	Socialist	Republican	RPR	
Extreme-left	34 ⎫	3	—	—	2
Left wing	52 ⎬ 86	17	—	—	13
Moderate left	8	52 ⎫	2	1	25 ⎫
Center	3	21 ⎬ 73	18	11	27 ⎬ 52
Moderate right	1	3	36 ⎫	28 ⎫	20
Right wing	—	1	28 ⎬ 64	38 ⎬ 66	8
Extreme-right	—	1	10	17	1
No answer	2	2	6	5	4
Total	100	100	100	100	100

SOURCE: SOFRES surveys, February 1978. Unpublished.

political parties in almost every domain: defending special interests, protecting freedom, reducing inequality, and maintaining the economy.[6] The Socialist party, as opposed to the Communist party (which was too clearly left wing) and the Majority parties (too clearly right wing), corresponded to the center-left policy supported by a large majority of the electorate (see Table 2–9).

Despite its internal quarrels, the left did not seem to lose its edge in the voting-intention surveys. On the contrary, its position continued to improve, as if the breakdown of the Common Program had actually been beneficial to the Socialist party. IFOP opinion polls placed the left as much as ten points ahead of the Majority (see Table 2–10), while Louis Harris France surveys put it ahead by seven points and SOFRES by six. With final scores varying between 26 percent and 29 percent, the Socialists promised to become the new dominant party. And yet the French did not believe the left would win, all the survey results and most expert opinion notwithstanding. At the beginning of March, 31 percent expected the left to win, as compared with 37 percent who forecast a Majority victory.

[6] See Jean-Luc Parodi, "L'union et la différence: les perceptions de la gauche après la crise de septembre 1977" [Unity and strife: perceptions of the left after the crisis of September 1977], SOFRES, L'opinion française en 1977 [French public opinion in 1977] (Paris: Presses de la Fondation Nationale des Sciences Politiques, 1978), pp. 72-74.

TABLE 2–10

Voting Intentions, September 1977–March 1978

(in percentages)

	Date of Survey					
Intended Vote	August 22–27, 1977	November 17–23, 1977	January 27– February 1, 1978	February 17–20, 1978	February 24–28, 1978	March 3–6, 1978
Communist party	19	21	20	21.5	21	20.5
Extreme-left	3	4	2	2	2.5	2
Socialist party	28	24	28	27.5	28	29
Leftist Radicals		2	2	2	2	2
(total left)	50	51	52	53	53.5	53.5
Other left	—	—	2	1	1	1
Ecologists	5	4	2	2	2.5	2.5
UDF (Republican party, Centrists, Radicals)	20	18	20	20	19	18.5
RPR	22	24	22	21	20	21
Other right	3	3	2	3	4	3.5
Total	100	100	100	100	100	100

Source: IFOP surveys cited by Jean-Luc Parodi, "L'échec des gauches" [The defeat of the left], *Revue politique et parlementaire*, no. 873 (1978), p. 16.

The Vote

On the eve of the first ballot the president of the republic made his last attempt to convince the electorate that reelecting the Majority was the "right choice." But according to the surveys, the left would be clearly ahead, at least on the first ballot. The second ballot (which is the decisive one under the French electoral system) was still uncertain since it was not known whether Communist candidates who received fewer votes than their Socialist rivals would withdraw in favor of the latter in accordance with the "republican discipline" reestablished in 1962.

MAP 1
THE FRENCH DEPARTMENTS

The First Ballot: March 12, 1978. The voters claimed to be less interested in the parliamentary elections of 1978 than in the presidential elections of 1974.[7] Nevertheless, the turnout for the first ballot was exceptionally high for a parliamentary election (see Table 2–11). The electorate seems to have regarded this election as the return match of the 1974 elections, and in the months following the municipal elections the number of citizens registering to vote rose. In metropolitan France,[8] the number of registered voters increased from 33,100,000 in 1977 to 34,400,000 in 1978. Part of this increase

---

[7] See the chapter by Roland Cayrol in this volume.

[8] Metropolitan France—continental France plus Corsica—comprises ninety-six departments. It does not include overseas departments or territories (see Map 1).

TABLE 2–11

ABSTENTION IN FRENCH PARLIAMENTARY ELECTIONS SINCE 1945

(in percentages)

Election	Abstention
Fourth Republic	
October 1945	20.1
June 1946	18.1
November 1946	21.9
June 1951	19.8
January 1956	17.2
Fifth Republic (first ballot)	
November 1958	22.9
November 1962	31.3
March 1967	19.1
June 1968	19.9
March 1973	18.7
March 1978	16.8

NOTE: The figures are for metropolitan France only.
SOURCE: Computed from official election returns.

can be ascribed to the natural increase in the population and to the recent registration of French citizens living abroad. However, a large number of these new voters (800,000) had been of voting age at the time of preceding elections but had not registered.[9] The first ballot, held on March 12, set a record for the postwar period: only 16.8 percent of the population did not vote. This percentage is all the more surprising in that the young, whose numbers had increased within the electorate, are more prone to abstain than older people.

The geographic distribution of abstention in 1978 followed the pattern typical when turnout is high: it ranged between 15 and 20 percent over more or less the entire country (see Map 2). The major exceptions to this rule were the North and the southwestern portion of the Massif Central, both regions where turnout is traditionally high (the Somme again set the record in 1978), and the Mediterranean coast, where nonvoting is more widespread than elsewhere (especially in Corsica and Bouches-du-Rhône).

---

[9] On this point see Alain Lancelot, "L'échec de l'alternance et les chances du renouvellement. Les élections des 12 et 19 mars 1978" [The defeat of change and the chances for renewal: the elections of March 12 and 19, 1978], *Projet*, June 1978, pp. 718-731.

MAP 2
ABSTENTION, MARCH 12, 1978

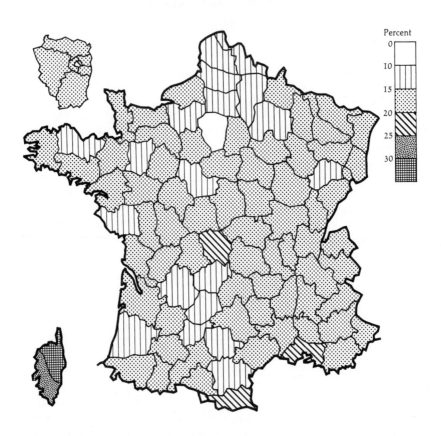

The left-right balance. The Socialist party beat the RPR by fewer than 50,000 votes in metropolitan France; if the overseas votes are counted, it becomes apparent that the PS actually lost its much desired status as France's largest party. The fortunes of the left, which had peaked in the cantonal and municipal elections, were on the wane— and French voting intention surveys registered their first major defeat since their appearance in 1965. The balance of power between the two large coalitions that emerged from the elections was much the same as it had been in 1974, but in 1978 it favored the left. In fact, the left had a 2.94 percentage-point lead over the Majority, although this advantage shrinks to 1.52 points if the "other right" and "extreme-right" categories are taken into account (see Table 2–12).

TABLE 2-12
The Left-Right Balance on the First Ballot, Metropolitan France, 1978

Party Group	Popular Vote	Percentage of Valid Vote
Left		
Union of the Left (PCF, PS, and MRG)	12,802,809	45.56
Extreme-left and other	1,086,503	3.87
Total left	13,889,312	49.43
Center and right		
Majority (UDF, RPR, and other)	13,063,517	46.49
Extreme-right and other	400,909	1.42
Total center and right	13,464,426	47.91
Ecologists and other	747,576	2.66
Total	28,101,314	100.00

NOTE: The differences between some of these totals and those found in other tables in this book are due to differences in the classification of candidates. This problem is explained further in Appendix A.
SOURCE: Computed from official election returns.

The Ecology candidates, who ran on an apolitical "quality of life" platform, had done surprisingly well in the municipal elections in various large cities; in Paris they had won 10.1 percent of the valid votes cast. In the parliamentary elections they ran candidates in a little more than two out of five constituencies and obtained a total vote of 2.04 percent (more than 7 percent in some fifteen constituencies). Their relative success, and the votes given to a variety of other minor parties not easy to classify, prevented the left from crossing the psychologically decisive threshold to an absolute majority.

In the past there have been periods when the left predominated (1945–1956) and periods when the right predominated (1958–1973), but an even balance between left and right is new in French politics (see Table 2-13). The nationalization of electoral behavior is also new. The difference between the most left-leaning departments and the most right-leaning ones has lessened considerably in the past ten years (see Table 2-14). The left has remained fairly stable within its traditional fiefs and is gaining some ground in the right-wing departments, without, however, obtaining the percentage of votes that would allow it to win a large number of parliamentary seats.

TABLE 2–13

ELECTORAL FORTUNES OF THE FRENCH LEFT SINCE 1945

(in percentages of valid votes)

Election	Total Left	Communist Party	Socialist Party
Fourth Republic			
October 1945	60.5	26.2	23.4
June 1946	58.6	25.9	21.1
November 1946	57.1	28.2	17.8
June 1951	51.5	26.9	14.6
January 1956	52.4	25.9	15.2
Fifth Republic			
November 1958	43.4	19.2	15.7
November 1962	44.2	21.7	12.6
March 1967	43.5	22.4	18.7[a]
June 1968	41.0	20.0	16.5[a]
March 1973	45.7	21.4	20.7[b]
March 1978	49.4	20.6	24.9[b]

[a] Federation of the Democratic and Socialist Left.

[b] The Socialist party and the Leftist Radicals.

SOURCE: Computations from official election returns.

Competition on the left. The major contenders in the elections were the Union of the Left and the Majority, but within each of these coalitions the elections precipitated a leadership struggle. From this point of view 1978 had a historic meaning for the left: for the first time since 1945 the Socialist party came out of an election ahead of the Communist party (see Table 2–13). With the help of its allies,

TABLE 2–14

BEST AND WORST SHOWING OF THE LEFT, 1967, 1973, AND 1978

(in percentages; differences in percentage points)

	Vote for the Left		
	1967	1973	1978
10 most leftist departments	62.0	61.6	62.3
10 least leftist departments	20.4	27.5	35.0
Difference	41.6	34.1	27.3

SOURCE: Author's computations from official election returns.

the Leftist Radicals, it improved on its 1973 performance by 4.2 percentage points and obtained the highest share ever in the history of French socialism. The Communist party, on the other hand, just barely passed the 20 percent mark; the largest party in France at the time of the Liberation, the Communists came in last of the four major political groups in 1978. A comparison of the results of the Communist and Socialist parties in each constituency shows that competition between the two actually favored the latter. The Communists did worse than the Socialists in two out of three constituencies whereas ten years before they had been ahead in more than half (see Table 2–15).

In the past few years the Communist party has adopted tactics that have allowed it to capture Socialist votes in areas traditionally belonging to the SFIO (the Section Française de l'Internationale Ouvrière, the French Socialist party founded in 1905 as a branch of the Second International). As Table 2–16 shows, the Communist party often does better than any other group of the left in departments such as Aude, Bouches-du-Rhône, Haute-Vienne, and the mining district of Nord–Pas de Calais, especially when a Socialist deputy retires. Originally attracted to the Socialist party on the basis of the SFIO's anti-Communist position, many voters have been put off by the reform of the party, its candidates, and its political line.

On the other hand, in some regions traditionally committed to the right, the Socialists have improved their position and the Com-

TABLE 2–15

PARTY LEADING THE LEFT AT THE LOCAL LEVEL, 1967–1978

(in number of districts)

Party Leading the Left	1967	1968	1973	1978
Socialist party[a]	212	217	276	321
Communist party	258	253	197	153
Total number of districts[b]	470	470	473	474

[a] In 1967 and 1968, the Federation of the Democratic and Socialist Left (FGDS); in 1973 and 1978, the Socialist party and the Leftist Radicals.

[b] In 1967 the FGDS did not compete in forty-eight districts, in 1968 in forty. In 1973 and 1978 the Socialist party and the Leftist Radicals did not compete in two districts.

SOURCE: Adapted from Gérard Le Gall, "A gauche toujours le rééquilibrage" [On the left, a shifting balance of forces], Revue Politique et Parlementaire, no. 873 (1978), p. 36.

TABLE 2–16

SOCIALIST LOSSES AND COMMUNIST GAINS IN SOME TRADITIONAL
SFIO DISTRICTS, 1967–1978

(in percentages of valid votes; change in percentage points)

| | Socialist Vote | | | | Communist Vote | | | |
District	1967	1973	1978	Change 1967–78	1967	1973	1978	Change 1967–78
Aude no. 2	49.8	36.7	30.0	−19.8	23.3	25.4	28.2	+ 4.9
Bouches-du-Rhône no. 8	33.7	31.6	24.8	− 8.9	27.0	27.7	31.3	+ 4.3
Bouches-du-Rhône no. 11	39.3	27.0	23.2	−16.1	31.1	38.0	37.3	+ 6.2
Nord no. 16	37.8	28.9	22.8	−15.0	26.2	29.8	29.8	+ 3.6
Nord no. 22	37.4	23.7	20.5	−16.9	31.8	30.1	36.2	+ 4.4
Pas-de-Calais no. 5	32.1	28.4	25.6	− 6.5	28.4	31.7	33.5	+ 5.1
Pas-de-Calais no. 14	44.8	32.0	30.2	−14.6	29.8	36.1	42.7	+12.9
Haute-Vienne no. 1	34.9	27.7	27.8	− 7.1	31.9	32.2	34.2	+ 2.3

SOURCE: Author's computation from official election returns.

munists have declined (see Table 2–17). This has been particularly obvious in the Catholic departments of eastern and western France. All around, the Communist vote, whose stability long astounded students of French politics, is now undergoing strong fluctuations—increases in departments with long Socialist traditions and losses to the Socialists in areas where the right is strong as well as in some departments (including several in the Paris region) where it used to monopolize the leftist vote.

Competition on the right. Having lost the presidency in 1974 and the prime ministership in 1976, the Gaullists also lost the leadership of the Majority. Although Jacques Chirac's Rally for the Republic (RPR) won more votes than the UDF and maintained its status as the strongest party in France, the Gaullists were no longer the majority in the Majority, for the first time since 1962; indeed, as the following figures show, in the five parliamentary elections since 1962, the Gaullists' percentage of the Majority's vote steadily declined:

TABLE 2–17
SOCIALIST GAINS AND COMMUNIST LOSSES IN TRADITIONALLY RIGHT-WING AREAS, 1967–1978

(in percentages of valid votes; change in percentage points)

District	Socialist Vote				Communist Vote			
	1967	1973	1978	Change 1967–78	1967	1973	1978	Change 1967–78
Calvados, no. 1	14.6	22.0	31.0	+16.4	18.7	15.0	12.9	− 5.8
Côtes-du-Nord, no. 2	a	29.3	38.1	—	23.7	16.3	11.0	−12.7
Finistère, no. 2	8.8	18.7	29.8	+21.0	18.0	16.1	13.9	− 4.1
Mayenne, no. 3	a	15.2	27.7	—	9.9	7.1	4.7	− 5.2
Moselle, no. 5	10.2	19.7	24.0	+13.8	16.6	13.5	12.3	− 4.3
Moselle, no. 6	5.4	11.7	24.4	+19.0	16.6	11.2	9.9	− 6.7
Savoie, no. 2	a	19.9	25.7	—	26.2	25.1	22.6	− 3.6
Vienne, no. 1	17.8	18.8	33.7	+15.9	14.9	18.0	13.1	− 1.8
Vienne, no. 2	a	15.0	25.9	—	29.9	23.2	18.0	−11.9

a No Socialist candidate ran.

SOURCE: Author's computation from official election returns.

1962, 89.4; 1967, 81.5; 1968, 80.4; 1973, 70.2; and 1978, 49.1. In 1973 the UDR was still the party of seven out of ten Majority voters. In 1978 the RPR represented a little under one out of two. The RPR claims a Gaullist lineage for its organization, its ideology, and its electorate. In fact, however, there is no direct relation between General de Gaulle's electorate and the RPR's. In the eight departments where de Gaulle did best in 1965 Jacques Chirac's party took between 10 and 38 percent of the valid votes; moreover, the UDF did best of the Majority parties in five of these departments (see Table 2–18).

The closeness of the vote for the RPR and the UDF (see Table 2–12) might lead one to believe that the competition between these two parties at the district level must have been lively. The fact is that the division of the Majority electorate into Gaullists and Giscardians cannot be explained by any clearly definable political, geographic, or sociological criteria. Instead, the Majority vote is closely linked to the reputation of the individuals running for office

TABLE 2–18

STRENGTH OF THE RPR AND THE UDF IN 1978 IN THE EIGHT MOST
GAULLIST DEPARTMENTS OF 1965
(in percentages of valid votes)

Department	de Gaulle, 1965[a]	1978[b]	
		RPR	UDF
Bas-Rhin	63.7	38.1	17.4
Haut-Rhin	59.1	28.4	30.1
Manche	57.4	22.1	37.0
Moselle	57.2	23.7	25.6
Corsica	56.5	33.3	12.9
Meuse	55.5	10.0	37.1
Morbihan	53.2	13.7	38.2
Haute-Marne	52.6	30.0	21.5

[a] First ballot, presidential election of December 1965.
[b] First ballot, parliamentary elections of March 1978.
SOURCE: Official election returns.

(see Table 2–19). When the RPR ran candidates who were much better known than those of the UDF (for example, incumbents) it had an average lead of 21.5 percentage points and represented about 70 percent of the Majority electorate. But RPR candidates who were only a little better known than their opponents (incumbent department councillors, for example) still had an average lead of 10.3 percentage points and took 60 percent of the Majority votes. The results were almost exactly the opposite when the UDF candidates were better known, yet the votes were almost evenly split if the candidates were equally well known. This pattern had already emerged in the 1977 municipal elections in Paris:[10] personality mattered more than party in the first-ballot "primaries" between the RPR and the UDF.

The UDF, which continues under the Giscardian label the traditions of the Radicals, the Christian Democrats, and the conservative right wing, is really more an ad hoc alliance than a homogeneous political party. In order to counterbalance the influence of the RPR, the president's advisors decided to present candidates under a group label, but the results of the elections indicated that the voters had

---

[10] See, in particular, Elisabeth Dupoirier, "Une ou deux droites à Paris? Les élections municipales de 1977 et la restructuration du bloc conservateur" [One right or two in Paris? the municipal elections of 1977 and the restructuring of the conservative bloc], *Revue française de science politique* (December 1977), pp. 848-883.

TABLE 2–19

Average Lead of the UDF over the RPR, March 12, 1978, by UDF Candidate's Previous Party Label and Saliency of RPR and UDF Candidates

(in percentage points)

Saliency of UDF and RPR Candidates	All UDF Candidates	UDF Candidate's Previous Party Label			
		Republican	Centrist	Radical	None
UDF candidate much better known than RPR candidate	+24.0	+24.2	+27.2	+35.8	+15.1
UDF candidate slightly better known than RPR candidate	+10.5	+12.2	+12.9	+ 2.8	+ 5.0
UDF and RPR candidates equally well known	−0.8	− 0.5	+ 1.3	− 5.3	−15.0
RPR candidate slightly better known than UDF candidate	−10.3	− 6.8	−13.5	−22.3	—
RPR candidate much better known than UDF candidate	−21.5	−17.5	−22.7	−29.7	—

NOTE: The entries show the average margin between UDF and RPR candidates; + indicates that the UDF candidate was ahead of his RPR opponent, − that he was behind. Saliency is a function of the candidate's previous political office (deputy, department councillor, mayor, and so on).

SOURCE: Author's calculations from official election returns.

actually been guided by the candidates' partisan origins, whether Republican, centrists, or Radical. As may be seen in Table 2–19, personalities previously associated with centrist and Radical party politics ran well ahead of little-known RPR candidates. On the other hand, in constituencies where the Gaullists' prestige was stronger, the UDF's results varied significantly and showed a clear advantage for candidates previously associated with the president's Republican party.

The geography of party support. A breakdown of the election results by department completes this picture, pointing out the continuities in French politics. Despite the slight advantage of the left in the nation as a whole, the nationalization of electoral behavior, and the improvement of the Socialists' position in the more conservative regions, the traditional geographic patterns of support for left and right remained valid.[11] Thus, as Map 3 shows, the Communist party is very weak in certain areas which have long resisted Communist penetration, but these alternate with areas of permanent Communist strength such as the region from Paris to the Belgian frontier, the northern and western border of the Massif Central, and the Mediterranean coast.

On the other hand, the corresponding map for the Socialist party and the leftist Radicals shows that this group has taken root all over the country (see Map 4). Only rarely have its results fallen outside the 20 to 30 percent spread. There are also traditionally strong Socialist areas such as the Southwest (Gironde, for example) and the belt stretching from Aquitaine all the way to Territoire-de-Belfort passing through Lot, Puy-de-Dôme, Saône-et-Loire, and Doubs. The map of Socialist gains and losses between 1967 and 1978 (Map 5) shows strong gains (in some cases more than fifteen percentage points) in the east and west, once strongholds of the Christian Democrats. On the other hand, the Socialists lost votes in the southwest Massif Central, where they were competing with Jacques Chirac himself, and along the Mediterranean seaboard (in particular Bouches-du-Rhône), where they lost votes to the Communist party.

The sixth map, showing the vote for the Majority, holds no surprises: it follows the traditional geography of the right in France. The areas of greatest strength are the southeast Massif Central (Lozère in particular) and the western interior (Manche, Orne, Mayenne, Maine-et-Loire, and Vendée). With only a few deviations, such as Corsica and Alpes-Maritimes, the geographic distribution of right-wing support follows closely the geographical distribution of church-going.

The maps of RPR and UDF support, meanwhile, illustrate the "clientele" phenomenon that currently characterizes relationships within the Majority. There are very few clearly delineated areas or contiguous dominant positions with the exception of the southern part of the Massif Central, where the RPR controls the west and the

---

[11] For a comparison see Marie-Thérèse Lancelot and Alain Lancelot, "A Cartographic Approach to the Presidential Election, May 1974," in Penniman, ed., *France at the Polls*, pp. 137-173.

MAP 3
The Communist Vote, March 12, 1978

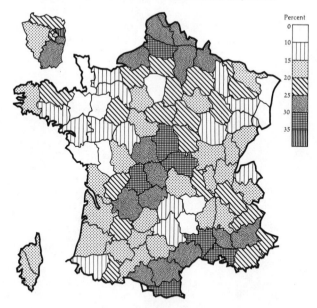

Percent
0
10
15
20
25
30
35

MAP 4
The Socialist and Leftist Radical Vote, March 12, 1978

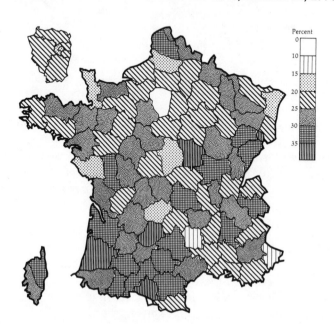

Percent
0
10
15
20
25
30
35

MAP 5
CHANGE IN THE SOCIALIST VOTE, 1967–1978

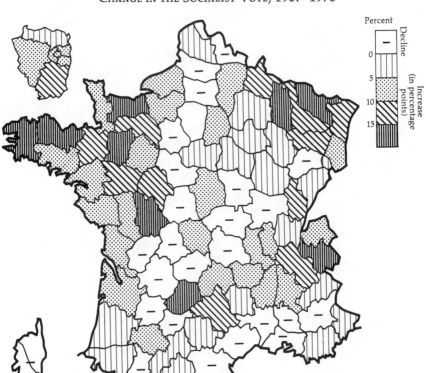

NOTE: The largest drop in the Socialist vote between 1967 and 1978 was 12.7 percentage points, in Corrèze. No Socialists ran in Pyrénées-Orientales in 1967.

UDF the east. The pattern of support for Giscard, however, is closer to the overall distribution of the Majority, whereas the geographic characteristics of the RPR are quite different from those of Gaullism. By comparison with the UDR, the Gaullist party of the 1960s, the RPR's losses are conspicuous in the north and in certain departments in eastern France like Haut-Rhin, Meuse, and Meurthe et Moselle.

Sociological analysis of the results. A postelectoral survey carried out by SOFRES for *Le Nouvel Observateur* using a sample of 2,000 people confirmed the left-right split of the French electorate (see Table 2–20). The Majority and the various center movements clearly led in the over-fifty age categories, in the agricultural sector, and among the inactive. The left, on the other hand, won, at times by a sub-

MAP 6
THE MAJORITY VOTE, MARCH 12, 1978

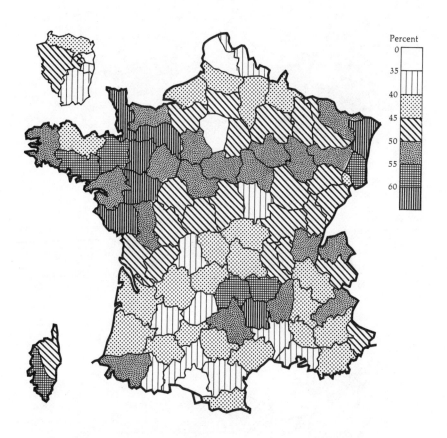

stantial margin, among the young, blue-collar workers, employees, and the middle-management and technical category. Contrary to general opinion, the postelectoral survey proved the stability of the practicing Catholics' vote: only 16 percent of those regularly attending mass voted for the left. If the Socialist party gained votes in traditionally Catholic areas this was probably because the number of practicing Catholics had decreased rather than because voting habits among Catholics had changed.[12]

---

[12] For an analysis of the Catholic electorate, see Christel Peyrefitte, "Religion et politique" [Religion and politics], in SOFRES, *L'opinion française en 1977*, pp. 117-134.

MAP 7
The UDF Vote, March 12, 1978

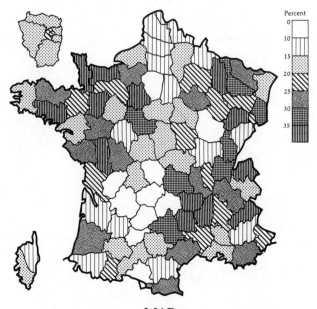

MAP 8
The RPR Vote, March 12, 1978

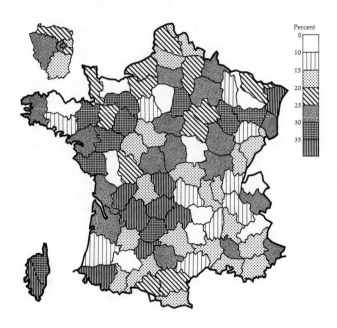

TABLE 2–20

SOCIOLOGICAL ANALYSIS OF THE 1978 ELECTORATE
(in percentages of respondents in the stated category)

Category	Extreme-Left	Communist Party	Socialist Party and Leftist Radicals	Ecologists and Others	UDF	RPR	Various Majority and Right
Total electorate	3	21	25	3	21	22	5
SEX							
Men	3	24	25	3	19	20	6
Women	2	19	25	3	22	24	5
AGE							
18 to 24	9	28	25	4	17	15	2
25 to 34	5	26	24	6	18	17	4
35 to 49	3	19	25	3	20	24	6
50 to 64	1	20	24	3	22	23	7
65 and above	—	15	25	—	27	28	5
OCCUPATION OF HEAD OF FAMILY							
Farmers and agricultural workers	1	9	17	6	33	31	3
Shopkeepers and craftsmen	—	14	23	5	25	26	7
Executives, industrialists, professionals, businessmen	5	9	15	4	27	30	10

(Table continued on next page)

TABLE 2–20 (continued)

Category	Extreme-Left	Communist Party	Socialist Party and Leftist Radicals	Ecologists and Others	UDF	RPR	Various Majority and Right
Middle management, technicians, and white-collar workers	6	18	29	5	14	20	8
Blue-collar workers	4	36	27	2	16	14	1
Inactive, retired	—	17	26	1	25	26	5
OCCUPATION OF RESPONDENT							
Farmers and agricultural workers	1	6	19	8	29	33	4
Shopkeepers and craftsmen	—	14	22	3	28	25	8
Executives, industrialists, professionals, businessmen	4	12	15	6	25	28	10
Middle management, technicians, and white-collar workers	7	20	31	5	14	17	6
Blue-collar workers	5	37	26	2	15	14	1
Inactive, retired	1	18	24	1	24	26	6
MONTHLY HOUSEHOLD INCOME							
Less than 2,000 francs	3	22	26	2	22	20	5
2,000 to 3,000 francs	3	26	27	3	18	21	2
3,000 to 5,000 francs	3	25	28	2	18	19	5
More than 5,000 francs	4	16	20	3	23	24	10

EDUCATION

Elementary	1	24	26	2	21	22	4
Secondary	4	15	21	4	22	27	7
Technical or commercial	5	27	26	2	14	21	5
Higher education	9	10	19	5	26	20	11

RELIGION

Catholic, devout	1	2	13	4	39	31	10
Catholic, practicing occasionally	—	11	20	3	28	33	5
Catholic, nominal	3	24	30	2	17	20	4
None	6	49	29	4	4	6	2

LEFT-RIGHT SELF-PLACEMENT

Extreme-left	10	61	23	4	1	1	—
Left	3	32	50	3	5	6	1
Center	2	4	19	5	35	27	8
Right	—	3	7	1	40	42	7
Extreme-right	—	—	5	3	30	49	13
Marais[a]	5	11	25	4	23	27	5

1974 VOTE (Second ballot)

Giscard d'Estaing	1	2	8	2	37	39	11
Mitterrand	3	42	44	3	5	2	1

[a] Includes respondents who were unable to place themselves on a left-right axis or who claimed to be centrist but uninterested in politics.

SOURCE: SOFRES survey carried out from March 28 to April 5, 1978, for Le Nouvel Observateur.

The findings of this survey should be interpreted with care when it comes to the losses of the Communist party. The PCF retained its working-class character but attracted much younger voters as well. In fact, the Communist party ranked ahead of the Socialist party among the working class and those under thirty-five. On the other hand, the Socialist party is not in direct competition with the Communist party since it is the only party that appeals across classes: it has much the same level of support in all sex and age groups and strong roots in all social categories, though it remains stronger in some than in others. As far as the right is concerned, the consequence of its "clientele" electorate is that both the RPR and the UDF recruit from the same social base. The Gaullists even lost their lead over the Giscardians in working-class districts.

In the past few years the right has lost a conspicuous amount of ground among the under-thirty-five age group and among white-collar workers, middle management and technicians, upper management, and executives. The most striking development, however, is the evolution of the female vote, which is moving ever closer to the patterns of the male electorate. The vote for the right among men and women in the elections since 1967 is as follows (in percentages of valid votes):[13]

	Men	Women
1967	48	65
1973	50	59
1974	47	54
1978	45	51

The Second Ballot: March 19, 1978. In 1978, as in the previous elections, recourse to a second ballot was the rule. In fact, only 68 candidates won enough votes to be elected on the first ballot, 56 in metropolitan France and 12 in overseas territories. A week later, on March 19, a second ballot was held in 423 districts (including a few where only one candidate met the requirement of 12.5 percent of the possible votes).

Polarization and mobilization. After the fierce intracoalition battles that take place on the first ballot, the second ballot reestablishes a bipolar situation. Within both the Majority and the left, candidates strictly observed their promises to withdraw in favor of whichever candidate on their side had won most votes in the first round. Thus there were 409 left-right duels on March 19 and only one three-way

---

[13] SOFRES surveys.

fight. Ninety-six percent of the duels were Majority-opposition contests, even more than the previous record of 85 percent in 1968.

This polarization brought the electorate up against hard choices. How was a Socialist to vote if the alternatives were a Communist and a UDF candidate? What was a UDF supporter to do when his options were a rather moderate Socialist and an RPR candidate of the old Gaullist tradition? Yet the French were undeterred: indeed, turnout increased. The abstention rate for the second ballot was only 15.3 percent as compared with 16.7 percent for the first ballot, and in twenty-three constituencies participation increased as much as four percentage points between the first and second rounds.

The Socialists' lack of discipline. The postelectoral survey permits us to measure vote transfers between the first and second ballots in the various types of contests (see Table 2–21). Within the Majority, RPR and UDF voters behaved much the same way: nine out of ten voted for the party opposing the Communists and eight out of ten for the party opposing the Socialists. Within the left, and despite the endless wrangling of the months preceding the elections, almost all Communists transferred their votes to Socialist candidates on the second ballot. Some of the Socialists' unexpected defeats (such as Creuse and Côtes-du-Nord) seem to have been caused by the defection of new voters rather than by a withdrawal of Communist support. On the other hand, Socialist voters were quite undisciplined. Only 65 percent voted for the Communist party when faced with a choice between the PCF and the UDF, and 73 percent did so in PCF-RPR races. These figures are no lower than those of 1973, but the left's lead after the first ballot was far too slight to compensate for this kind of loss.

If the first ballot had seen the "rise of the center"—the Socialist party and the UDF[14]—the second ballot saw the revenge of the extremes: the Communist party and the RPR. Thanks to the Socialists' advance in the first ballot and to Socialist voters' willingness to continue supporting the left in the second round, the Communists were rewarded with more seats than they had ever won since the beginning of the Fifth Republic, while the Gaullists retained their position as the largest parliamentary group. The mobilization of the moderate voters and the Socialists' lack of discipline magnified the opposition's defeat. In fact, the left managed to win only 201 seats

---

[14] The expression is borrowed from Jean-Luc Parodi, "L'échec des gauches" [The defeat of the left], *Revue Politique et Parlementaire*, no. 873, 1978, pp. 9-32.

TABLE 2–21

VOTE TRANSFERS BETWEEN THE FIRST AND SECOND BALLOTS, 1978

(in percentages)

PCF–UDF Races at the Second Ballot:

First-Ballot Vote	Second-Ballot Vote		
	PCF	UDF	Neither
PS	65	23	12
RPR	2	91	7

PCF–RPR Races at the Second Ballot:

First-Ballot Vote	Second-Ballot Vote		
	PCF	RPR	Neither
PS	73	10	17
UDF	3	90	7

PS–UDF Races at the Second Ballot:

First-Ballot Vote	Second-Ballot Vote		
	PS	UDF	Neither
PCF	98	—	2
RPR	4	87	9

PS–RPR Races at the Second Ballot:

First-Ballot Vote	Second-Ballot Vote		
	PS	RPR	Neither
PCF	94	3	3
UDF	4	83	13

SOURCE: SOFRES survey, March 28 to April 5, 1978, for *Le Nouvel Observateur*.

(just 18 more than it had held before the elections) and was still far from having an absolute majority in the National Assembly.

Why did the left lose again? In 1977 the left was a victim of the system instituted by the Fifth Republic under which parliamentary elections function as a return match after a presidential ballot. An

TABLE 2–22

Voters' Attitudes toward Communist Participation in Government,
February 1978
(in percentages)

Effect of Communist Participation on:	Good	Bad	No Opinion
Small and middle-sized businesses	34	39	27
Freedom	34	45	21
The recovery of the French economy	32	44	24
The role of France in the world	29	45	26
The stability of the Government	28	47	25

Note: The survey question was: "Do you think that the presence of Communist ministers in the Government would be a good/bad thing for [the categories listed above]?"
Source: SOFRES opinion polls, February 1978.

opposition victory would have called Giscard d'Estaing's mandate into question, just as the election of an opposition president in 1974 would have entailed the dissolution of the National Assembly. The Socialists and Communists tried to remove the president's influence from the electoral campaign, but Giscard, bolstered by his popularity and the public's desire to see him remain in office, intervened twice to recommend "the right choice" to the nation.[15]

In addition, a parliamentary election under the Fifth Republic is primarily an *élection de désignation*, not an *élection de représentation*. The electoral system functions in such a way that, at the crucial second ballot, the voter is really choosing between alternative governing coalitions instead of between a multiplicity of parties; he designates a Government for the nation, not a representative for his district. It was in this political context that the incessant quarrels between the Communist party and the Socialists (to which must be added the strong anticommunism of the French) destroyed the left's credibility as an alternative governing coalition. An important segment of public opinion felt that Communist participation in a Government would have negative effect in many areas (see Table 2–22). Only 21 percent of the French thought that the left would be able to form a stable Government, while 63 percent thought it would not.

---

[15] To the SOFRES question, "If the left wins the parliamentary elections, do you think Mr. Giscard d'Estaing should serve out his term or should he resign?" asked from February 14 to 17, the responses were: serve out his term, 68 percent; resign, 23 percent; and no opinion, 9 percent.

The Majority's electoral situation has become more precarious with the passage of time, yet the disunity of the left and the Majority's own renewal allowed it to win the sixth parliamentary elections of the Fifth Republic. The left's long march did not end in 1978.[16] Once again the Socialists were faced with the enigma of a strong Communist party. The question remained: How is the Socialist party to maintain its identity and strength outside the Union of the Left? And within the Union of the Left, how can it come to power?

---

[16] See the chapter by Serge Hurtig, "Never So Near Victory: The United Left's Long Road to the 1974 Elections," in Penniman, ed., *France at the Polls*, pp. 113-135.

3

The Majority

Jean Charlot

Since 1958 France has had a single-member-majority voting system with two ballots. To be elected on the first ballot a candidate must obtain an absolute majority of the votes cast; to be elected on the second he must simply top the poll. In 1978 only 68 of the 491 seats, or 13.8 percent, were filled on the first ballot. The first time around the voter has nine or ten candidates to choose from, and he casts his vote for the candidate who comes nearest to sharing his opinions. On the second ballot his choice is restricted to two, occasionally three, candidates, partly because no candidate may go forward to the second ballot unless at the first ballot he has won at least 12.5 percent of the registered voters, partly because the major parties on the left and on the right generally agree that their lower placed candidates will stand down in favor of the candidate who has done best. The voter's choice is thus greatly clarified—there is usually one candidate on the left and one on the right at the second ballot—and he chooses the lesser evil. But the second round hardly puts an end to political debate. French national politics seems geared toward an ever-postponed "third ballot," for hardly is one election over than preparations for revenge begin, even if the next election is actually months or years away.

Immediately after Valéry Giscard d'Estaing was elected president of the republic on May 19, 1974, preparations began for the general election still four years off. Two questions were to dominate French politics during this period: Would the Union of the Left (the PCF, the PS, and the MRG) win the election in March 1978 and take the place of the Majority (the CDS, the PR, and the RPR)? And would the president's party manage to reduce the proportion of Gaullists in the new Parliament, itself becoming the major force within the right-wing coalition? It was generally assumed that the answers to both would be yes—that the left would win and that the president's party would crowd out all but the hard core Gaullists. In fact, of course, the left lost and the Gaullists remained the most numerous group in Parliament.

The Struggle for Power

Reversals. Between 1974 and 1978 the parties within the Majority experienced a series of spectacular role reversals. To begin with, in June 1974 Jacques Chirac, then prime minister, was greeted by the members of the Central Committee of his party, the UDR, in icy silence and invited to take a seat, not on the platform but on the floor like any other party activist. His colleagues found it difficult to forgive Chirac for having supported Giscard against Jacques Chaban-Delmas on the first ballot of the presidential election.[1] Chirac reminded them that he had been "born, politically, within the Gaullist movement" and that no mere "tactical differences lasting a few weeks" could cast doubt on his deep attachment to Gaullist ideals and principles.[2] But the Gaullists remained wary, fearing that Chirac's ambition was to "Giscardize" their movement. By March 1978, however, the tables had turned. Jacques Chirac, mayor of Paris, uncontested leader of a strong Gaullist party, was looked on as the president's rival, the warmest defender of the Gaullist movement and of Gaullist ideas. The center party, meanwhile, was to know a similar volte-face. On two occasions, in June 1974 and in May 1977, Center party activists prevented their leader, Jean Lecanuet, from uniting their party—the Democratic Center, then the Social Democratic Center (Centre Démocrate and Centre des Démocrates Sociaux)—with Giscard's Independent Republicans, then Republican party (Républicains Indépendants and Parti Républicain) which they deemed too right wing. On the eve of the March 1978 general election, however, a federation was born, the Union for French Democracy, or UDF (Union pour la Démocratie Française), with Jean Lecanuet as its president: it brought together the centrists, the Giscardians, and the right-wing Radicals.

One reason for events like these is that the voting system encourages a struggle on two levels, first within the two camps—

[1] See Jean Charlot, "The End of Gaullism?" in Howard R. Penniman, ed., *France at the Polls: The Presidential Election of 1974* (Washington, D.C.: American Enterprise Institute, 1975), pp. 75-79.

[2] *La Lettre de la Nation*, June 10, 1974. *La Lettre de la Nation* is the Gaullist daily newsletter, which in 1974 replaced the Gaullist daily newspaper, *La Nation*.

majority and opposition—and then between them. At the first balloting in 1978 the struggle was between Communists and Socialists on the one hand, Gaullists and Giscardians on the other. At the second ballot it is usually between left and right. If either camp faces a three-cornered struggle at the first ballot, it runs the risk of seeing none of its candidates qualify for the second ballot. If either camp is divided at the second ballot, it gives a clear advantage to the other. So broadly speaking, polarization is the rule both between the coalitions and within them.

Up until the presidential election of May 1974 it was the political division between opposition centrists (the Democratic Center and the Radical party) and centrists sympathetic to the Majority (the Center for Democracy and Progress, Centre Démocratie et Progrès) that prevented the non-Gaullist wing of the Majority from uniting against the powerful Gaullist element. But after the presidential election the political climate favored a closer alliance, as did the electoral system. The parties that belong to what has sometimes been called the presidential majority, that is, those parties nearest to Valéry Giscard d'Estaing, were naturally tempted, under the benevolent eye of the president, to try and tip the balance of power within the Majority away from the Gaullists. The Giscardians hoped to cash in on the victory of their former leader and at the same time to give him added strength. The centrists wanted above all to put an end to what they called the UDR state, the majority within the Majority. Everything thus coincided to encourage the non-Gaullist parties within the Majority to unite against the Gaullists. It took them four years to actually do so, and even then only the threat that the Gaullist party would be strengthened finally prompted them to act.

During the first six months of Giscard d'Estaing's presidency, from June to December 1974, the Gaullist party was in a sorry state: it had no leader, no strategy, no policy, and it questioned its own future. Because of the strength of the Left, however, the president of the republic could not take advantage of the situation by dissolving the Assembly[3] and thus breaking up the Gaullist party, which was too weak to remain united and defend its position within the Majority. The Union of the Left was pegging 51 percent in the opinion polls on voting intentions, and if Giscard dissolved the Assembly it would

---

[3] The president of the republic has the power to dissolve the National Assembly (art. 12, 1958 Constitution) as and when he wishes, with two limitations. He cannot dissolve it while art. 16—conferring special exceptional powers—is in force or during the first year following a dissolution.

probably win the election. In this context each non-Gaullist party within the Majority was tempted to play its own game.

By December 1974 things had changed. Giscard's party had been unable to develop an organization of its own and win over supporters from its rivals within the Majority.[4] The centrists, torn between three potential leaders—Jean Lecanuet, Jean-Jacques Servan-Schreiber, and Michel Durafour—and unable to decide whether to swell the ranks of the left or the right, were split into five or six groups. In December 1974 Jacques Chirac, then prime minister, was elected general secretary of the UDR and managed to breathe new life into the party. The UDR needed a leader who could restore its self-confidence—while Chirac needed a party that could consolidate his position within the Majority. In June 1974, Chirac dropped from his Government—exactly twelve days after it had been formed—Jean-Jacques Servan-Schreiber, who had publicly spoken out against France's nuclear deterrent. The Gaullists saw this as proof of Chirac's capacity to defend Gaullist positions, and his leadership of the movement was thereafter a matter of course.

Gaullism was back on the rails. It gained electoral momentum gradually, putting its poor showing in the presidential election of May 1974 behind it. The Giscardians and the centrists on the other hand saw their potential vote—the 33 percent Giscard had carried on May 5, 1974—draining away. In October 1975 the gap between the Giscardo-centrists and the Gaullists in the voting intention surveys was still seventeen points (31 percent to 14 percent); in March 1976, when the left won a decisive victory in the cantonal elections, the gap closed slightly, dropping to fourteen points (see Figure 3–1). The rise of the Gaullist party was accelerated by Jacques Chirac's resignation as prime minister on August 22, 1976. The reason he gave was that he could not lead a Government when he was not given the power to do so. On December 5, 1976, he organized the spectacular transformation of the UDR into the vast Rally for the Republic or RPR (Rassemblement pour la République) and the party's star continued to rise. By September of the following year the gap between Gaullists and Giscardians was a mere five points (20 percent to 25 percent), and in November 1977, when the opinion polling institutes tested the popularity of actual candidates as opposed to party labels, the RPR outstripped all its rivals and allies.

---

[4] See Jean Charlot, "Cinq partis, et quelques autres . . . pour une nouvelle Majorité" [Five parties and then some . . . for a new Majority], Projet, June 1975, pp. 639-652.

FIGURE 3–1

VOTING INTENTIONS FOR THE MAJORITY PARTIES, 1975–1978

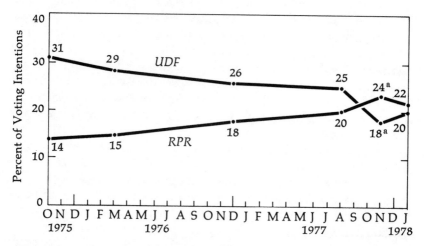

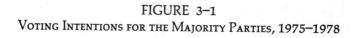

[a] First opinion poll on actual candidates.

SOURCE: IFOP.

Primaries. Since the creation of the Fifth Republic, the word "primaries" has been used to designate the contest that occurs at the first ballot between candidates belonging to the same political bloc in districts where no common candidate is chosen.[5] In general, primaries are the rule on the left: both Communist and Socialist (and sometimes Leftist Radical) candidates run in the first ballot, then whichever does best competes in the second ballot, while the remaining candidates on his side stand down. Thus it is the strongest candidate of the left who confronts the right. For the Majority, on the other hand, primaries were the exception until 1973. The Giscardians were in favor of primaries in theory, but in practice, faced with a strong rival in the Gaullist UDR, they preferred on the whole to reach a general

---

[5] In France the term *primary* or *primary election* refers to the first round of an election when there is a private agreement between two or more parties that the candidate among those sponsored by the agreeing parties who receives the most votes in the first round will be supported by all of the parties to the agreement in the second round; their remaining candidates, including those who receive enough votes to be eligible to run in the second round, will withdraw from the race. In the United States the primary is an election within a political party to determine who shall represent that party in the general election. The aspirant receiving the most votes becomes the party's candidate. Although they are internal party elections, American primaries are administered by the various state governments.

agreement with their allies and rivals and share out districts before the first ballot. But the Gaullist candidate, Jacques Chaban-Delmas, was defeated in the first round of the 1974 presidential election when two serious candidates from Majority parties ran, and by 1974 the center, previously opposed to the Government, had swelled the ranks of the Giscardians. From 1974 to 1976 the Giscardians used the threat that they would insist on primaries across the board to keep the Gaullist deputies in line in Parliament: the president would only endorse those deputies who had supported the Government consistently. Later, when the opinion polls were running in their favor, it was the Gaullists who favored primaries in the hope of keeping their supremacy in Parliament. The turning point seems to have come in May 1976. With the blessing of Prime Minister Chirac, who was already seriously thinking of leaving the Government, Yves Guéna, the general secretary of the Gaullist party, came out publicly in favor of holding primaries within the Majority at the forthcoming general election. Although they did not actually say as much, the Gaullist leaders considered primaries a means of counterattacking those who wanted to reduce the power of the Gaullists within the Majority before the voters had their say. If only one Majority candidate ran in each constituency on the first ballot, after all, it would be the president of the republic who would arbitrate between the parties, and he would use this power against the Gaullists. The Gaullists decided to fight back. Immediately the non-Gaullists, meeting on May 23, 1976, in Rennes,[6] reactivated the idea of an alliance between the centrist and Giscardian parties put forward by Jean Lecanuet with Giscard's blessing. The alliance was rejected in the end, but the seeds of the UDF, which would blossom on the eve of the 1978 election, had been sown.

The left's decisive defeat of the Majority in the municipal elections of March 1977[7] undermined the strategy of the Giscardians, who had been in favor of widening their movement to the left. It also consolidated the Chirac strategy of attacking the left and appealing to the traditional Majority electorate. At this point no one in the Majority save Jean-Jacques Servan-Schreiber dared attack the Rally for the Republic directly. Chirac was in command. He decided that the RPR would put up 400 candidates for the 491 seats and held out

---

[6] This was the first conference of the CDS, the Social Democratic Center, which united the Democratic Center and the Center for Democracy and Progress. The latter had broken away from the Democratic Center in June 1969 to support Georges Pompidou in the presidential election.

[7] The Communists and Socialists won in 159 of the 221 towns of over 30,000 inhabitants; Jacques Chirac won in Paris, where he beat the Giscardian candidate, Michel d'Ornano.

an olive branch to his allies and rivals within the Majority. He informed the Giscardians that he was willing to refrain from opposing any of their sixty-five sitting deputies, and he let it be known that he was ready to help Lecanuet's centrists win thirty seats, the quota necessary for the formation of a parliamentary group. The least anti-Gaullist of the Radicals, those associated with Edgar Faure, he offered the support of the RPR, trying thus to bring them into conflict with the president of their party, Servan-Schreiber. The National Center of Independents, or CNI (Centre National des Indépendants), close ally of the Gaullists in Paris, supported Chirac's tactics, which aimed at making him the real leader and arbiter within the Majority by dividing his allies and rivals. Right up to the autumn of 1977 it looked as if Chirac would succeed in imposing his will on the Majority, even on the president's Republican party, despite the fears of the president and the prime minister.

On May 18, 1977, Chirac proposed an electoral pact laying down rules of conduct for the campaign for all the parties within the Majority. On June 24 he gave a more detailed account of his proposals in a letter to the leaders of the four other Majority parties, Lecanuet (CDS), Jean-Pierre Soisson (PR), Servan-Schreiber (Radical), and Bertrand Motte (CNI), and suggested that they meet to seal a "Majority pact." "Such an agreement should in its preamble insist on the fundamental principles governing the free society we defend," Chirac's letter said.

It would include the following points:

- the natural, legitimate diversity of our groups
- the principle of "primaries"
- the possibility of running joint candidates when we consider that circumstances make it necessary
- a code of conduct regulating the relations of our candidates with all the parties within the Majority
- an honor code binding each candidate prior to his official nomination to stand down in favor of the candidate within the Majority who has the highest tally at the first ballot and to support him unreservedly at the second ballot in all cases where a primary has taken place.[8]

Events from then on followed Chirac's plan. On July 19 an electoral pact was signed by the CDS, the PR, the CNI, and the RPR,

---

[8] *Le Monde*, June 26-27, 1977. Chirac sent a copy of this letter to Prime Minister Raymond Barre, who was invited to send a member of his cabinet to the meetings. He did not take advantage of this offer since it would have amounted to an official admission that he was not the real leader of the Majority.

at a Majority summit meeting. Only the Radical party, at Servan-Schreiber's instigation, refused to take part. The four parties reaffirmed "their profound agreement with the principles and institutions of the Fifth Republic," then declared their intention to draw up a joint manifesto. They also adopted a certain number of rules of conduct to be observed by their candidates:

> Except in those cases where a decision has been taken in common to present a single candidate, primary elections will be organized as follows:
> (a) candidates belonging to the Majority will agree not to campaign against each other;
> (b) lower placed Majority candidates will automatically stand down in favor of the one who wins the most votes; and
> (c) all will actively campaign at the second ballot for the single candidate of the Majority. These obligations must be publicly subscribed to by all candidates prior to their formal endorsement by any group.[9]

The representatives of the four parties that signed the electoral pact met on several occasions after July 27 to draw up the manifesto, which was released to the press on September 14, and to reach agreements concerning 118 joint candidates and 373 primaries, which they finally managed to do on November 10 and December 7. On the surface everything went as RPR President Chirac had hoped. Neither the president of the republic nor the prime minister intervened; instead, the agreement was negotiated by the parties concerned. Primaries would be held in three-quarters of the constituencies (instead of one out of ten as in 1973) and the parties had agreed upon the candidates, avoiding both internal strife that would have been prejudicial to the Majority at the second ballot and the atmosphere of interparty hostility that had arisen in the presidential election of May 1974 and the Paris municipal election in March 1977. Last but not least, no official anti-RPR front had been organized by the other parties within the Majority.

But beneath the surface things were more complicated. Jean-Jacques Servan-Schreiber, having refused to take part in the Majority summit, revealed on September 7 that parallel to their negotiations with the Rally for the Republic, the Republicans and the CDS had "over the last four months" held a dozen or so discreet meetings with his Radical party to nominate joint Majority candidates who would run against Gaullist candidates as representatives of a "reformist front."[10]

---

[9] *Manifeste de la Majorité* [The Majority's manifesto], p. 2.
[10] *Le Monde*, September 9, 1977.

Servan-Schreiber had threatened to put up Radical candidates in all constituencies if the Giscardians and centrists did not reach an agreement with him. His revelations were aimed at detaching the non-Gaullist majority parties from the RPR.

Giscardians and centrists tried to play down the incident. They assured Jacques Chirac that they were in favor of union and remained faithful to the Majority pact. They had no intention of creating an anti-Gaullist front, they said, and to prove it they and the RPR signed a joint communiqué on September 14, 1977, the day the Majority's manifesto was published. In this statement the parties declared: "The agreements reached between them commit them wholly and without question and they will under all circumstances, while respecting their separate individualities and their diversity, form a resolutely united front."[11]

Confronted by Servan-Schreiber's reformist front, the Majority remained to all appearances united. But once again this was not the whole story. A few days later, during a broadcast, the general secretary of the Republican party, Jean-Pierre Soisson, declared that the "understanding" between the Majority parties did not "mean uniformity," and he admitted that his party and the groups closest to it (the CDS and the Radical party) had made arrangements "so that for the general election only one candidate represented our various groups at the first ballot."[12] Soisson denied that this constituted in any way an anti-RPR front, and the RPR did not react. On November 10 and December 7, representatives of the RPR, the PR, and the CNI put their signatures on common lists of candidates, which were ratified by the Central Committee of the RPR on December 10.

The struggle between Gaullists and non-Gaullists within the Majority came back into the limelight at the beginning of January 1978, when the non-Gaullist parties asked the prime minister to arbitrate between them in an effort to reduce the number of candidates they were putting up in constituencies where there were to be first-ballot primaries. In a statement released on January 3, Soisson, Lecanuet, and Servan-Schreiber clearly stated their aim: "In order to avoid a multitude of candidates and to enable the voters to make a clear choice, the leaders of these parties have agreed to put up and support a single common candidate in almost all constituencies" holding first-

---

[11] The statement was signed by Jacques Barrot (CDS), Jacques Chirac (RPR), Bertrand Motte (CNI), and Jean-Pierre Soisson (PR); *Le Monde*, September 16, 1977.

[12] Jean-Pierre Soisson, during a broadcast on the radio station Europe no. 1, reported in *Le Monde*, September 20, 1977.

ballot primaries.[13] Servan-Schreiber declared that he hoped the non-Gaullist parties would unite under a common banner and form a "front." His partners refused because they feared the reactions of the RPR. Soisson tried to reassure the Gaullists by suggesting that all the parties revise the lists already established with a view to reducing the number of candidates and putting up, wherever possible, a single candidate for the Majority. The Gaullists remained hostile to these proposals, and on January 11 at a meeting convened in all haste, Gaullists and non-Gaullists clashed violently.

The Gaullists could not reproach the PR and the CDS with having broken the electoral pact since they had not revised in any way the list of 118 joint Majority candidates (54 of whom were RPR members) agreed upon in December. As for the primaries, it had always been on the cards for any party to change its candidate at will, on condition that its partners were informed. It was obvious that the minor parties within the Majority could not afford to be divided among themselves at the first ballot, for if they were they would simply pave the way for the major parties, in particular the RPR. On the other hand the Gaullists could—and did—blame the PR and the CDS for the deviousness of the whole affair and more particularly for having concluded an agreement with a party that had not supported the Barre Government's general policy statement on April 28, 1977, and had refused to pledge its support at the second ballot for whichever Majority candidate did best at the first. Soisson, conscious of the validity of the RPR's complaints, persuaded Servan-Schreiber to publicly endorse the general agreement concerning the withdrawal of candidates at the second ballot, which he did on January 29, 1978. The non-Gaullists, however, continued to play fast and loose with the Gaullists. On January 12 the general secretary of the PR claimed that for the Majority non-Gaullists there was "no question, for the moment, of fighting under the same banner";[14] on February 1, when they published a definitive list of 405 candidates, the Giscardian, centrist, and Radical leaders declared that the candidates could "present themselves as belonging to the Union for French Democracy" or UDF (Union pour la Démocratie Française), echoing the title of Giscard d'Estaing's *Démocratie Française* published in 1976.[15] Thus, a month before the election the UDF was born. By reducing by about 35 percent the number of non-Gaullist candidates in the primaries, the UDF greatly increased the non-Gaullist candi-

---

[13] *Le Monde*, January 5, 1978.

[14] Ibid., January 14, 1978.

[15] Ibid., February 3, 1978.

dates' chances; by invoking Giscard as the Gaullists in the past had invoked de Gaulle or Pompidou, the UDF created a positive image for its candidates and at the same time cemented the bond between its various components.

The Leader of the Majority: Giscard, Chirac, or Barre? The power struggle between Gaullists and non-Gaullists was, over and above the problems of candidates and primaries, a struggle for the leadership of the Majority. Who was to be the recognized leader: Prime Minister Raymond Barre, whom the president of the republic had designated to lead the campaign, or Jacques Chirac, former prime minister and leader of the most powerful parliamentary group within the Majority? The president had declared at his press conference on January 17, 1977, "The public makes up its mind according to what the Government has done and according to whether or not it wants to change the Government. That is why the prime minister will head the national campaign during the 1978 election."[16] Since not everyone saw things this way, the president restated his opinion in an interview in May.[17] If precedents were anything to go by, his decision was justified: in 1967 and 1968 under General de Gaulle and in 1973 under President Pompidou, the prime minister had been invested with supreme authority for the general election. He had announced the aims of the Majority and had cited its achievements. Each time the Giscardians had fully accepted the arbitration of a Gaullist prime minister. But Jacques Chirac and the RPR saw things differently. Precedents were, they declared, of no account in a new situation. General de Gaulle and President Pompidou had both been, in their time, the uncontested leaders of the Majority. President Giscard d'Estaing was not in the same position in 1977. As Chirac put it:

> When he said—as he was entitled to—that whatever the result of the election he would remain in power, he gave up his position as leader of the Majority since he disassociated himself from its destiny. From then on, contrary to what had happened before, he could not expect to delegate to his prime minister a power he had already adandoned.[18]

So the RPR obstinately refused to relinquish its freedom of action, whether by designating joint candidates or by signing a joint mani-

---

[16] Ibid., January 19, 1977.
[17] Interview in *L'Express*, May 9-15, 1977.
[18] Interview in *Le Point*, June 20, 1977.

festo. It favored an understanding between the partners within the Majority and resolutely rejected the very notion of arbitration by the prime minister. The struggle for power within the Majority was on.

The three potential leaders of the Majority had unequal hands. The president drew advantage from his office; the general public readily attacks political parties and leaders, but it sees the presidency as immune. Moreover, Valéry Giscard d'Estaing himself was more popular than his Majority and his Government—and during this period his popularity was on the increase despite the left-wing parties' rising scores in the opinion polls. Chirac was not in a position to attack the president head on. He could not afford to be seen as responsible for any divisions within the Majority. As he put it, speaking before the Central Committee of his party in December 1977: "As far as the president of the republic is concerned, we are deferential. As far as our allies within the Majority are concerned, we are loyal. As far as the electorate is concerned, we are—and we shall remain—true to ourselves."[19] On two separate occasions the president of the RPR tried unsuccessfully to win Giscard over to his side. On December 1, 1977, he asked for an immediate appointment with the president and stressed the danger facing the Majority on account of both internal divisions and the Government's political inactivity. Chirac wanted above all to prove to the public that he was the Majority leader closest to the president. In this he failed, judging by the report of the interview carried a week later in *La Lettre de la Nation*, the Gaullist daily newsletter:

> The President of the RPR thinks he has made his point, which has given him a certain satisfaction. He must have spoken rapidly, for the President of the Republic had an appointment at UNESCO which prevented him from granting more than a short audience to his visitor. The President's timetable is obviously extremely full and it was further loaded yesterday when the Elysée announced that within the next week Jean Lecanuet, Jacques Chaban-Delmas, and Jean-Pierre Soisson would be received . . . . So that no one would feel left out, at the Council of Ministers meeting yesterday the President of the republic congratulated the prime minister "on his courage and on his action to rejuvenate the French economy."

Then during a luncheon Giscard held for eighty leaders of the Majority on January 16, 1978, Chirac tried once more to impress the

---

[19] *La Lettre de la Nation*, December 12, 1977.

president with his misgivings about the anti-Gaullist front within the Majority. The "problems of the political parties" were not, declared the president, to be discussed at such a time or in such a place. And when, a little later, Chirac attacked Jean-Pierre Soisson, his host reminded him again that the Elysée should not be made into a battlefield.[20]

In fact, although he was careful not to intervene directly in internal party controversies, the president followed developments within the Majority closely. Jean Riolacci, the member of his cabinet who dealt with the elections, was present at all the meetings between Giscardians, centrists, and Radicals leading to the creation of the UDF; Michel Pinton, political advisor to the PR and the inventor, as it were, of the UDF, was readily received at the Elysée. It was also from the Elysée that the impetus came, when the moment was ripe, for the launching of secret negotiations between the non-Gaullist Majority parties in mid-1977, or again, for the choice of a common banner in early 1978 and the organization of a poster campaign unofficially linking the non-Gaullist Majority to the president of the republic. Throughout 1977 the president hesitated to allow his troops to do as they wished, fearing that he would expose himself by linking his fate too clearly to that of a specific faction within the Majority. He claimed for instance in his press conference on January 17, 1977, that "the President of the Republic must not have preferences, even if he once belonged . . . to a particular party within the Majority." Giscard went on to evoke a Majority of many parts:

> There is the UDR, which has recently become the RPR. There are the RI, the CDS, the Radicals. It is imperative that each of these political groups express its personality, make known its proposals, thus arousing the interest and support of that particular part of the French electorate that shares its views. Thus there is no uniformity within the Majority. But there is an understanding within the Majority. . . .[21]

Some might say that since the president was unable to impose his will on the various Majority parties he publicly emphasized their diversity, like a general who must follow his troops to remain at their head. Jacques Chirac repeatedly quoted Giscard's statement, the better to justify his own action in favor of several organizations within the Majority. But Giscard changed his tune. In an interview published in the May 9, 1977, issue of *L'Express* he no longer spoke in

---

[20] *Le Monde,* January 18, 1978.
[21] Ibid., January 19, 1977.

terms of several parties, but of polarization within the Majority: "It is imperative to show that the Majority is an entity in which those who want a certain transformation of French society can express themselves and in which those who on the contrary want to keep things as they are will also be heard, so that the two may complement one another." Thus Giscard—using Servan-Schreiber's magazine as his forum—presented the Gaullists as conservatives and the other parties within the Majority as reformers. Even as he attacked the leaders of the RPR he added that the Majority could only win the elections if it were seen as united. In this, Giscard echoed Servan-Schreiber, who had made these points at a time when the president's own party, the PR, had had no desire to do battle with the RPR.

Michel Pinton had a hard time persuading the Giscardians to take on the Gaullist party. His argument was simple: the election was going to be decided by floating voters of the center-left; they had supported Giscard in the past but were now tempted to vote for the Socialists. The RPR had too right-wing an image to attract these new Socialist voters. The solution therefore was to appeal to them by differentiating between Gaullists and Giscardians and by showing the latter to be in favor of reform. It was in November 1977 that the Giscardians decided to stress their distinctiveness and to organize the non-Gaullists within the Majority. The first set of opinion polls carried out for Michel Pinton by SOFRES on the public image of the Republican party worried the Giscardians, for it showed that the Gaullist party had a powerful, dynamic image. It did, however, prompt them to change their strategy. And it showed that the PR was the only other Majority party beside the Gaullists that seemed to the public to have a real organization and to be attractive enough to stand a chance of overtaking the Gaullist candidates in the primaries.[22] What really made the Giscardians decide to act, however, was the fear that, given the strength of the RPR, centrists and Giscardians would be routed in the election if they were divided. The opinion poll published by IFOP-*Le Point* at the beginning of November 1977—the first poll on voting intentions that named the candidates, not simply the parties—gave the RPR 24 percent of the votes, as against 18 percent for all the non-Gaullist parties put together. There is no doubt that this poll cemented the alliance of the non-Gaullists.

---

[22] The first series of SOFRES opinion polls was undertaken for the Republican party between September 15 and 19, 1977; the second between December 15 and 20, 1977; and the last between February 14 and 17, 1978, after the official creation of the UDF. The PR also had the IFOP do a major study of new Socialist voters.

Jacques Chirac for his part had only one trump card in the battle for the leadership of the Majority, and that was the strength of his party. On December 5, 1977, only a year after the Rally for the Republic had been launched, the Gaullist revival was a fact. The party had doubled its membership, bringing it up to half a million, according to the general secretary of the RPR, Jérôme Monod. After the Communists, the Gaullists had the best party machine at both local and national levels. Chirac had a numerous brain trust, full of ideas, and his potential electorate had risen to around 25 percent, from less than 15 percent in May 1974. This meant that the RPR could fight its Majority rivals at the first ballot to good effect, even where they were united.[23] The RPR had proved in the Paris municipal election that it was capable of carrying the day even when the president and the prime minister threw their support to other candidates. So Jacques Chirac had a powerful means of intimidation within the Majority: would it not be better for the PR and the CDS to negotiate with the Gaullists, as he suggested, than to be obliged to run against them at the first ballot? Was the president prepared to run the risk of presiding over an anti-RPR front? When the UDF project was under discussion Chirac used all the means at his disposal to sink it before it could be launched. In mid-January he even threatened to go back on the electoral agreements he had concluded with the PR and the CDS in the winter of 1977 and to run RPR candidates in all 491 constituencies, underlining the risks of an anti-Gaullist front for the president himself: "More serious still," he said, "this maneuver compromises the institutions of the Fifth Republic for it reduces the president to endorsing sectarian behavior and serving a faction. That is what I told the President of the Republic in a letter on January 9 last."[24]

However, when the non-Gaullist Majority parties decided to go ahead with their plans, Chirac found himself deprived of any means of retaliation. His dilemma was that he had to show due respect to the president and could not appear to be the divisive partner within the Majority—especially at a time when the left seemed united and on the verge of winning. Since he could not attack the president himself, Chirac attacked his entourage: "When the course of history wavers . . . as in a Shakespearean tragedy, no trumpet sounds to warn the courtesans and the buffoons that they must leave the stage before fate's will is done."[25] Since Chirac was unable to break the alliance

---

[23] On the state of the RPR a year after it had been launched, see Jérôme Monod's report in *La Lettre de la Nation,* December 6, 1977.

[24] Vierzon, *La Lettre de la Nation,* January 17, 1978.

[25] Ibid.

between the PR and the CDS, he simply added a few token candidates to the RPR list in districts where the UDF candidate was otherwise unopposed on the right. Unable to prevent the creation of the UDF, he ridiculed it: "Our problem is to outdistance the right—the UDF for instance, which I have never heard of at the grass-roots level."[26]

But Chirac gave RPR candidates and campaign workers strict instructions: "Do not mistake your enemy. The only enemy is the opposition. Do not indulge in polemics of any sort with allied groups within the Majority."[27] The battle was joined with the Union of the Left, and internal quarrels had to be put aside.

Prime Minister Raymond Barre tried, for his part, to extricate himself from a difficult position. The president asked him to lead the Majority, but he could not do so since the major component of the Majority was hostile to him. Giscardians, centrists, and the president himself begged Barre at least to lead the non-Gaullist group, but he would not be persuaded. In his opinion the prime minister—responsible to Parliament for the whole of the Majority—could not lead a faction. He was, however, in favor of the agreement between the non-Gaullist parties, and once the UDF was created he did not hide the fact that for him it was both useful and desirable. In a television interview, for example, Barre said:

> It was normal for the two major groups within the Majority to be organized. . . . It was both useful and desirable, for the UDF represents a certain ideology which may attract people who have until now been in the opposition. . . . To lead such a group is another matter. As I am prime minister and as the Majority which supports me includes the two groups, I do not see why, during the election, I should become leader of one of them.[28]

Every prime minister of the Fifth Republic has had one eye more or less on the presidency, and perhaps for this reason Raymond Barre decided to conduct his own campaign on behalf of the Majority:

> Mine is the prime minister's campaign. I conduct it without belonging to any party. I am going to come out in favor of an understanding within the Majority, of an opening up of the Majority, and I am going to beg the French people not

---

[26] Television interview, Antenne 2, February 8, 1978, reprinted in *La Lettre de la Nation*, February 10, 1978.

[27] Speech to RPR candidates and officials in Paris, January 22, 1978, *La Lettre de la Nation*, January 23, 1978.

[28] Television interview, "Spécial Evènement," TF1, February 21, 1978, reprinted in *Le Monde*, February 23, 1978.

only to criticize and condemn the Common Program but also to turn towards a France that is the answer to their hopes and their desires. . . .[29]

During the long struggle for power that preceded the March 1978 elections, each of the three major protagonists suffered blows and each scored. If Giscard failed to impose Barre's leadership, he nevertheless managed to inspire the creation of the UDF as a counterweight to the Gaullists. Jacques Chirac, for his part, could not prevent the organization of an anti-RPR front, yet his remained the major party within the Majority, and he succeeded in eliminating the prime minister and safeguarding the autonomy of the RPR. He also forced the other parties within the Majority, including Servan-Schreiber's Radicals, to conclude an electoral pact with him; the PR and the CDS even reached agreement on a minimal program. Finally, Prime Minister Barre, though not able to lead the Majority's campaign as previous prime ministers had, had encouraged the creation of the UDF without tying his own destiny to its success or failure.

Platforms and Campaigns

The Majority parties were united in their rejection of the left's Common Program, but they had a harder time agreeing on their own. The process of drawing up the manifesto of the Majority, signed by Gaullists, centrists, and Giscardians, showed how fragile was the understanding between the Majority parties. In particular, the Gaullists' refusal to simply ratify the Blois Program, which had been drawn up under the eye of the prime minister, made the most important cleavages plain. In the end the Majority parties organized not one but three separate election campaigns: a Gaullist one led by Jacques Chirac; a Giscardian one, of which Raymond Barre's personal campaign was one element; and the president's major speeches.

The Manifesto of the Majority. The manifesto of the Majority was drawn up on July 19 at the first summit of the leaders of the RPR, the CDS, the PR, and the CNI, at Jacques Chirac's instigation. Its contents were strongly influenced by the most powerful party of the Majority and by the platforms of the RPR and the CDS. Although it outlined objectives for the next legislative session, the manifesto was not a real program for a Majority Government. The non-Gaullist Majority parties could not discuss such a program in the

---

[29] Ibid.

absence of the prime minister, whom Giscard had charged with determining "the objectives for future action to be presented to the country in March 1978,"[30] but the Gaullist party would not hear of the prime minister's taking a leading role. The purpose of the manifesto, therefore, was to underline "the essential values" shared by the parties within the Majority and to describe their basic orientation in important policy areas.[31]

On August 10, 1977, during the four parties' first working session together, the RPR presented a four-page draft drawn up by the director of the party's election department, Jacques Toubon. He had adapted the document from the RPR manifesto and had retained verbatim chapter headings referring to "a free society in an independent France," a "responsible society," and a "just society" committed to "fighting privilege." On August 16 a preamble was added defining the real issue of the March election—the choice between "the society of freedom and progress" and "the constraints of collectivism and bureaucracy"—and mentioning the achievements of the first twenty years of the Fifth Republic. The following day, the CDS presented a counter-proposal, virtually a summary of the first draft of its own program.[32] As for the PR, it put forward no proposals at all. Its own manifesto, *Le Projet Républicain*, was not to be published until two months later, in December 1977. The Giscardians at this stage tried to delay things so as to give the non-Gaullist parties time to organize and the prime minister time to draw up the Government's program.

On August 17, Jacques Douffiagues, representing the PR, protested the fact that the manifesto was being discussed before the nominations and suggested that the two should be examined at the same time—which, of course, would have slowed down the whole process. Yves Guena, the RPR representative, insisted that the manifesto be drawn up first, and he was supported by the representative of the CNI, Jacques Fouchier, who underlined the importance of publishing the Majority manifesto *before* the left-wing parties met in mid-September to revise their Common Program. The Gaullists obtained satisfaction, mainly because the representative of the CDS, André Fosset, thought it would be possible to conclude the discus-

---

[30] Carpentras, July 8, 1977. *Le Monde*, July 10, 1977.

[31] Preamble, *Manifeste de la Majorité*.

[32] "Trente Minutes avec le CDS" [Thirty minutes with the CDS]. This brochure was intended to give a rapid overview of the party's history and aims. The CDS manifesto, *L'Autre Solution* [The other solution], was not published until October 1977 (by Hachette, in Paris).

sions within a week or at most a fortnight. The discussions took place at the end of August and the final text, drawn up on September 5, was signed on September 14, 1977.

The centrists and the Gaullists were the main participants in the negotiations. Both made concessions. The centrists refused to permit allusions to "twenty years" of achievement under the Fifth Republic since they had only been in the Majority for the last four years; the Gaullists gave in, settling for vaguer formulas like "in less than a generation." André Diligent, the centrists' spokesman, also asked for some passages to be toned down. Instead of declaring that the welfare system introduced by de Gaulle was "the most humane and best in the world," the final draft spoke of "one of the most humane and all-inclusive [systems] in the world." Similarly, the energy crisis and the lack of raw materials were said to have brought about "unemployment" where the first draft had spoken of "slight unemployment." For its part, the CDS agreed to eliminate a reference to nationalization that the RPR considered ill-timed[33] and to couch the references to Europe in Gaullist terms—to speak of "an independent Europe on the confederate model," rather than "the peoples of Europe" electing a European Parliament.[34]

Hardly had it been signed and released than the Majority manifesto was forgotten. While the left-wing parties battled over their Common Program, the Majority parties, having shown themselves capable of reaching agreement, could henceforth concentrate on their differences. Nevertheless, they had formulated their agreement about what was at stake in the election:

> The country must decide whether it chooses the society of freedom and progress that we defend or the constraints of collectivism and bureaucracy that the signatories of the Common Program would relentlessly impose. . . . You must not be led astray by the suicidal demagogy of the Common Program. You must bear in mind, when the time comes, that the real issue, IS YOUR FREEDOM.[35]

The different parties within the Majority—newcomers and old timers alike—also agreed on the major achievements of the Fifth Republic:

> What has been achieved is fundamental. No one can deny that the Fifth Republic has deeply changed our country and

---

[33] The CDS declared that it considered nationalization to be a democratic means of managing industrial monopolies.

[34] The unpublished information on the negotiations between the parties is taken from interviews conducted by the author.

[35] *Manifeste de la Majorité*, p. 2.

bettered our living conditions. The institutions have proved stable—more so than those of any other democratic regime France has had. We have managed to ally democracy with efficiency. France has achieved greater dignity throughout the world thanks to its institutions; to its economy which has been overhauled . . . and to its defense, which—thanks to the nuclear deterrent—ensures its independence. . . . In less than a generation the purchasing power of the French people has doubled.[36]

Last but not least, the Majority program stressed the "values" the parties shared and their "plans for the future," for "a society of freedom, a society of responsibility, and a society of justice." "We say: the individual must come first . . . the institutions the French have chosen must be respected . . . there must be dialogue . . . communication with the world."[37]

The Blois Program. Even before the Majority manifesto had been signed, Jean Pierre Soisson declared that the PR felt the Government should define precise objectives.[38] Jacques Chirac, meanwhile, had warned the Elysée and Matignon that the Gaullists would "under no circumstances" put their signatures to a program drawn up by the Barre Government: "Less than a hundred days before the election, the Government in office is by definition a doomed Government and as such cannot make pledges for the future."[39] This did not prevent the prime minister from drawing up a program for the next legislative session, as the president had instructed him to. On November 15 he held a meeting of the whole Government to define his objectives for the next five years. On January 6, 1978, at a round table held at the Château de Rambouillet and presided over by the president of the republic, the Government finalized its "future objectives for individual freedom and justice." Raymond Barre announced the 30 objectives and the 110 proposals that were henceforth to be known as "the Blois Program" in Blois on January 7.

We choose reform, not upheaval; evolution, not revolution. We propose objectives that can be achieved. I ask all the French men and women who are going to vote and all those who are standing as candidates—without excluding anyone

---

[36] Ibid., p. 3.

[37] Ibid., pp. 8-9.

[38] August 24, 1977.

[39] Jacques Chirac to the Central Committee of the RPR, December 10, 1977. *La Lettre de la Nation*, December 12, 1977.

—to unite, over and above their legitimate differences around these objectives for the pursuit of individual freedom and justice. . . . I ask you today to remain full of hope. We shall not lead France into a hazardous political and economic experiment.[40]

Giscardians, centrists, and Radicals immediately expressed their agreement with the Blois Program. The Gaullists, however, remained true to themselves. The Government's objectives did "include some interesting points," they said, adding:

But, over and above the intentions the Government has expressed, the RPR declares once again that to bring France out of the crisis it faces the new mandate expressed in the March general election must lead to the formulation of a new economic policy aiming at ensuring first the revival of growth, the adaptation of the existing structures, and full employment. The RPR has drawn up its own proposals especially in this field. It will develop and complete them during the campaign.[41]

The Socialist-Communist program entailed modifying France's economic and social structures; it was expensive and the taxpayer would have to pay. The Blois program, on the contrary, was resolutely liberal, clearly capitalistic, and limited both in its ambitions and in its cost. It aimed at giving a new impetus to private industry, competition, and profit making in a liberal economy; it defined priorities in the field of welfare, in particular for the poorest categories (those earning the least, the elderly, women living alone, large families). The Common Program was costed by the prime minister at 65 billion francs for its first year; the Blois Program in five years would cost the nation no more than 22 billion. This was to be a major theme of the prime minister's campaign.

Three Campaigns in One. When the prime minister's campaign was finally launched several weeks before the creation of the UDF, the Gaullist campaign had been in progress for some time. Already in September Jacques Chirac had urged the Gaullists to conduct a serious, separate campaign.

We shall remain true to ourselves for we shall stand under our own banner. Our candidates will neither seek nor accept

---

[40] Prime Minister Raymond Barre, in Blois, January 7, 1978. *Le Monde*, January 10, 1978.

[41] Yves Guéna after the joint meeting of the RPR Political Council and parliamentary bureau, January 9, 1978; *La Lettre de la Nation*, January 11, 1978.

> any endorsement other than that of the movement—except where our candidate is by agreement the joint representative of the Majority. Our candidates will defend our objectives and support no other program.[42]

At the beginning of October 1977 the president of the RPR began a marathon campaign which was to take him in less than five months into virtually all 491 constituencies. Personal contact with the people and interaction with opinion leaders seemed to Chirac more productive than a centralized national campaign relying on the mass media, which, out of sympathy either for the left or for the Giscardians, consistently portrayed Chirac as driven by ambition and right-wing authoritarianism. In an election campaign, they were sure to distort his message.

His staff in Paris, who prepared his speeches and organized his trips, and the leaders of the regional federations of the party gave Chirac sound support. At the grass-roots level too he had help from a great number of party workers. He was no doubt the only leader within the Majority to have both the time and the political resources necessary for a major tour. By the beginning of March 1978 he had traveled 50,000 kilometers in seventy-eight departments, had held sixty-nine rallies with average audiences of 5–6,000, had made 292 speeches and met local officials at 112 meetings—not to mention the innumerable contacts he had had with individual party members and activists.[43] The pattern of these trips was always the same. First Chirac met the people in the streets and markets. He talked to passers-by, did a little shopping, kissed children, ignored the handful of hecklers. Next he met with the local Gaullist activists, usually at a buffet luncheon or dinner and praised their work, declaring himself as shocked as they were by the blows below the belt being delivered by their so-called allies. Then came meetings with the local press—usually either a press conference or a dinner at which Chirac would drop a few carefully calculated confidential remarks. Finally Chirac would meet the voters at vast public rallies where he would speak for an hour or more, taking up over and over again the specifically Gaullist themes—those that in the RPR's opinion revealed a fundamental difference between the RPR and the other parties within the Majority: "We are more intransigent where the independence of France and the security of the French are concerned. We are more

---

[42] Jacques Chirac, parliamentary group meeting, Menton, September 29, 1977. *Le Monde,* October 1, 1977.

[43] See *La Lettre de la Nation,* March 1, 1978, and *Le Monde,* March 4, 1978.

ambitious for the economy, more conscious of the intolerable nature of unemployment, more eager for social progress."[44]

Accused of secretly hoping for a victory of the left to carve out a promising future for himself as leader of the opposition, Chirac defended himself by citing the vigor of his campaign efforts: "I was the only Majority leader to be on the hustings all day every day, . . . holding six to eight meetings a day, a meeting every evening in a different department or constituency, the only leader to fight on all fronts exclusively against the opposition."[45]

Gradually the Gaullist themes became clear:

- Refusal to give up and contemplate seriously a victory of the left. Whether Communists and Socialists agreed on a Common Program was immaterial. The peril was the same in the eyes of the Gaullists; the Socialist adversary was no less dangerous than his Communist counterpart. The Gaullists led the fight for the victory of the Majority, differentiating themselves from the "lukewarm partisans and believers in compromise."
- A new economic policy based on planning and the revival of growth through investment, denying the inevitability of unemployment.
- A constant, determined desire for the independence of France, and hence rejection of European integration in any form and great attention to defense policy—in particular the maintenance of the nuclear deterrent.
- The upholding of the institutions as they were; categorical rejection of proportional representation and of any innovation leading to a presidential regime.
- A firm commitment to ensuring the security of the individual and of property, to a free society in which those who wield authority have not abdicated their responsibilities.
- The reiteration of the importance of participation, the elimination of bureaucracy, and the creation of a "day-to-day democracy."[46]

These themes, apart from the last, were all defensive, aimed at preserving what the Fifth Republic had created under de Gaulle and Pompidou.

---

[44] February 11, 1978, Jacques Chirac in Paris, Porte de Pantin. *Rassemblement Actualité*, February 23, 1978.

[45] Jacques Chirac, France Inter, January 19, 1978. *La Lettre de la Nation*, January 20, 1978.

[46] For further details see the RPR manifesto, *Propositions pour la France* [Proposals for France] (Paris: Stock, 1977).

The climax of the Gaullists' campaign was an enormous rally held in Paris at the Porte de Pantin on Saturday, February 11—the "most enormous rally ever organized in Paris by a political party," according to *Le Monde*.[47] In the huge spaces of an old beef market, 260 meters long, 60 meters wide, and 30 meters high, on an icy day, some 130,000 Gaullist supporters gathered to listen to speeches by Michel Debré and Jacques Chirac, to see the RPR candidates, and finally to sing the "Marseillaise," led by Line Renaud. This was no time for subtleties; it was a general mobilization of troops. Debré was in his element: "It is in battle that we are most true to ourselves," he declared, "for it is in battle that we are important and assert ourselves. It is our willingness to join battle that underlies our political worth."[48] Chirac led the charge: "Yes, we must win. Yes, we are going to win. Together we shall win this battle of France. Long live the Republic! Long live France!"[49] The RPR played up this grassroots campaign even in its national television broadcasts, featuring, in between speeches by Chirac, interviews with local Gaullist activists.

The Giscardian Campaign. However one looks at it, the Giscardians' campaign was exactly the opposite of the Gaullists'. First, it started much later: the prime minister gave the kick-off when he announced the Blois Program on January 7, and the UDF was finally constituted on February 1, only forty days before the first ballot. The non-Gaullist Majority parties' campaign, above all, relied more on mass television audiences than on major political rallies. The weakness of their party organization and the limited time they had in which to reach the voters gave them no choice. The three parties that made up the UDF ran coordinated poster and television campaigns but otherwise campaigned separately. The PR, for instance, brought out a manifesto that made "twenty-one concrete proposals," some of which were very concrete indeed: universal home ownership, manual training at school, retirement à la carte, free telephones for the elderly, and so on. Others were simply headings under which a policy remained to be formulated: the reform of national service, a consumer protection code, a national ecological charter, a code for the wives of shopkeepers and artisans, and so on. The CDS was the most inno-

---

[47] *Le Monde*, February 14, 1978.

[48] Michel Debré, former prime minister, Porte de Pantin, February 11, 1978. *Rassemblement Actualité*, February 24, 1978.

[49] Jacques Chirac, president of the RPR, Porte de Pantin, February 11, 1978. *Rassemblement Actualité*, February 23, 1978.

vative in its use of the media, presenting its program in the form of a comic strip, the better to be understood by Everyman.[50]

The CDS, the PR, and the Radicals delegated the responsibility for their major effort, their television broadcasts, to the "father of the UDF" Michel Pinton. This gave their media campaign a certain unity—as did the unofficial patronage of the president of the republic. An enormous poster of Valéry Giscard d'Estaing seen in profile associated the UDF with the president. The television campaign was designed to express the Giscardians' reformist message while stressing the notion of renewal by showing young people, new faces, and a new tone. The UDF tried less to put forward a program of its own—since in fact its program was the Government's—than to strike public opinion by conveying the impression that something important was happening on the center-left.

Raymond Barre's campaign complemented this effort. It was essentially a poster campaign, featuring pictures of the prime minister and the slogan *"Barre-confidence."* In a series of television broadcasts and public meetings covered at length by the radio and television networks, Barre and Chirac were presented as the only champions of the Majority against the left and the Common Program. Making the most of his background as a professor of economics, Barre depicted the economic chaos that, in his opinion, would immediately flow from a Socialist-Communist victory:

A burden would be placed on the economy amounting to 227 billion francs. The question is not what measures have been proposed, but how they will be financed. There is in fact only one solution: unless the solution is inflation, the creation of money by the Bank of France to finance the new expenditures, the only possibility is increased taxes. What is being offered to the French people today is, in fact, at least the doubling of their taxes.[51]

The President's Campaign. Although Giscard's contribution was limited to fewer than a dozen speeches over the year preceding the election, it played a decisive part in the result. All of the speeches were announced well in advance except the last, which struck public opinion all the more forcefully. On January 17, 1977, the president promised that he would make known his view of what was the right

50 *L'Autre Solution pour la France* [The other solution for France], available at CDS headquarters.
51 Raymond Barre, "Spéciale Législatives 78" [The legislative election special] Antenne 2, February 13, 1978. *Le Monde*, February 15, 1978.

choice, *le bon choix*, for France: "The President of the Republic, chosen by universal suffrage, cannot remain a silent figurehead," he said. "Every time the question crops up, that is, every time that there is a fundamental choice to be made for France, I shall indicate what is, in my opinion, the right choice for France."[52] A year later, on January 27, 1978, at Verdun-sur-le-Doubs, Giscard clearly and gravely announced his support for the Majority and his rejection of the Common Program: "In 1974, during the presidential campaign I spoke to you of the Common Program and you followed my advice. My opinion has not changed nor is it simply linked to the coming election."[53]

When he announced in Washington, on May 21, 1976, that he would remain in office as he was entitled to until 1981 even if the left won the general election, Giscard took the risk of reassuring hesitant Socialist voters. Should serious difficulties arise, they might think, the president would always be there. At Verdun-sur-le-Doubs he corrected this impression when he told the voters they must assume their responsibilities: "You can choose the Common Program. You have the right to do so. But if that is your decision it will be abided by. Make no mistake, the president of this republic has not the means to oppose it."[54] It was generally thought that the president would take no further part in the election campaign. But the results of the opinion polls—which remained unpublished, under the new law—continued to give the parties of the left a clear victory, and the president was pressed to speak out again on the eve of the election, as de Gaulle and Pompidou had done in former years. The prime minister, Raymond Barre, seems to have advised Giscard not to intervene, but the major leaders of the UDF urged him to make a speech, and the leaders of the RPR declared to anyone who would listen that the president's silence would be a desertion of his troops in the face of danger. After much hesitation the president decided, on March 8, to tell "the truth to the French people" one last time and to show them clearly that they must assume their responsibilities.

His speech was broadcast live on Saturday, March 11. "I am speaking to those who hesitate," he said, "and who want to be quite sure what the right choice is. It is my duty to warn you, so that you cannot say later that you were deceived."[55] The alliance of the parties

---

[52] Press conference, Elysée, January 17, 1977.

[53] Verdun-sur-le-Doubs, January 27, 1978.

[54] Ibid. On the question of the president's tactics see Jean Charlot, "Le mimodrame de la gauche au pouvoir" [Psychodrama of the left in power], *Projet* 109 (November 1976), pp. 1005-1019.

[55] *Le Monde*, March 14, 1978.

of the left, Giscard said, was incapable of forming a stable, lasting Government based on sincere agreement. If the Government were to keep the numerous and tempting promises made by the Common Program, the French economy, still recovering, would rapidly be reduced to a state of crisis. The independence and the dignity of France and the building of Europe would be empty phrases. Concluding, Giscard said: "My dear French women, my dear French men, I have not addressed you in the language of partisanship, but in the language of common sense. . . . I have no interest to defend, no ambition to satisfy, I am preoccupied with the fate of France, which you hold in your hands."[56]

The Results

Motivations. It is difficult to isolate the impact of a single event, such as the president's final speech, among the mass of appeals and speeches that constitute an election campaign. Yet the fact remains that the electorate swung over to the Majority at the very last moment. After the election 5 percent of the voters said they had changed their minds shortly before the first ballot, 4 percent in favor of the Majority, 1 percent in favor of the left. And among these eleventh-hour converts, roughly half said they had changed their minds during the very last days—15 percent on the last day, when Giscard made his final speech on television, 35 percent "at the last moment."[57] At the very least, Giscard's address accompanied and magnified a decisive shift of opinion during the final days of the campaign—a campaign that had lasted many months during which the victory of the left had seemed beyond challenge.

Opinion polls give a fairly clear idea of the motivations of the voters who supported the Majority. The major reasons given by respondents were negative: a vote for the Majority was a rejection of the left, based on fear of seeing the Communist party dominate a left-wing Government, fear of the economic risks that the Common Program of the left would entail if it were applied, or a belief in the incapacity of the parties of the left to form a solid, stable Government. Half-Giscardian, half-Gaullist, the Majority voter was above all frankly anti-Communist, suspicious of the Socialist party, and not ready to risk the benefits of today's society in the name of the better tomorrow promised by the left. But these negative motives were

---

56 Ibid.
57 SOFRES Opinion Poll, *Le Nouvel Observateur*, April 24, 1978.

TABLE 3–1
Voters' Reasons for Supporting the Majority, February 1978

Reason	Percentage of Respondents
Negative Reasons	
Objections to the Communist party; anticommunism	22
Objections to the Socialist party; suspicion of the Socialists	7.5
Positive Reasons	
In favor of Gaullism	
Approval of General de Gaulle's work	12
Approval of the institutions of the Fifth Republic	9
Appeal of Jacques Chirac	7
In favor of Giscardianism	
Approval of President Giscard d'Estaing	13
Agreement with the ideas expressed by Valéry Giscard d'Estaing in *Démocratie Française*	8
Appeal of Raymond Barre	2.5
Appeal of Jean Lecanuet	2
Appeal of Jean-Pierre Soisson	1
Other	
Approval of society as it is	7.5
Other	4
Don't know	4.5
Total	100.0

NOTE: The survey question was, "Give the major reason why you prefer the Majority."
SOURCE: *Le Quotidien de Paris*, February 6–10, 1978.

underpinned by a positive belief in the values of Gaullism and Giscardianism, in their leaders, and in the political system of the Fifth Republic (see Table 3–1).

At the first ballot, although the Majority shrank in relation to 1973, it did not suffer as much as had been expected. Indeed, the Majority did far better in the election than anyone had believed possible and the left was defeated (see Tables 3–2, 3–3, and 3–4).

The Strength of Gaullism. With 22.43 percent of the votes cast in metropolitan France and 154 deputies elected, the Gaullist party remained the largest single party, though it did less well than in 1973. As a percentage of votes cast, its 1978 score was among its best in

TABLE 3-2

1978 ELECTION RESULTS, FIRST BALLOT, METROPOLITAN FRANCE

Party	Percentage of Votes Cast	Popular Votes
Majority		
RPR	22.43	6,303,611
UDF	20.42	5,738,938
(PR)	(10.78)	(3,028,810)
(CDS)	(4.99)	(1,402,018)
(Center-left)	(2.88)	(808,577)
(Other Majority)	(3.15)	(884,480)
Total right and center	46.17	12,973,072
Total left	48.86	13,729,494
Ecologist and other	4.97	1,395,547
Total	100.00	28,098,113

NOTE: The differences between some of these totals and those found in other tables in this book are due to differences in the classification of candidates. This problem is explained further in Appendix A.

SOURCE: Author's adaptation of the Ministry of Interior's electoral statistics, published in *Les Elections Législatives de 1978* [The legislative elections of 1978] (Paris: Imprimerie Nationale, 1978).

TABLE 3-3

1978 ELECTION RESULTS, DECISIVE BALLOT, METROPOLITAN FRANCE
(in percentages of votes cast)

Party	Vote
Majority	
Rally for the Republic	25.9
Union for French Democracy	23.0
Other	2.2
Total	51.1
Left	
Socialist party and Movement of Leftist Radicals	29.7
Communist party	18.3
Other	0.4
Total	48.4

NOTE: These figures are based on the results of the "decisive ballot" in each district—the first ballot in districts where the deputy was elected by an absolute majority on the first ballot, the second ballot in the remaining constituencies.

SOURCE: Jean-Luc Parodi, "L'échec des gauches," *Revue Politique et Parlementaire*, no. 873, p. 23.

TABLE 3–4

Outgoing and Incoming Majority Deputies, by Party, 1978

Party	Outgoing Deputies Number	%	Incoming Deputies Number	%	Change (in seats)
RPR	173	35.2	154	31.3	−19
UDF					
PR	(61)		(71)		(+10)
CDS	(28)		(35)		(+ 7)
Radicals	(7)		(7)		
Total UDF	119	24.2	123	25.2	+ 4
Other	15	3.1	13	3.0	− 1
Total Majority	307	62.5	292	59.5	−15
Total Opposition	184	37.5	199	40.5	+15
Total Seats	(491)	(100)	(491)	(100)	

Source: Compiled by the author from the lists of members released by the different parliamentary party groups.

those general elections where it faced competition on the right: the Rally of the French People (Rassemblement du Peuple Français) had only obtained 21.2 percent in 1951, and the Union for the New Republic (Union pour la Nouvelle République) 19.5 percent in 1958. There had been times, of course, when the Gaullist movement had done considerably better—1968 (37 percent), 1967 (32.2 percent), 1962 (31.9 percent), or even 1973 (25.7 percent)—but in all these elections the Gaullists had concluded pacts with other Majority parties before the first ballot and had obtained the lion's share of joint Majority nominations. The main lesson to be drawn from the 1978 election was that—despite the defeat of Jacques Chaban-Delmas, the Gaullist candidate, at the first round of the presidential election in May 1974, the loss of the direction of the Government in August 1976, when Raymond Barre became the first non-Gaullist prime minister of the Fifth Republic, and the rivalry of its allies in three-quarters of the constituencies—Gaullism remained one of the major components of the French party system. It has often been prophesied that the Gaullist movement was about to be wiped out—in 1962 when the Algerian war ended, in 1969 after General de Gaulle left power, in 1970 after his death, in 1974 when Chaban-Delmas lost to Giscard. Each time events belied the prophesy, and again in 1978 Gaullism was shown to be an important, lasting political force. As its leaders

TABLE 3–5
PERFORMANCE OF THE RPR AND THE UDF IN THE FIRST BALLOT,
1978, METROPOLITAN FRANCE

	RPR		UDF	
Category	No. of districts	% of districts	No. of districts	% of districts
Party heading the Majority list	248	52.3	226	47.7
Candidates elected in the first ballot	25		27	
Single Majority candidates in the second ballot	223		199	
Winners of Majority primaries	186	55.5	149	44.5

SOURCE: Compiled by the author.

immediately underlined: "The Gaullist movement is once again the major political party in France, both in the number of votes cast in its favor and in the number of deputies it elected. Since 1974 the durability of the Gaullist movement has been questioned. Today its existence is unequivocally confirmed."[58]

If we take into account the fact that the RPR presented no candidate in seventy-six constituencies which it left to its allies, and that there was no UDF rival in fifty-four constituencies, we must adjust the RPR score to obtain a better estimate of its potential strength in the electorate. This comes out at roughly 25 percent of the votes cast. Clearly, then, the Gaullists had overcome the negative effects of the presidential defeat in 1974 (when their strength fell to 15 percent) and had recovered the position they had occupied in 1973. In the primaries the RPR scored well (see Table 3–5). In 55 percent of the races it did better than the UDF. When faced with a Republican or CDS rival the Gaullist won exactly half the time; when faced with a Radical opponent the Gaullist won two contests out of three.

Even so, the Gaullists' position was less safe than it was in 1973. If we consider the thirty-four constituencies in which there

[58] *La Lettre de la Nation*, March 22, 1978.

were Majority primaries in both 1973 and 1978, the Gaullist candidates came first twenty-five times (73 percent) in 1973 and only sixteen times (47 percent) in 1978. It is true that between the two elections the Giscardians' ranks had been reinforced by the former opposition centrists. At the second ballot, contrary to certain Giscardian statements during the campaign, the RPR did as well against the Socialists as the UDF. In the fifty-two constituencies where the left had obtained 46 to 49.9 percent of the votes cast at the first ballot, the RPR candidate beat the Socialist at the second ballot in eighteen out of twenty-five cases (72 percent), the UDF candidate in twenty out of twenty-seven (74 percent).

The Making of the UDF. The essential function performed by the UDF in the end was to give some consistency and credibility to the non-Gaullist parties in the Majority by putting them on a level with the three major parties—the Gaullists, the Socialists, and the Communists. Had they run separately in 1978 the three parties that made up the UDF would not have been thought of as winners by a long stretch. The largest of them, the Republican party, with its 10.78 percent of the votes and seventy-one seats, would have cut a sorry figure for a party that had elected a president only four years before; it had been winning more than 20 percent in the voting intention polls in 1974 and 1975 and its leader, Jean-Pierre Soisson, had believed it capable of reaching 21 percent in the general election. It must be remembered, of course, that the Republicans ran only 186 candidates in the end—further proof, perhaps, of their inadequacy as the sole representatives of Giscardianism at the first ballot.

The CDS and the Radicals, for their part, could not boast either: when the reformist center had been in opposition it had polled some 13 percent of the votes cast, and when it joined the UDF it brought with it just over half its electorate—some 8 percent of the votes. Together under the UDF banner, however, these parties came close to the RPR in votes and in seats. They served as a rallying point for Giscardian voters and captured some left-of-center floating voters as well. The maneuver was so obviously successful that, despite the hesitations of its founders, the UDF, which had started off as a mere electoral alliance, became a permanent alliance and a parliamentary group after the elections. Moreover, it seemed full of promise. The political pendulum had not swung to the left after all, and the bright young newcomers to the National Assembly were not the Socialists everyone had expected, but the Giscardians.

Conclusion

For the Majority, once the wonderful surprise of victory was over, the aftermath of the general election of March 12 and 19, 1978, was not without bitterness. Uncertain of their fate within the new UDF alliance, Radicals, centrists, and Giscardians were frustrated by the fact that the Gaullists had remained strong (almost 53 percent of the Majority deputies were theirs), and this in their opinion would put a brake on the policy of reform and relaxation that the president wanted to further. Some centrists and even some Giscardians were not happy with the extension of Raymond Barre's austerity plan or with the cure that was prescribed for the country after the election—namely economic liberalism, resulting in rising prices in the name of the true costs. The Gaullists, for their part, vaguely felt that they had been cheated out of their victory by the Government, which had proceeded as if nothing had happened and the Gaullists did not exist. They will, no doubt, be all the more tempted to provoke a Government crisis to remind both the Government and the country of their existence. The differences of opinion between Gaullists and Giscardians that had been apparent throughout the campaign, were even clearer afterwards when the left, stunned by defeat, no longer constituted enough of an immediate threat to compel the Majority to unite.

Several major issues intensify the differences between the two major components of the Majority: they differ in their attitudes towards widening the European Economic Community, reinforcing the power of the European Parliament, and promoting economic revival and full employment. Neither the president of the republic nor the president of the RPR seems to put his faith in conciliation and collaboration between the parties within the Majority. Once the election was over it rather looked as if both were waiting for the right moment or the right issue to fight the "third round"—this time between Gaullists and Giscardians. As long as neither had won or lost, the institutions of the Fifth Republic remained stable. In a country where ideological divisions are the rule and where the parties are many and the differences between them acute, the electoral system forces the parties to form alliances, and the authority of the president and of the state are consequently reinforced. Indeed, some unrepentant Gaullists would go so far as to say that the real winner in the March 1978 election was General de Gaulle, the spirit behind the constitution of the Fifth Republic.

4

The Union of the Left's Defeat: Suicide or Congenital Weakness?

Georges Lavau
and
Janine Mossuz-Lavau

The parties of the left, which had been divided since 1947, joined in an electoral pact for the presidential election of December 1965. This alliance, renewed for the legislative elections of March 1967 and June 1968 (though not for the presidential election of June 1969), was never complete. On the one hand, it was only partially applied during the 1971 municipal elections: in many cities the Socialists maintained tight alliances with the center parties that dated back to the cold war. On the other hand, the old Radical party and a faction of the Socialist party refused to commit themselves to too strict an electoral alliance with the Communist party.

In the late sixties, the sole aim of this electoral alliance was to grab as many seats as possible from the Gaullist coalition in the second round of voting. The allied parties had neither a common program nor an agreement that would serve as the basis for forming a Government if the left should win a majority. The alliance became more cohesive and complete, however, when the Common Program (Programme commun de gouvernement) was signed in June 1972 by the Communist party (PCF), the Socialist party (PS), and the Movement of Leftist Radicals (MRG, Mouvement des Radicaux de Gauche). With this program, the three parties pledged to coordinate their campaigns and, if they should win, to form a Union of the Left Government. The Common Program set forth the general objectives of such a Government as well as specific measures it would adopt during the legislature's five-year session. Between 1972 and 1977 the Communists, the Socialists, and the Leftist Radicals adhered to the Common Program and campaigned as the Union of the Left. They did so for the legislative elections in 1973, the presidential election in 1974, the cantonal elections in 1976, and the municipal elections in March 1977.

Though relations between the two principal partners, the PCF and the PS, had worsened, it was reasonable to assume that the Union of the Left would make it through the legislative elections of March 1978 in the same way. Since 1973, the Socialists and Communists had always patched up their differences on the eve of an election; it seemed likely that when the time came they would compromise and reaffirm the alliance to achieve the victory that appeared imminent. The left had lost every important election since 1958, but between May 1974 and March 1977 its position had substantially improved. Its margin of defeat in May 1974 had been small, and since 1976 it had been beating the Majority (Giscardians, Gaullists, and centrists) in the voting-intention polls.

In addition, there were two external factors that seemed likely to induce the parties of the left to overcome their differences for the sake of victory. The first was the lowering of the voting age from twenty-one to eighteen in July 1974. All of the surveys clearly showed that the eighteen to twenty-one year olds favored the Union of the Left. These young voters formed only a small fraction of the electorate (and many of them would forget to register)—but the left had taken 49.2 percent of the vote in May 1974 and even a small advantage might turn this into a majority. The second factor was the persistence and deepening of the economic crisis. Potential leftist voters were particularly sensitive to this problem, which would probably also weaken some of the right and center's traditional support.

But the reconciliation everyone expected did not take place. During the seven months leading up to the elections, the Union of the Left was split by incessant disputes between the Socialists and the Communists. In the early months of 1978, even the purely electoral alliance (the agreement to withdraw lower-placed leftist candidates in favor of the one who did best on the first ballot), which had functioned without snags from 1967 to 1973, seemed in question. The Communist party refused to make a firm commitment. At the last minute, on March 13, 1978, the day after the first round, amid much fanfare, the Socialists and Communists reestablished their electoral alliance, but the move came too late: the leftist parties (especially the Socialist party) had not won enough votes in the first round to hold out against the intensive mobilization of abstentionists which the right would certainly seek for at the second ballot.

The two essential reasons for this final defeat were the strong performance of the Majority parties in the last few weeks of the campaign and the disintegration of the Union of the Left. While the latter had begun in the fall of 1974, it had not seemed seriously to jeopardize the left's chances for victory in 1978.

The Roots of the Split

Misunderstandings and Ulterior Motives. The roots of the split go back to the very origins of the Union of the Left. In May 1972, the signers of the Common Program probably shared but one object: to put an end to thirteen years of Gaullist hegemony. They sought to accomplish this by forming a strict alliance and pledging to govern together, if elected, according to a definite contract. In addition, each of the partners had its own perspective on the Union of the Left and the Common Program.

The Socialist party, led by François Mitterrand since 1971, saw the Union of the Left as the only possible means of escaping the slow erosion to which the old Socialist party, the SFIO (Section Française de l'Internationale Ouvrière, founded in 1905), had succumbed under the Fourth and Fifth Republics when it had tried to remain independent of both the right and the Communists. The Socialist party hoped that the reconstruction of a Popular Front comparable to that of 1936 would broaden its support and compel the Communist party to accelerate the "democratization" process it had initiated in 1965. It was for this reason that Mitterrand, anxious to conclude the alliance and under pressure from the left wing of his party (the Socialist Studies and Research Center, CERES), agreed to a Common Program not basically different from the one the Communist party had proposed a few months before.[1] It is probable that Mitterrand and most Socialists considered the Common Program something less than a binding contract: it was the price they had to pay to develop their party's strength and enter the next electoral consultations on an equal footing with the PCF. If the left should win, experience would soon show whether or not the Common Program could be implemented.

The Movement of Leftist Radicals, a faction of the old Radical party, had not participated in the negotiations but rallied in the end and signed the Common Program. Its interest in the alliance was clear: since 1967, the MRG had consistently sided with the Socialists, and its candidates could only be elected if they had Socialist and Communist votes in the second round. The moment the Socialists struck a firm alliance with the Communists, the MRG was forced to join in. Whatever its ideological reservations, signing the Common Program was the price the MRG had to pay for electoral survival.

---

[1] The Communist party's program, adopted at the end of 1971, was published in its entirety under the title *Changer de Cap* (Paris: Editions Sociales, 1972). The Socialists' program, adopted a short while later, was published under the title *Changer la Vie* (Paris: Flammarion, 1972).

For its part, the Communist party needed the Common Program to break out of its political isolation and to obtain some guarantee that its allies, the PS and the MRG, would remain loyal. It also needed to ensure that the contents of the Common Program were as close as possible to its own program. The PCF had no illusions about its partners' sincerity; it did not doubt for a moment that once victory was achieved—thanks mostly to the votes of PCF supporters—they would break the alliance and try to govern with some of the center parties. At the time, however, the PCF had no choice: all it could do was remain vigilant and see to it that its partners signed the strictest possible Common Program. By June 1972, the Communists appeared satisfied with the alliance; at least they expressed no apprehensions about it in public.[2] They were also pleased to see the leftist forces that had so loudly criticized the Common Program and the PCF—the Trotskyists, the Unified Socialist party (PSU), and the non-Communist labor union, the CFDT (Confédération Française Démocratique du Travail)—left out. Isolation could only hurt them.

The Union of the Left built around the Common Program was riddled from the start with latent misunderstandings and disagreements. These did not become evident until the end of the summer of 1974. The 1973 legislative elections were contested by all three parties in an atmosphere of unity,[3] as was the May 1974 presidential election, even though, as we will soon see, Mitterrand and the Socialist party had begun to stray from the Common Program. It was not until the fall of 1974 during preparations for the twenty-first PCF congress on October 24–27 that the Communists suddenly launched a violent campaign against the Socialist party. Despite temporary truces and certain platform changes, this campaign continued until March 13, 1978, and was resumed after the second round on March 20, 1978. The Communists accused the PS of wanting to abandon the Common Program and its commitment to the Communist party, while reaping the benefits of alliance in the form of votes. They also accused the PS of seeking a rapprochement with big capital and with the right.

---

[2] Georges Marchais's report to the Central Committee meeting on May 29, 1972, asking the committee to adopt the Common Program was not made public, until July 1975. Marchais severely criticized the Socialist party's attitude and its reservations about accepting the Common Program.

[3] The left did no better in the March 1973 elections than it had in the election of 1967. Nevertheless, despite the predictions of the surveys taken immediately before the first round, the Communist party won a slightly higher percentage than the PS and the MRG combined.

Three Factors in the Split. It is difficult to understand what happened inside the Union of the Left between 1974 and 1978 unless three major points are brought to light.

(1) The first point is the importance of the economic crisis, which was not perceived until 1974. The more it seemed that the Union of the Left could win elections (between May 1974 and February 1978), the more the spokesmen for the Majority argued that the Common Program would bring inflation, indebtedness, production drops, trade deficits, and monetary slumps—that it would be, in fact, the worst possible answer to the crisis. Forced to defend their plan, the PCF and the PS expressed divergent views of the nature of the crisis and of the appropriate remedies. According to the PCF, the crisis had but one real cause: big business's lust for profits. The remedy was to "make the rich pay," to nationalize the principal production and credit sectors, and to increase consumption by increasing buying power. The Socialists, whose voters were mostly middle class and who knew that if the left should win they would assume the principal responsibilities of governing, were much more hesitant and divided. Some of their leaders thought the Common Program ill-adapted to conditions of economic crisis and advocated combining it with economic austerity measures. This position, though far from unanimous inside the PS, was frantically attacked by the Communists.

(2) The second fact behind the deterioration of the Union of the Left was the Socialist party's growth from the fall of 1974 until 1977, when its support stabilized at the level it maintained through the first round of the 1978 elections. During this period the whole of the left grew, finally surpassing the Majority in the polls. But on the left, it was the Socialist party that grew fastest. This trend was confirmed in every election between September 1974 and March 1977, as well as in every voting-intention survey. By March 1, 1978, the polls showed the PS seven points ahead of the PCF (see Table 4–1). The Socialist party's growth in terms of voting intentions was not matched by an equally spectacular increase in membership, yet the PS seemed to be the party on the rise during this entire period: journalists focused on it, and well-known public figures rallied to it, including some deserters from the Majority but also some former CFDT and PSU leaders. No one doubted that in the event of a Union of the Left victory, the PS would play the major role and would be in a position to impose its conditions upon the Communist party.

The rise of the PS weakened the Union of the Left in several ways. First of all, some Socialist leaders and party activists became overconfident. They underestimated the PCF's ability to catch up and

TABLE 4-1

VOTING INTENTIONS, DECEMBER 1972–MARCH 1978
(in percentages)

Party	1972 Dec.	1973 Feb.	1974 June	1976 Jan.	Mar.	June	Oct.	1977 May	June	Sept.	Oct.	Nov.	Dec.	1978 Jan.	Feb. 7	Mar. 1
PCF	21	19	21	20	21	21	21	20	20	20	21	21	21	21	20	21
PSU and extreme-left	2	3	3	3	2	2	3	3	3	2	2	2	2	2	2	2
PS and MRG	22	24	27	30	30	28	28	30	30	31	27	26	27	28	28	28
Left, total	45	46	51	53	53	51	52	53	53	53	50	49	50	51	51	51
Ecologists and various center-left[a]	—	—	—	—	—	—	—	—	—	—	3	4	3	5	5	4
Center[b]	15	13	12	8	9	8	9	8	6	5	5	6	7	7	9	—
RI	40[c]	39[c]	24	24	22	24	22	19	19	19	21	20	18	16	14	23
RPR	—	—	13	15	16	15	17	20	22	23	21	21	22	21	21	22
Majority, total	40	41	49	47	47	47	48	47	47	47	47	47	47	44	44	45

[a] Voting intentions for Ecologists were first reported in October 1977. Voting intentions for various center-left groups were negligible (less than 1 percent).

[b] In 1972 and 1973, the center called itself "Mouvement des réformateurs" and did not support the Majority or the left. In 1974 and after, the center joined the Majority.

[c] In 1972 and 1973, the Gaullists (RPR) and the Giscardians (RI) were tightly allied and seldom ran rival candidates.

SOURCE: IFOP survey, December 16-21, 1972, in Le Monde, January 5, 1973. IFOP survey, February 9, 1973, Le Nouvel Observateur, February 19, 1973. SOFRES surveys, in Jean-Luc Parodi, "L'échec des gauches," Revue Politique et Parlementaire, no. 873, 1978.

overestimated the drift of center and right voters towards their party. In the second place, the party's successes made it apparent that the PS of 1975–1977 was not the party that had signed the Common Program in 1972: in particular, it comprised a number of people with strong prejudices against the PCF and the Common Program (many of them former members of the CFDT and PSU). In addition, the "cadres"—high civil servants, professors, "experts"—exerted greater influence within the party than they had in 1972. Many of the PS's new voters saw the PS not as the Communist party's ally and a signer of the Common Program but as a centrist opposition party, one that placed greater emphasis on social justice, perhaps, than the Majority parties, but otherwise not radically different from them. The third consequence of the Socialists' success between 1974 and 1978 was the extreme concern it caused the Communist party. The PCF absolutely had to destroy whatever mechanism was making it possible for the PS to take the lead on the left—a position the PCF had occupied without interruption from 1945. At all costs, it had to prevent the PS from straying from its commitments and assuming that it could impose its will on the PCF merely by threatening to dissolve the alliance and leave the Communists as isolated as they had been from 1948 until 1965. This is why the PCF fought so hard for dominance on the left.

(3) The third factor in the split was the quadripolar structure of French politics since the election of Valéry Giscard d'Estaing as president—that is, the internal division of the two major coalitions, the Union of the Left and the Majority, into two groups also equal in size. On the left, the Communist party faced the non-Communist leftists (Socialists and Leftist Radicals); on the right, the Gaullist party (the UDR, which in the fall of 1976 would become the RPR) confronted the Giscardians (Independent Republicans, Social and Democratic Center, and Radicals), and within each coalition the two components vied for leadership as well as for votes.[4]

This internal rivalry was much more damaging to the Union of the Left than to the Majority, for two main reasons. First, even if relations between the leaders of the Majority's two groups were tense, their voters were similar enough that the consequences would not be serious as long as the leaders did not strain the electoral alliance to the breaking point. Gaullists and Giscardians had the same basic out-

---

[4] See Jean-Luc Parodi, "L'union et la différence: Les perceptions de la gauche après la crise de septembre 1977" [Alliance and rivalry: perceptions of the left after the crisis of September 1977], in SOFRES, *L'opinion publique française en 1977* (Paris: Presses de la Fondation Nationale des Sciences Politiques, 1978), pp. 69-86.

look and would probably vote in both the first and the second rounds for the candidate of *either* group who appeared to have the best chance of winning. By contrast, PCF, PS, and MRG voters were profoundly different and between 1975 and 1977 their differences showed up more and more strongly in the opinion polls.[5] Socialist voters in particular had a deep mistrust of the PCF. The more was made of this, the more serious was the risk that some voters, especially non-Communist ones, would refuse to vote for their partner's candidates in the second round, especially if, in the first round, the partners had fought each other as fiercely as they had fought their common adversaries.

The second reason why internal rivalry was deadlier to the Union of the Left than to the Majority is simply that it was incomparably more intense. Most but not all of the blame lies with the Communist party. The PS and the PCF finally went so far as to accuse each other of wanting the Majority to win.

Three Years of Rivalry

The Left's Indian Summer, May–October 1974. Without previously consulting the other Union of the Left parties, François Mitterrand announced his candidacy for president in the election brought on by Georges Pompidou's death. The announcement came during his party's special congress on April 8, 1974.[6] The PCF and the MRG immediately backed Mitterrand. Indeed, early on the Communist party even tried to portray Mitterrand as the "Common Program's Common Candidate," but it was soon forced to abandon the pretense that it had sponsored Mitterrand's candidacy.

Also on April 8, Mitterrand announced the five themes on which he would base his campaign—"freer men, a more just society, a stronger currency, a more fraternal people, a nation more active on the international scene." At a press conference on April 12 he developed them, proposing in addition three complementary plans for dealing with the economic crisis: (1) immediate steps to be taken over a period of six months, (2) an eighteen-month plan that would remedy the structural causes of inflation and social inequality, and (3) a five-year plan designed to encourage a new type of growth and a reorientation of production. To be sure, this platform drew on the Common Program, but it did not duplicate it. Mitterrand and his advisors had put together something new.

---

[5] Cf. Roland Cayrol, "Les attitudes des électeurs de gauche" [The attitudes of leftist voters], in SOFRES, *L'opinion publique*, pp. 45, 49.

[6] The PS's Special Congress in Suresnes.

During the campaign Mitterrand spoke of the Common Program only when pressed to justify having signed it. The Socialist party's instructions to its campaign workers specified that their efforts must focus exclusively on the candidate's platform, which, the party explained, was "perfectly compatible with the Common Program," adding, "since we are in the midst of a presidential election, which is completely different in nature from legislative elections, our candidate's program is not the Common Program."[7] After the first round of voting, Mitterrand announced a "program for environmental protection" in an attempt to attract the votes that had gone to René Dumont, the ecologist candidate, in the first round. Again, neither the MRG nor the PCF was so much as consulted. Clearly, during those weeks Mitterrand was a very casual member of the Union of the Left. He conducted a highly personal campaign and scarcely even sought to associate himself with the Common Program—while the PCF unstintingly gave its support to his candidacy and never expressed reservations.

Shortly after the election, however, the Socialist party brought up a second bone of contention with the PCF. On May 25, 1974, Mitterrand and the Socialist party called on the supporters of the CFDT and on a fraction of the PSU led by Michel Rocard to join the Socialist party.[8] These were the groups that had previously criticized the Common Program and had refused to join the Union of the Left but had actively supported Mitterrand's candidacy. From that instant, it was clear that Michel Rocard and his followers would join the Socialist party, as would a large number of CFDT members and leaders. Since 1970, these groups and individuals had promoted the concept of worker control (*autogestion*) as an alternative to the "Socialist model" of national development (super-centralized, statist, and strongly oriented toward production) to which the PCF remained staunchly committed. The PCF, which had never mitigated its outspoken opposition to worker control, could not ignore a development that might strain relations with the Socialist party and even tempt the PS to stray from the Common Program.

For the time being, however, the Communist party appeared unperturbed. Georges Marchais refrained from criticizing the Socialists in any way during an important Central Committee meeting on June 10–11, 1974. "We completely understand," he declared, "that the parties with whom we are allied wish to reinforce their own ranks.

---

[7] Paris Federation flier, April 12, 1974.

[8] *L'Unité*, May 31, 1974.

TABLE 4–2

THE LEFT's FIRST-ROUND RESULTS, BY-ELECTIONS,
SEPTEMBER 29, 1974
(in percentages of valid votes; change in percentage points)

	PCF		PS-MRG	
Constituency	By-election 1974	Change 1973–74	By-election 1974	Change 1973–74
Ardèche, 2nd	12.47	−2.5	34.48	+11.30
Côte d'Or, 3rd	9.90	−3.73	40.45	+13.11
Dordogne, 1st	30.43	+3.16	22.52	+ 3.25
Loire Atlantique, 7th	7.0	−2.43	30.31	+12.95
Moselle, 8th	3.85	−1.10	9.17	+ 1.31
Savoie, 2nd	25.93	+0.84	31.42	+11.42

SOURCE: *Le Point*, no. 109, October 21, 1974.

I might add that for the success of our common battle this is a good thing. . . ." [9] Marchais's extremely moderate report at that meeting made it clear that, in order to increase the left's vote, the PCF would campaign on the theme "Union of the French People against monopolistic forces." The party called a special congress (a very rare event in the PCF's history) for the end of October 1974. According to Marchais, this Congress would have "one and only one point on the agenda: the Union of the French people." [10] Certainly there was no reason to think it would let loose a wave of hostility toward the Socialists.

But at the end of September 1974, the PCF received another blow. The first round of six by-elections began on September 29. In four of these, the PCF fell an average of three percentage points behind its 1973 result. On the other hand, the Socialist party (or the MRG) improved its showing in all six constituencies, in four by more than eleven percentage points (see Table 4–2). This disappointment came just as comment leading up to the special congress was beginning to appear in the Communist press. The discussion papers by PCF militants and local cadres published at this time expressed dissatisfaction and concern.

[9] *L'Humanité*, June 12, 1974.
[10] Ibid.

The Strategy of the PCF. At the time of the twenty-first congress, the March 1978 legislative elections were more than three years off, and no major confrontation was expected during this interval. The cantonal elections due in March 1976 and the municipal ones in March 1977 were relatively unimportant politically. The PCF predicted that the Socialists would make new gains but calculated that the electoral agreement binding the PCF, the PS, and the MRG, as well as its own voters, would prevent a defeat in the local elections. The key would be forcing its partners to respect the electoral accords. In effect, the PCF had at its disposal more than three years in which to alter the balance of power between itself and the Socialist party and become the most powerful party on the left. Its goal was to retain a free hand in determining its own course and perhaps even impose its will on the Union of the Left. The PCF was prepared to commit all of its resources to this battle for hegemony and to strain the alliance, if need be, up to the very brink of rupture. At this early stage, the PCF seemed to think it would be able to reverse its tactics a few months before the 1978 elections. It probably also thought it could demoralize its partners, provoking splits and dissension at the heart of the Socialist party and among its supporters. Even as late as the summer of 1977, when it became evident that these hopes were vain, the PCF persisted with this strategy.

To attain its principal goal—namely to be the most powerful member of the Union of the Left—the PCF proposed to reaffirm its own identity more emphatically than ever. This was a central theme at the twenty-first congress, at the Central Committee meeting on April 14–15, 1975, and at the twenty-second congress in February 1976. The Communists had realized that the party's image had been blurred by its merging into the Union of the Left and giving precedence to common action over independent action. The decision to support François Mitterrand in 1974 rather than wage a campaign of its own was a key case in point. Henceforth, the PCF would spare no efforts in making known its irreducible differences with the Socialist party. The latter was "reformist" and by nature "contradictory," the PCF was by nature "revolutionary," guided by a scientific theory.[11] By taking autonomous action, the PCF would show how much more determined, audacious, and revolutionary it was than the Socialist party.

---

[11] This theme is tirelessly reiterated in the two-volume *L'histoire du réformisme en France de 1920 à nos jours* [History of reformism in France from 1920 to the present] (Paris: Editions Sociales, 1976), a collaborative work by Communist historians.

One of the best ways for the PCF to underline its own identity was to zealously reaffirm its absolute domination of the organized, militant sector of the working class. To this end, the PCF made an immense effort to multiply its cells in factories, to intensify their struggles, and to set up political demonstrations in factories and offices. After the twenty-second congress, the party reinforced (again) its control over the CGT and channelled all of its activities into the struggle against the Socialist party.[12] The other way for the PCF to recoup its position was to develop its organization and membership: beginning in April 1975, the party made an intensive recruitment effort, shooting for a membership of one million. At the end of 1977 membership reached 630,000.[13]

The whole strategy of reaffirming the party's identity and differentiating it from the Socialists involved two serious risks for the PCF. The first was that it would be interpreted as a sectarian retrenchment, a falling back on the working class; the other, that the PCF would be accused of Stalinism and reversion to the Bolshevik model.

To forestall the first, the PCF made "the Union of the French People" the central theme of its appeal to the public. The idea was simple: since big capital and the right depend on the exploitation of *all* social classes except the "narrow caste that runs the economy and the state, the immense mass of French people who live by their work" must unite to defend themselves, forming the Union of the French people around the working class and the PCF.[14] The union was open to intellectuals, artists, small businessmen, the military, women, youth, and Christians, to supporters of the center and to Gaullists.[15] It was in everyone's interest, the party claimed, to join this vast union where "each retains his own personality and independence in the reciprocity of rights and duties."[16] The call for union was designed to prove that the PCF would not isolate itself in a working-class ghetto but, on the contrary, advocated an even broader political alliance than the Socialists.

---

[12] Cf. Georges Lavau, "Les voies du PCF" [The paths of the PCF], *Etudes*, March 1977.

[13] It is true that today the PCF does not screen potential members as closely as in the past: anyone who is more or less a sympathizer is invited to join and no one is turned away.

[14] Resolution adopted by the twenty-first congress, in *XXIeme Congrès. Le Parti Communiste propose* [Twenty-first congress, the Communist party proposes], Paris, November 5, 1975, published by the PCF, p. 118.

[15] Ibid., pp. 118-122.

[16] Ibid., p. 122.

From the fall of 1975 on, to escape the "return to Stalinism" charge the Communist party was careful never to miss an opportunity to express its reservations about the Soviet Union and Eastern European communism. During the twenty-second congress (February 1976), it solemnly abandoned the notion of "the dictatorship of the proletariat," and it became one of the champions of Eurocommunism.

Finally, the PCF set itself a goal to which it would remain faithful to the end: to reject any policy requiring or engendering economic austerity. Thus, it tirelessly opposed the policies with which the Chirac and Barre Governments attempted to deal with the economic crisis, but also the remedial measures outlined by the Socialist party's economists and leaders. It was enough that the latter were not in strict compliance with the Common Program: the PCF denounced the Socialists as traitors. Meanwhile, it devoted all of its efforts to systematically defending the unemployed and the salaried workers, indeed, all of the groups hit hardest by the crisis; the solution, it declared, was to develop consumption and production and to make "the rich and only the rich" bear the burden. It was this strategy that in the last months before the election brought the negotiations over the Common Program to a standstill and caused the de facto rupture of the Union of the Left—the prelude to electoral defeat.

Assault on the Socialists, 1974–1975. A few days before the PCF's special congress, the PS sponsored a conference on socialism (*"les assises du socialisme"*) which ended with a faction of the PSU and the most influential members of the CFDT joining the Socialist party. The statement they issued was permeated with the idea of worker control and made no reference whatever to the Common Program.

Although Mitterrand's defeat a few months earlier had been a near miss, the French public was still prejudiced against the Union of the Left. A majority of the respondents in one survey doubted that the union would last long in office, and distrust of the Communist party was still widespread. Even more worrisome for the PCF, the people who said they favored the Socialist party had more or less the same views on most subjects as the rest of the sample (see Table 4–3).

Marchais's address to the twenty-first congress (at Vitry, October 24–27, 1974) dealt mainly with the Union of the French People, but it also contained a long passage formulating three charges against the Socialist party:[17] (1) Ever since the *"assises du socialisme"* meeting, the PS had been trying "to replace the Common Program with

---

[17] Ibid., pp. 64-69.

TABLE 4–3

VOTERS' VIEWS ON PCF PARTICIPATION IN GOVERNMENT,
OCTOBER 1974
(in percentages)

Area Affected and Respondent Group	The Effect of PCF Participation in Government Would Be:		
	Good	Bad	Don't know
The economy			
All respondents	37	33	30
Socialists	52	24	24
Social policy			
All respondents	54	20	26
Socialists	69	13	18
Individual freedom			
All respondents	25	43	32
Socialists	36	34	30
National security			
All respondents	23	40	37
Socialists	34	32	34

NOTE: In the same survey respondents were asked whether they would expect the Union of the Left to last if it came to power. The results were:

	All respondents	Socialists
It would last	19	29
It would soon split		
because of the Communists	27	22
because of the Socialists	25	28

SOURCE: IFOP poll, in Le Point, no. 109, October 21, 1974.

its own rather incoherent program, which would not bring the workers the concrete and important reforms that the Common Program guarantees them."[18] (2) The Socialist party had not always respected its commitment to the Union of the Left. In numerous municipalities, the PS had remained allied with parties of the right, "camouflaged or not by the centrist label."[19] This ambiguity was no longer tenable. And (3), the Socialist party would be prepared to collaborate with President Giscard d'Estaing in a supposedly leftist Government, which, like Chancellor Helmut Schmidt's in West

---

[18] Ibid., p. 65.
[19] Ibid., p. 66.

Germany, would "loyally oversee" the interests of the capitalist bourgeoisie. To bring this about, the Socialist party (under pretext of adjusting the balance of power on the left) wanted "to reduce the Communist party's influence" and "grow in strength, to the detriment of the PCF, so that it can then impose its will." In short, the Socialist party wanted to be the chief decision maker within the Union of the Left.[20]

From the twenty-first congress on, the PCF waged an intensive campaign against the Socialist party. This went through many stages, the first of which lasted from October 1974 until the fall of 1975 and reached its culmination in the spring and early summer of 1975. The charges against the PS were spelled out at some length at an important Central Committee meeting on April 14–15, 1975, when Georges Marchais revealed part of a previously unpublished report he had presented to the Central Committee three years before, on May 29, 1972, the night before the signing of the Common Program.[21] In this report, Marchais had accused the PS of being a reformist social-democratic party, ever ready to compromise with big capital and willing to collaborate with all classes, a party the working class could never trust.

At the end of this first phase, the balance sheet certainly did not favor the Communist party. Not only did the PCF's frantic campaign against the PS fail to split the Socialists (on the contrary, it gave Mitterrand a reason for reasserting discipline and authority over the party), but its quasi-Stalinist tone served as a foil for the moderation of the PS, actually improving the party's image in the mass media. At the end of 1974, according to a survey conducted by IFOP, only 18 percent of the electorate intended to vote for the PCF whereas 34 percent were ready to vote for the PS-MRG bloc.[22]

At this time, the image of the international Communist movement and Communist parties everywhere was damaged by the behavior of the Portuguese Communist party, which adopted a Leninist strategy in an attempt to hold on to power after a serious electoral defeat. The PCF gave the Portuguese Communists its full support, as did the Soviet Communist party, meanwhile indignantly

---

[20] Ibid., p. 67-68.

[21] The complete text of this report was not published until July 1975, when it appeared as an appendix to a brochure by Etienne Fajon, *L'Union est un combat* [The struggle for union] (Paris: Editions Sociales, 1975). Marchais's report to the Central Committee on April 14-15, 1975, was carried in *L'Humanité*, April 17, 1975.

[22] Survey partially published by *Le Point*, no. 123, January 27, 1975, p. 30.

condemning Socialist leaders like Mario Soares, François Mitterrand, Helmut Schmidt, and James Callaghan, all of whom, it claimed, would support American imperialism, big capital, and the forces of the right against the masses. Unfortunately for the PCF, the Portuguese Communists were removed from power and entirely discredited.

Another embarrassment for the PCF during this period was the Soviet party's definite hardening against Eurocommunism, the "liberal" tendency spreading through the parties that were most independent of Moscow.[23] The next European Communist Parties Conference was due in June 1976 in Berlin. At first, the PCF was sympathetic to the pro-Soviet, anti-Eurocommunist position, but as public opinion in France swung toward what soon became an extraordinary infatuation with Eurocommunism, especially the Spanish and Italian Communist parties, the PCF changed its tune.

First, it attempted to moderate its attacks on the Socialist party and made deliberate efforts to back them up with better arguments. It also, quite abruptly, began to portray itself as the perfect Eurocommunist party. Georges Marchais and Enrico Berlinguer met in Rome in November 1975 to sign a joint declaration in which the two parties proclaimed their total agreement. What was more, during the Berlin conference, the PCF sided with the most resolute adversaries of the Soviet party. After the conference, the PCF was preoccupied with the preparations for its twenty-second congress, at which it strongly affirmed its attachment to liberty, democracy, and the victory of the Union of French people over forces of monopoly capitalism.

The Second Phase, Autumn 1975–Spring 1977. In the second phase of its campaign against the Socialist party, the PCF was more methodical, applying incessant and intense pressure designed to drag the PS into line. Where it failed to obtain submission, it was prepared to denounce the PS for "treason."

A year before the date set for the 1977 municipal elections, the Communist party began pressing for a sweeping national agreement with its partners on the left. Its two key proposals were: (1) the three Union of the Left parties would run common lists across the board in the municipal races and (2) the number of candidates from each party on a given list and the choice of a candidate to head the list (and become mayor if it won) would be determined on the basis of the results obtained in the municipality by the three parties not

---

[23] On all of these problems, see Lavau, "Voies du PCF." Also, Lilly Marcou and Marc Riglet, "Du passé font-ils table rase?" [Are they obliterating the past?], *Revue française de science politique*, vol. 26, no. 6 (December 1976), pp. 1054-1079.

only in the 1973 legislative elections but also in the 1971 municipal elections. The purpose of the first stipulation was to prevent any new Socialist gains from being clearly distinguished as such; the purpose of the second, to lower the Socialists' relative standing, since in 1971 they had polled fewer votes than the PCF.

The PS and the MRG preferred a looser agreement, one that would leave room for exceptions, but the Communists protested and remained intransigent. In some constituencies, they did not hesitate to side with the MRG (which was not a threatening partner) in skirmishes with the PS; in many, they succeeded in dictating their own terms. In the end, after difficult negotiations, the PCF and the PS agreed on common mayoral candidates; of the cities with populations over 30,000, there were only five where the two parties ran separate lists. As a result, both did very well.[24]

The PCF exerted further pressure on the Socialist party in the area of foreign affairs and defense policy. It relentlessly denounced the influence that Socialists from the Federal Republic of Germany, the Low Countries, and Great Britain exerted on the PS through the Socialist International, and it portrayed the meetings that took place between French Socialist leaders and the foreign affairs departments and heads of state of NATO members as signs of an inclination to abandon France's independence. The PCF, meanwhile, defended the principle of national independence more and more stubbornly. Finally on May 11, 1977, the Central Committee announced that it favored an independent national defense policy: the maintenance of a French nuclear force ready to strike in any direction, not just at Eastern Europe (the famous "stratégie tous azimuts"), and rupture with the NATO systems of surveillance and communication.[25]

It was in the areas of economic and social policy, however, that the PCF, with full backing from the CGT, exerted the most formidable pressure on the Socialist party. During the years 1975–1977, the PS organized many symposiums and discussions on "the crisis" and measures for combatting it, and Socialist experts in fields like economics and planning were highly visible in the press, on the radio, and on television. The Communist party was unimpressed by the fact that most of these expressed views critical of the Government's

---

[24] In the 221 cities with more than 30,000 inhabitants, the PS won the mayorship in 81 (48 in 1971), the PCF in 72 (50 in 1971), the MRG in 2 (3 in 1971). The PCF's gains were principally due to a rise in the Socialist vote, since the Communist vote remained stable.

[25] Jean Kanapa, L'Humanité, May 12, 1977. Louis Baillot, "Défense Nationale: une politique pour la gauche au pouvoir" [National defense: policy for a Government of the left], Cahiers du Communisme, no. 7-8 (July-August 1978), p. 15-23.

policies and consistent with orthodox socialism. Whatever their content, the PCF always found three faults with the Socialists' proposals: under one form or another they required the workers to accept sacrifices to save capitalist profits, they called into question the whole Common Program, and they contradicted the PCF's analysis of the real nature of the economic crisis.

Only two facts counted for the Communist party, the profits being made by business with help from the state and the poverty of the working class. The PCF led some powerful campaigns against the oil companies' financial "racket" and the super-profits of some of the large corporate "trusts" (Dassault, Péchiney-Ugine-Kuhlmann, the Empain group, IBM, and so on). And it led a long and intelligent campaign against poverty, christened "operation truth-hope."

During the Central Committee meeting of March 31–April 1, 1977, Georges Marchais announced, "the Common Program is the only answer. . . . Everything else is subterfuge, demagogy." According to Marchais, "as the crisis gets worse, it becomes more urgent than ever that we apply the reforms called for in the Common Program. . . . Our program is more valid than ever."[26] Marchais proposed a high-level meeting with the PS and the MRG to tackle the problem of bringing the Common Program up to date.

On May 10, 1977, the PCF published in *L'Humanité* its estimates of the cost of applying this up-to-date Common Program. They were so high, the fiscal burden on business so heavy, and the upheavals for the economic and industrial structures so profound, that they left the public in a kind of stupor. Yet these estimates were published *two days* before a very important televised debate between Raymond Barre and François Mitterrand on the subject of economic policies for combatting the crisis. Mitterrand, irritated by the Communists' having taken this step, strove to disassociate himself from the PCF's positions, but Barre exploited them to the hilt.

The Socialists' Response. In the middle of 1974, three years after its founding congress, Mitterrand's Socialist party was still coping with the problems of organization. Around the remnants of the old Socialist party of Leon Blum and Guy Mollet, it had to unite an assortment of groups, which in turn had to learn to live and work together. It also had to integrate the new members who started joining in 1973 as well as the groups who came over from the PSU and the CFDT in October 1974. The party's organization was defi-

---

[26] For the text of Marchais's report, see *L'Humanité*, April 1, 1977.

cient and fragile, its membership incomparably less than the PCF's—around 130,000 at the end of 1974, with no significant increase until the end of 1977. Finally, its internal functioning was highly democratic; disagreements tended to be aired, and internal minorities participated in making party policy.[27]

If it never seriously threatened to split the PS, this internal democracy nevertheless weakened the party's unity—and may have done so in particular during the three difficult years 1974–1977. During this period the Socialist party often seemed to be drifting, its policies contradictory and hesitant. Paradoxically, this forced Mitterrand to become increasingly authoritarian. As the 1978 election approached, he had to assume two roles: he had to deal with the problems that confronted him as the leader of a heterogeneous and divided party sorely pressed from outside, but at the same time he had to convince the public that he was a potential prime minister, backed by a disciplined party. He also had to prove himself in the face of challenges from the right and left wings of his own party. The left-wing Socialist Studies and Research Center which considered itself Marxist and had been the staunchest advocate of the Common Program inside the Socialist party, had the support of about a quarter of the active party members; as the election approached, it was ready to make concessions to satisfy the Communist party. At the other end of the party, meanwhile, men like Michel Rocard and Jacques Delors repeatedly made statements that exasperated the Communist leaders and gave them new ammunition to use against the Socialists.[28]

By 1974, the possibility that the Union of the Left would win the 1978 elections was serious, and none doubted that in a Union of the Left Government the prime minister and the other key ministers would be Socialists. Obviously, given this expectation, alliance with the Communist party was a serious handicap for the PS, especially with the Communist party taking such a hard line. Mitterrand could neither deny that there would be Communist ministers in his Government nor ignore the PCF's electoral importance. With its organizational strength and the support of the CGT as well as of millions of workers, the PCF would be able to bring considerable pressure to

---

[27] On the Steering Committee and the Executive Committee of the party, the different "tendencies" are represented in proportion to their strength at the preceding congress. Only the Secretariat is a homogeneous organization, composed exclusively of representatives of the majority tendency.

[28] Delors, an economist, was one of the Prime Minister Jacques Chaban-Delmas's chief advisors from 1969 to 1972 and joined the Socialist party only in November 1974.

bear on a leftist Government. If the PS wanted to win the elections, it had to show that it possessed the ability and the will to withstand this pressure—that it could govern with the Communists while resisting them. It also had to try to outpoll the Communists. If the Socialist party could again become the biggest political party—if as Mitterrand imprudently put it, it could win over 3 million Communist voters—then the PCF would be obliged to behave like a reasonable partner. From the moment this dream seemed within reach, the PCF launched a vigorous reply.

But the alliance with the PCF was not the Socialist party's only handicap. In addition, unlike any other European Socialist party, the French Socialist party had never held the reins of government alone, and none of the rare experiments with a Socialist prime minister had lasted more than fifteen months or met with complete success. Furthermore, since the Socialist party had not been in power at all for more than two decades, it was short on potential governmental personnel. The closer the 1978 elections came, the more eager the Socialist party was to assure the public that it had the ability to assume the responsibilities of governing as well as if not better than the Majority. But this also forced it to spotlight those of its leaders who had special expertise and to adopt "responsible" positions, a necessity not to the liking of many activists.

One of the areas in which the Socialist party had to prove itself "responsible" enough to govern was foreign affairs and defense. Socialist leaders publicly reiterated the party's basic positions, carefully differentiating them from the president's, and established contacts with representatives of the Western nations in an attempt to reassure them about the party's policy. In addition, the Socialist party called a number of conventions at which its proposals in the area of defense policy were discussed. Yet these were the questions on which the Socialist party itself was most deeply divided. Mitterrand had to tread a fine line in order not to alienate the factions within the party that were hostile to the United States, to a thorough integration of France in the European Community, and to the party's nuclear defense policies.

The Socialists realized that if they came to power, it would be in the midst of an economic crisis. Rightly or wrongly, French Socialist leaders have always had the reputation of being poor economists and have been blamed for inflation, monetary slumps, drops in production, rising prices, the flight of capital, and ineffective economic controls. All of those charges might well be borne out if the Socialist party, severely pressed by the PCF and by its own left wing, attempted to implement a Common Program drawn up before the crisis. For all these reasons, Mitterrand's advisors concentrated on coming up with measures to combat the economic crisis as soon as his candidacy was announced, in May 1974, and continued to do so until the early summer of 1977. The party's economic spokesmen were in the spotlight—men like Michel Rocard, Jacques Attali, Jacques Delors, Pierre Uri, Christian Goux, and Laurent Fabius. Inevitably, not all of their statements had full backing from all of the party. Several times Mitterrand himself had to act as mediator and explain his party's economic policies even though this was the policy area in which he was least comfortable and convincing. Worst of all, the economy proved to be the problem that provoked the most internal dissension among the Socialists, as well as the most frequent attacks from both the PCF and the Majority.

The long-term strategy adopted by President Giscard d'Estaing and the center-right groups that were his staunchest supporters was first to seduce the MRG (assumed to be ill at ease in the Union of the Left), then to woo the Socialist party's more moderate, anti-Communist members. This the Giscardians attempted by adopting reform policies and a liberal political style; the president invited opposition leaders to the Elysée for informal talks (only the MRG accepted) and courted the common man by visiting with several ordinary French families, even once with garbagemen and prisoners. In short, the plan was to erode the Union of the Left by provoking increasing tensions first between the MRG and the PS, then inside the PS itself, and finally between the PS and the PC. Clearly the Communist party's campaign against the Socialists could only further this end.

This maneuver failed, primarily because Giscard was never able to rally any real support for it. Still, it could have been dangerous for the Socialist party, and Mitterrand had to remain extremely vigilant lest some Socialists succumb to the president's wiles. This would have placed the Communist party in a prime position to accuse the Socialists of treachery—even though once the PS was divided and the Union of the Left severely weakened, the right would very probably have ignored the Socialist traitors.

In 1976 the Majority suddenly realized that it was losing both time and opportunities by concentrating its attacks on the Communist party: it was the Socialist party that had to be fought above all, at its two weak points, the Common Program and the role of Communist ministers in a Socialist Government. By 1976 the Majority understood that it could no longer hope to split the Union of the Left; and when the left did well in the cantonal elections of March 1976 and the municipal ones of March 1977, the Majority noted that the Socialist party in particular had continued to gain new voters, most of them from the Majority electorate. Jacques Chirac and Raymond Barre became convinced that a change of strategy was the only possible means of avoiding defeat, and from the beginning of 1977 they made the Socialist party their main target. Always on the defensive, the Socialists were beaten into a corner. And the more they tried to justify their position on the Common Program and the presence of Communist ministers, the more they opened themselves up to vehement criticism from the Communists and to dissension within their own ranks.

Despite the surveys' finding that the Socialists had more supporters than any other party, the PS was beginning to tire. Its position worsened between June and November 1977 during the negotiations on bringing the Common Program up to date. The Communist party was more intransigent than ever, never missing a chance to denounce "the Socialist party's rightist leanings."

Combining Offense and Defense. During the whole period since 1974, the Socialist party consistently underlined that its *only* enemy was the Majority, its *only* objective the Union of the Left's victory in 1978; the defensive war it reluctantly waged against the Communist party was secondary. The Socialists were determined never to be outdone by the Communists in antiestablishment zeal. But leading the assault proved to be a difficult task for the Socialist party. The PS had neither the militant manpower nor the organizational resources of the PCF; it had no daily newspaper, no strong trade union network. Instead the Socialist party actively opposed the Government by participating in marches and demonstrations and campaigns, against the Government's anti-inflation policies and its educational policies and its wage freeze, against unemployment and French military intervention in Africa, against any erosion of civil liberties. Socialists spoke out more and more often on broadcasts and in the newspapers. In addition, from the spring of 1977 on, the new Parisian daily, *Le Matin*, though it had no formal ties with the PS, openly supported the Socialists.

Nevertheless, the PCF's incessant attacks forced the Socialist party to reply. Disconcerted by the violence of the Communists' campaign, the Socialists hesitated between self-defense and counterattack. On May 3–4, 1975, a Socialist Party National Convention analyzed the relationship between the two parties. Lionel Jospin, one

131

of the national secretaries of the PS, called for a firm reply to the Communists' accusations, including the demand that both parties commit themselves to a code of conduct and that they "reexamine the Common Program and engage in a thorough-going debate on the worldwide crisis of capitalism."[29] This unleashed the fury of the PCF—and left the Socialist party obliged to defend itself or strike back day after day on everything, from its analysis of the economic crisis to worker control,[30] from relations with the Socialist International, to defense policy, to electoral strategy for the cantonal and municipal elections.

Some of the Communist party's accusations were outrageous, incoherent, or clearly absurd. Even so, they were profoundly disturbing to the Socialists. For one thing, the Communist offensive brought home to them how great were the resources the PCF had at its command. In September 1977, for example, the PCF put out a special edition of *L'Humanité* (6 million copies were printed) on its proposals for the revision of the Common Program and the Socialists' treachery in rejecting them. The Socialists simply did not have the means of replying on a comparable scale. Then too, the Socialists were torn between the desire not to dramatize the quarrel on the left, which might alienate voters, and the desire to strike back hard, proving that they could not be intimidated and would resist the Communists when the left came to power.

While responding to the Communists' attacks, the PS was also working out the details of its economic policies. On January 27, 1976, François Mitterrand announced to the press a vast "industrial restructuring plan" defining France's policies in the new international division of labor and outlining a new direction for growth. He sought to take into account the fact that, more and more, big corporations shifted their plants from one country to another depending on where labor costs were lowest. For France, Mitterrand proposed economic growth oriented less toward consumption than toward improvement of public utilities and infrastructure. On April 26 of the same year in a speech to a group of businessmen, he tried to reassure his audience about the meaning of a "French Socialist experiment": "All

---

[29] *La Croix*, May 3, 1975.

[30] The Socialist Party National Convention adopted "Fifteen theses on Worker Control" on June 21-22, 1975. These recommended a reduction in the powers of the state and of central management in both private and public enterprises very much along the lines advocated by Michel Rocard (though Rocard himself is not a strong supporter of nationalization and tends to favor the maintenance of the market economy). The fifteen theses provoked severe disagreements in the inner circles of the Socialist party.

we are aiming for," he explained, "is control of key points in the economy through limited nationalization and planning, . . . but the market system will continue to rule the French economy."[31] This effort to inform the public about the Socialists' economic program intensified as soon as negotiations over the revisions to the Common Program began and the PCF announced its proposals.

An enormous part of the Socialist party's energy meanwhile was taken up by the numerous elections held between 1974 and 1977: frequent by-elections as well as Senate, cantonal, and municipal elections across the nation. Preparations for the legislative elections (especially candidate selection) began in the spring of 1977. Here again, electoral activity aggravated rivalries within the Socialist party and created multiple conflicts with the Communist party as well as less serious disputes with the MRG.[32] The PS's leaders, Mitterrand more than anyone, campaigned tirelessly.

Compared with the PCF and the Majority, and despite its relatively limited means, the Socialist party was well rewarded for its feverish activity. It did well in almost all of the races, even in regions where it had previously been weak.[33] Socialist and MRG candidates together obtained almost 27 percent of the votes cast in the first round of the cantonal elections. As for the voting intention surveys, we have already seen that during this whole period they consistently placed the Socialists ahead of the Communists, the Gaullists, and the various center parties (see Table 4–1), and the press was virtually unanimous in singling out the Socialists as the up and coming party.

---

[31] *Le Monde*, April 28, 1976. Under the Common Program, the credit system and nine industrial groups would be nationalized: Dassault, Roussel-UCLAF, Rhône-Poulenc, ITT-France, Thomson-Brandt, Honeywell-Bull, Péchiney-Ugine-Kuhlmann, Saint-Gobain, Pont-à-Mousson, and the Compagnie Générale d'Electricité.

[32] The selection of Socialist candidates for the municipal elections in Paris and Toulon, but also for the legislative elections in some constituencies, caused conflicts within the party. The conflicts with the PCF were mainly over the designation of candidates for the common lists in the municipal elections, the chief points of contention being the number of candidates from each party and the party of the common candidate for mayor. In certain cities, notably Marseille, the Socialists and the Communists ran separate lists. The MRG has very little chance of securing a significant number of votes if it runs a candidate against a Socialist in the first round; for this reason, it fights desperately to ensure that in a few districts the PS will refrain from nominating candidates to run against its own. In 1978, it obtained this concession from the Socialist party in thirty-three districts, half of which the Union of the Left had very little chance of carrying.

[33] For example, the Socialist party won the mayoralty in a number of cities in western France where it had long been weak, including Rennes, Brest, St.-Malo, Angers, Angoulême, Poitiers, Dreux, and La-Roche-sur-Yon.

Those who doubted that they would ultimately win power were few indeed; until September 1977, almost everyone believed that at the last minute the Communist party would become conciliatory and that the three parties would compromise to achieve victory. The more pessimistic commentators believed that the Union of the Left would face its worst crisis only after victory, when it would have to assume the responsibilities of power.

Final Breach and Defeat

Revising the Common Program. Despite the intensity of their quarrels, the three parties of the left agreed on May 17, 1977, to meet for the purpose of bringing up to date the Common Program of 1972. The negotiations were expected to be difficult. The Socialist party hoped they would wind up quickly (Mitterrand proposed a deadline of July 1) and that only the portions of the program that were really outdated would be revised. The Communist party, however, refused to be bound by a deadline and insisted that the Common Program be entirely reworked in the light of the economic crisis.

The fifteen negotiators nominated by the three parties worked through June and July. Not without difficulty, they reached agreement on a number of points, but they remained at odds on many others—in particular, defense policy, the scope of nationalization, compensation for shareholders of corporations taken over by the state, the means of choosing personnel to run the nationalized industries, the amount by which the lowest salaries and family allocations would be increased as soon as the Union of the Left Government was installed, a new tax on wealth, and the overall contraction of the wage scale.

A "summit" meeting of the three parties convened on September 14, 1977, to settle these disagreements. Since the beginning of the talks in May, the Communist negotiators' behavior and the tone of the Communist press had led observers to expect that the PCF would be uncompromising. The September 14 meeting was a failure: the MRG declared that the Communists' intransigence and excessive demands made agreement impossible. The three parties met again on September 21. In the interval, they tried to hit upon a mutually acceptable compromise; but late in the night of September 22, the negotiations ended in stalemate.

The PS Steering Committee unanimously authorized new proposals and concessions early in October; these the PCF denounced as a ploy, and the negotiations were never resumed. The PS and PCF each continued to maintain that it was ready to negotiate at any time as long as the *other* was willing to match the concessions it had made already and beyond which it could not go.

The major modification to the Common Program demanded by the PCF was a considerable expansion of nationalization. The PCF proposed to add the iron and steel industry and the Citröen-Peugeot automobile group to the list of enterprises to be nationalized contained in the 1972 text. It also insisted that all subsidiaries more than 50 percent controlled by listed parent companies be nationalized along with the parent companies. Thus, not only the shares and assets of businesses listed for nationalization would be transferred to the state, but a great many others would as well, by a sort of chain reaction. According to the PCF's economists, this process would result in the nationalization of somewhere between 729 and 1,451 companies; the exact number was the subject of interminable dispute.

The problem of nationalizing subsidiaries had never been dealt with, strange as that may seem, during the original Common Program discussions or during the five years since. The Socialist party agreed to the nationalization of shares in subsidiaries, but only those shares belonging to parent companies included in the list of companies to be nationalized. One of the concessions made by the PS on October 8–9 was the proposal that restrictions be imposed on companies in which the state held less than three-quarters of the shares, in particular preventing a minority of private shareholders (between 49 and 25 percent) from blocking decisions made by the majority: most important, such a minority could not forestall the implementation of economic policies being applied by the government in public and semi-public enterprises.

The quarrel over the number of companies to be nationalized was factitious but revealing. For one thing, it showed that between 1972 and 1977 the three parties to the Common Program had carefully avoided clarifying a number of crucial questions because they wanted an agreement and knew that, on these questions, agreement could not be reached. The Socialists (and even more the MRG) had probably thought they would never really be held to the Common Program. As for the Communists, they had probably assumed that when the time came they would choose to be either conciliatory or stubborn according to the circumstances of the moment.

The real question, of course, was not whether 1,450, 1,008, 729, or 227 enterprises should be nationalized but what *economic* necessity dictated any given nationalization, *in what way* it contributed to the structural reforms planned under the Common Program, and *what kind of socialism* it was supposed to prepare the way for. Since 1972, these basic problems had never been broached by the three signers of the Common Program; they had always settled for hollow and ambiguous formulas. When certain Socialists (like Michel Rocard, Jacques Attali, and Jacques Delors) had tried to bring them up in 1975 and 1976, they had run into a double barrier: the Communist party had contemptuously accused them of rushing to the aid of big capital, and all of the Socialist party's intransigent Marxists had attacked them.

The PCF attributed inordinate importance to the quarrel over the scope of nationalization. According to the PCF, the Socialists' rejection of its proposals could only mean that they would never really give the workers the means to break the capitalist monopolies' hold, and, furthermore, that they were turning their backs on commitments they had made in 1972—essentially abandoning the Common Program. From late November 1977 on, the Communist party no longer even bothered to spell out this reasoning, but its denunciations of the Socialists continued: the Socialist party, which had "strayed to the right," was trying to obtain a "blank check" from the "workers" (that is, from the Communist party) to form a Government without Communist ministers, supported by the right (like that of Mario Soares in Portugal), and soft on big capital.

The PCF also demanded that the presidents of nationalized companies' boards of directors be elected, without governmental intervention, by the boards themselves, one-third of whose members would in turn be elected by the employees from lists drawn up by the unions. The PCF's purpose here was twofold: on the one hand, to take advantage of the CGT's strength and give it a decisive voice on the boards of directors; on the other hand, to deny the Government the right to designate board presidents since the Socialists would probably control a Government of the left.

By proposing that, immediately upon taking office, a Union of the Left Government raise salaries, pensions, and family allowances, the PCF was trying to keep the Socialist party from applying the Common Program in steps and selectively in a way designed to prevent an abrupt rise in inflation and prices and the almost immediate bankruptcy of a number of small and medium-sized businesses.

Finally, on the matter of nuclear disarmament, the Socialist party eventually proposed that the nuclear arsenal be maintained until the voters could voice their opinion in a referendum if international negotiations for controlled universal disarmament failed. The Communist party, which suddenly became a staunch advocate of French nuclear armament, energetically opposed a referendum.

The Left Divided. At the beginning of October, the PCF still hoped to win over the Socialist party.[34] It calculated that the Socialists would yield to pressures from their own left wing (CERES), which expected the party to make concessions to the PCF and criticized the leaders' wariness and intransigence. The Communists also reckoned that sheer electoral necessity would sway the Socialists, who would want to make certain the Communists would withdraw in the second round wherever the PCF candidate was outdistanced by the PS or MRG contender.

But the PCF's hopes were disappointed. Thanks to Mitterrand's firm authority, the Socialist party managed to remain united until the end. The CERES continued to criticize its leaders but never dared provoke a split. As for the CFDT, in November 1977 it spoke out against all three parties (but especially the PCF) and published a "platform" that could be interpreted as a synthesis of the PCF's proposals and the PS's. But it went no further. The Communist party courted the CFDT more assiduously than ever,[35] even espousing the cause of worker control, the CFDT's pet theme which the Communists had always ridiculed in the past. Their flattery was to no avail: the CFDT doubled its criticism of the Communist party and even more of the CGT, whose leaders enthusiastically supported the PCF's campaign against the Socialists.[36]

But as election day approached, the problem of the Communist party's electoral strategy became more and more important. After the PCF's Central Committee meeting on October 8–9, it was clear that the Common Program negotiations would never be resumed. The three parties would fight the election without a Common Program—or rather, the Socialist candidates would run on the Common Program including all of the revisions accepted by the three parties as well as those proposed by the Socialist party and the MRG, while the Communist party would declare that this was in no way the *real* Common Program.

Even the status of the electoral alliance was in doubt. Mitterrand, who wanted to force the PCF into a definite commitment, spelled out the Socialists' position on September 28: Whatever happened and whatever the PCF did, the Socialist party would respect the Union of

---

[34] Marchais's long report and the Central Committee's resolution can be found in *L'Humanité*, October 7, 1977.

[35] See, for example, the PCF's declaration to the CFDT, *L'Humanité*, November 7, 1977.

[36] See, for example, Georges Séguy's declarations on the CGT's National Committee in *L'Humanité*, December 8 and 9, 1977.

the Left and the tradition of the left since the Third Republic. Socialist candidates would withdraw in favor of any Communist candidates who beat them in the first round. "I have no reservations about this," Mitterrand said. "We will apply the Union of the Left's discipline and we will work for the candidate of the left who gets the most votes. Whatever happens, this is what we will do...."[37] Mitterrand repeated his statement on October 2 at Angers, and the Socialist party's Steering Committee unanimously approved it on October 8–9.

The Communist party, on the other hand, had no intention of making its position unambiguous—for the simple reason that, by declaring firmly that its candidates would withdraw in favor of the PS and the MRG in all cases, it would lose its sole means of exerting pressure on its partners. The PCF refused to commit itself, pretending to consider the question premature.[38] As the Socialists pressed them on the electoral alliance during the fall and winter, the Communist leaders replied that "the discipline of the left" was as outdated as oil lamps, that the Socialist party was obsessed with obtaining a "blank check" from the Communist party, that all it wanted was to win—thanks to Communist votes—enough seats to impose its will and betray the workers' cause. According to the PCF, the only serious question was whether the Socialist party was ready to "return to the Common Program."

The PCF obstinately stuck to this attitude until the night of the first round of voting. It also invested the five and a half months from October 1977 until March 1978 in a major campaign effort. The first phase of this campaign stretched from October 1977 to the beginning of January 1978. The party and the CGT mobilized en masse and the Communist press went all out. The principal theme of this phase was the Socialist party's "straying to the right." Endlessly repeating their charges, marshalling the most varied arguments,[39] deliberately ignor-

---

[37] Europe no. 1 radio, September 28, 1977.

[38] At the end of his report to the Central Committee on October 5, 1977, Georges Marchais declared, "The Political Bureau considers that we should not open the electoral campaign prematurely, but should utilize the maximum amount of time to develop our unified effort on the bases that I have exposed." Thus, he proposed to postpone the party conference that was scheduled on October 21-22 to solve the electoral question until an unspecified date. "We propose," Marchais added, "to dedicate the weeks and months ahead to a major effort promoting the policies we are proposing." L'Humanité, October 7, 1977.

[39] L'Humanité of October 26, arguing from a draft electoral platform elaborated by the various Socialist parties of the European Community in preparation for the European Parliament's future elections, strove to show that this platform was completely out of keeping with the Common Program and that this proved that the PS had given its allegiance to German social democracy. The meeting

ing the Socialists' responses,[40] the Communists seemed determined to force the Socialist party to either break the alliance or give in to their demands for fear of losing the election. They obtained neither—and the public opinion polls continued to favor the Socialist party, even though it was now the principal target of both the Communists and the Majority.

The second phase began with the PCF's national conference on January 8, 1978.[41] After restating the case against the Socialist party and refusing to make a commitment on second-round withdrawals, Georges Marchais declared that the only way for the voters to ensure "real change" after the March 1978 elections was to give the Communist party every possible vote. The PCF launched a "Call to the French people," which read in part:

> There is only one way left to bring about change this year, one way of making the Socialist party return to an alliance based upon a sound program after the legislative elections: namely, to give massive support to the Communist party on March 12, to its proposals and to its candidates. If our support is strong enough, the scales will tip in the right direction. . . . Change depends on you.[42]

In the official campaign, which began a little while later, the Communist party tirelessly repeated: "For real change, vote Communist," "To guarantee real change, there must be Communist ministers in the government," and "Everything is still possible if you back the PCF."

But what did the PCF expect from this intensely emotional appeal for votes? It certainly did not hope to outdo the Socialist party in the first round: all of the surveys showed that this would not occur. What then? During the party conference in January, Georges Marchais imprudently told reporters: "If we could take 25 percent of the votes, it would be good; if we only get the 21 percent that the surveys

---

between President Carter and François Mitterrand in Paris on January 6, 1978, was further proof for the Communists. The President declared that Mitterrand was playing "a beneficial role for France." The Communist party, indignant at this "interference" by a foreign head of state, suspected Mitterrand of having solicited this declaration from President Carter to encourage voters to defect from the right.

[40] For example, when Mitterrand agreed (against the advice of some of his economic advisors) to include an increase in the minimum wage (to 2,400 F/month) in his program, the PCF dismissed this concession—which it had previously demanded—as worthless.

[41] The text of Marchais's report and of resolutions adopted at this conference, as well as a long analysis of the discussions, can be found in *L'Humanité*, January 9 and 10, 1978.

[42] *L'Humanité*, January 9, 1978.

show it will not be enough." Later Marchais tried to deny having said this. In fact, the PCF probably knew perfectly well it had little chance of getting more than 21 percent; what it absolutely wanted was to make sure of holding any of its regular supporters who were still hesitating and, on the other hand, try to prevent the Socialist party from improving its position by detaching its potential and wavering supporters. In fact, it is difficult to dismiss the hypothesis that the PCF's whole strategy was based on a fantastic miscalculation: too confident of the surveys' accuracy, the PCF thought that the PS would take close to 30 percent of the votes and the PCF scarcely 20 percent. It was terrified that such a gap would entitle the PS to consider itself the victor and dictate its terms to the other parties of the left, and so the PCF went all out to turn the tide.

There remained one unknown. If, despite this offensive, the PS-MRG bloc succeeded in taking between 26 percent and 30 percent of the votes, what would the PCF do? Would it refuse to withdraw its candidates and thus voluntarily help the Majority win in the second round? All of its past behavior suggested it would. If the PCF did well in the first round and the PS poorly, on the other hand, the Communists would be much more conciliatory and would be prepared to respect the Union of the Left's discipline. This is exactly what happened when the first round produced mediocre PCF outcomes but also a relative failure for the PS-MRG bloc.

It must be noted that from December 1977 until the elections, the Socialist party's behavior had been both firm and prudent. It rejected the PCF's offer to resume negotiations over the Common Program, saying that the three parties would meet only after the first round to see if an agreement were possible. Until then, it was up to the Communist party to take an unequivocal stand on the withdrawal question. In addition, the Socialist party tried to the last to prevent the campaign from becoming any more bitter than necessary so as to preserve the chances for a final accord after the second round. Its own campaign was relatively low key. Indeed, the Socialists seemed slightly ill at ease though all of the polls were favorable right up until March 6, 1978.

On March 13, the three parties met and, to everyone's surprise, the Communist negotiators proposed an extremely vague agreement mentioning almost none of the demands they had been holding out for since the summer of 1977. The text was bland enough that it could be quickly accepted by all with virtually no change. The three partners had only one thing on their minds: the second round. The news photographers duly recorded the handshakes and beaming faces, and the next day *L'Humanité,* overlooking three years of bitter quarrels, ran a two-inch-high banner headline: *"Ça y est!"*[43]

The very night the second-round results were announced, when it became known that the Union of the Left, with practically the same number of votes as the Majority, was still sadly behind in seats, the three parties went back to bickering as noisily as ever. On March 19, the president of the MRG declared that he considered himself free of all obligations to the Union of the Left. The next day, the Socialist party's Executive Bureau accused Georges Marchais of having "helped the right and retarded the time for change" by his attacks on the Socialists, and it urged the workers to "learn a lesson from his behavior."

Finally, on March 29, the secretaries of all of the PCF departmental federations met in Paris. One of Georges Marchais's main assistants, Charles Fiterman, presented a long report in which he revived all of the accusations the PCF had made against the Socialist party back in October 1974. Fiterman insisted that the PCF could not have acted differently, yet his report sounded painfully like an attempt at self-justification.[44] The PCF leaders knew that the left's defeat, which had seemed so unlikely as recently as December 1977, had left Communist voters and activists feeling betrayed. In the name of the Political Bureau, Fiterman asked that in every cell and section members of the party launch a serious "discussion" of their party's past actions and of their duties for the future. Meanwhile, of course, Fiterman's report supplied all the answers, making plain what conclusions were to be reached. The departmental secretaries, to whom it was addressed, would make very sure that the "discussions" in their departments conformed.

Epilogue

After the defeat of March 1978, none of the three parties—not even the MRG—was willing to take responsibility for admitting that the Union of the Left had broken down or to draw the necessary conclusions by fundamentally revising the left's strategy. If certain official statements were to be believed, all of the parties remained faithful to the Union of the Left. In fact, however, each implicitly accepted that

---

[43] On the night of March 12, when the first round results had become known, television audiences had seen Georges Marchais surrounded by the whole Political Bureau solemnly read a declaration calling for an electoral alliance of the Union of the Left parties.

[44] *L'Humanité,* March 30, 1978.

they were no longer bound by the Common Program. Furthermore, it was clear that the congresses of the PS and the PCF scheduled for the spring of 1979 would have to make important decisions concerning the future strategies of the two parties. Increasingly, the presidential election of May 1981 would have to be considered. Meanwhile, in both parties, but particularly within the ranks of the PS, opinions favoring modification of the 1974–1978 strategy began to emerge.

Within the Socialist party, a twofold debate was developing, focused on the party's leadership and on its ideological direction. As it concerned the party leadership, the issue was also twofold: would Mitterrand remain the general secretary, and would he be the candidate for the presidency? Party members tired of or in disagreement with Mitterrand's leadership hoped that Pierre Mauroy (the mayor of Lille) would be chosen as general secretary and that his ally Michel Rocard would eventually be the Socialist candidate for president. However, since these militants were conscious of the fact that their proposals would offend the rank and file who were grateful to Mitterrand for services rendered, they refrained from attacking Mitterrand directly and contended that the only serious issue was ideological. Should the PS remain faithful to the type of socialism that the Common Program had represented, or should it reject this constricting model and opt for a non-Marxist, decentralizing, antiauthoritarian socialism? The latter orientation, advocated by Michel Rocard and his friends, was a minority view.

Rocard and Mauroy committed some tactical errors, whereas Mitterrand maneuvered with great skill. As a result, when the congress convened in Metz on April 6, 1979, the outcome was already certain: Mitterrand won out easily over the supporters of Rocard and Mauroy (who, shortly before, had quarrelled among themselves) and also over the CERES. Mitterrand's victory signified that a majority within the party refused to modify the ideological orientation adopted in 1972. The problem was that this orientation presupposed a Communist party ready and willing to cooperate and ally itself with the Socialists—which was not, and is not, the case.

In April 1978, the PCF began to establish its new line. Since the Socialist leaders no longer wanted a united strategy and in fact were aiming at an alliance with the Giscardians, the Communists would have to "reconstruct unity at the grass-roots level." Of course, the Communists knew very well that Socialist militants and voters would not be seduced by Communist appeals: they were not ready to accept the PCF version of events and bring pressure to bear on the PS leadership. In other words, the PCF decided to play the card of final breach. It had chosen to make the most of every charge it could bring against the PS, to fight it on any ground. By unscrupulously exploiting every possible grievance against the Socialists, the PCF would attempt to win as many votes as it could in both the elections for the European Assembly (June 10, 1979) and the more distant presidential election of 1981 (in which the party announced it would present its own candidate). This strategy received clear confirmation at the party's twenty-third congress, held on May 9–13, 1979.[45]

The question most often asked in the immediate aftermath of the 1978 election was: had the PCF deliberately chosen to block a dangerous rival (to whom the alliance had been much more beneficial than to the Communists themselves) and attempted to provoke a schism within the ranks of that rival in order to remain the principal opposition party? Were the Communists really content with this sterile supremacy—or had the PCF expected its partners to yield to pressure at the last moment and itself to emerge as the moving force in a victorious united left?

In any case, the decisions reached at the PCF's twenty-third congress show that the party's decision not to yield, while it may have backfired in 1978, was a deliberate strategic choice. The PCF would rather fight its battles in opposition than renounce its ambition to dominate the Socialist party. In this it remained faithful to the direction it has chosen over and over again since 1920.

---

[45] The resolution adopted by the twenty-third congress is very critical of the role supposedly played by the Common Program: its existence was held to have nourished illusions among party militants and played a part in weakening their combativeness. In addition, at the congress the party leadership made no concessions to the numerous members who, after the defeat, had expressed their reservations about the leadership's strategy.

5

The Mass Media and
the Electoral Campaign

Roland Cayrol

An electoral campaign for legislative elections in France officially begins two weeks before the first round of voting. In addition to this two-week period there is a week of campaigning between the two ballots, which brings the official campaign to a total of three weeks. During this period the state provides the candidates with billboards for use within their electoral districts and meets the cost of printing their campaign posters and form letters, which are sent free of charge to every registered voter in the district.[1] In addition, the candidates are permitted to organize meetings in public schools. Finally, the major parties receive free radio and television time every evening during peak listening and viewing hours—an especially important privilege in a country where private television does not exist and where neither political parties nor candidates can buy time on the radio and television to use for their campaigns.

An Interminable Campaign

Traditionally the official campaign is preceded by a preliminary campaign that may last several weeks or even months, during which the political parties and the candidates are pitted against each other in the national and local media. In 1978 the unofficial campaign was longer and more intense than ever before.

Indeed, it was interminable. It might even be said to have begun as early as May 1974, immediately after the presidential election, with Valéry Giscard d'Estaing's narrow victory (50.8 percent of the votes cast) over the leftist candidate, François Mitterrand. The

---

[1] Candidates who do not manage to win 5 percent of the votes cast are required to pay the printing costs of their campaign posters and form letters.

144

left, frustrated by an unexpected loss, staked everything on the subsequent legislative elections. The campaign for these elections reached an unequaled intensity as the opinion polls began to show a steady advance for the left; they were confirmed by the March 1976 cantonal elections and the March 1977 municipal elections, from which the left emerged as the strongest political force in the country. A victory of the left in 1978 seemed probable, and the main institutional and political problem ahead, in the eyes of the commentators, became whether a conservative president could coexist with a leftist majority in Parliament. As the campaign progressed, the country became ever more polarized—and both camps expected the left to win.

Because it was long, the campaign was extremely repetitive. By Christmas 1977 both camps had stated and restated their basic positions many times over. The left had publicized its proposals for achieving social justice and combatting inequality, partly through a state takeover of key sectors of the economy. The Majority, on the other hand, had tried to impress upon the public how well it had managed the nation and how important its social reforms—the liberalization of laws governing contraception, abortion, and divorce, the lowering of the voting age to eighteen, and so on—had been.[2] It concentrated its attacks on the Communist party, dismissing the Socialists as little more than hostages to the Communists. The Majority depicted itself as the sole defender of liberal values.

Certainly, the falling out between the Socialists and the Communists that occurred on September 22, 1977, and the highly polemical exchanges that followed altered the lines of battle. Yet the opinion polls recorded little change: still favorable to the left, they suggested that the split had had limited impact on public opinion. Likewise, the Communists' attempt to focus the debate on inequality—in particular their proposal (supported by the PS) to raise the minimum wage to 2,400 francs a month—failed to get the campaign off to a fresh start.

The campaign had lost its momentum long before the election. This might explain why survey respondents, asked at the beginning of March 1978 how closely they were following the campaign, showed far less enthusiasm than the voters polled during the presidential election of 1974 (see Table 5–1).[3] Almost a quarter of the

---

[2] It must be pointed out that most of these measures required the support of the leftist members of Parliament in order to pass.

[3] Unless otherwise indicated, the poll data in this chapter were gathered by the author with the help of Louis Harris France and have not been published elsewhere.

TABLE 5–1

VOTERS' INTEREST IN THE CAMPAIGN, MAY 1974
AND MARCH 1978
(in percentages)

Respondent followed the campaign:	May 1974	March 1978
Every day or almost	59	30
From time to time	32	48
Not at all	9	22
Total	100	100

SOURCE: For 1974, Jay G. Blumler, Roland Cayrol, Gabriel Thoveron, *La télévision fait-elle l'élection?* [Does television swing the election?] (Paris: Presses de la Fondation Nationale des Sciences Politiques, 1978), p. 288; for 1978; unpublished Louis Harris France poll conducted by the author.

voters were totally uninterested in the campaign, and only 30 percent said they followed it daily—half as many as in 1974. On the other hand, the social characteristics, level of interest in politics, and voting intentions of those respondents who followed the campaign closely were more or less the same in 1978 as in 1974 (see Table 5–2).

Once again, we find that a general interest in politics underlay interest in the campaign. More men than women followed the campaign closely, but the breakdown by age was inconclusive, showing no significant differences from one age group to another. Interest was greater among the more well-to-do (as well as among the retired and the inactive, who have more free time) than among shopkeepers, craftsmen, and industrial and agricultural workers. Following an electoral campaign on a daily basis is, in many ways, a luxury available only to the privileged. On the other hand, it is also a sign of a more definite involvement with politics: Communist voters were relatively more likely than other voters to follow the daily vicissitudes of the electoral campaign.

The Voters and the Media

Which media did the voters follow during the campaign? Which did they consider most useful as they tried to make up their minds how to vote? These questions were asked of a national sample of voters in March 1978. The respondents were asked to select those they had found most helpful from a list of media, both printed and audiovisual, that also included conversations, polls, and traditional

TABLE 5-2

INCIDENCE OF HIGH INTEREST IN CAMPAIGNS IN VARIOUS SOCIAL
AND POLITICAL GROUPS, MAY 1974 AND MARCH 1978
(in percentages)

Group	May 1974	March 1978
Sex		
Men	64	36
Women	54	24
Age		
18–24	54	24
25–34	53	29
35–49	53	31
50–64	65	33
65 and over	68	30
Occupation		
Industrialists, executives and upper management, professionals, merchants	73	43
Middle management, and technicians, white-collar workers	61	35
Shopkeepers and craftsmen	46	20
Blue-collar workers	50	24
Agricultural workers and farmers	53	21
Retired and inactive	69	34
Interest in Politics		
Great interest in politics	87	73
Some interest in politics	62	37
Very little interest in politics	52	12
No interest in politics	25	6
Voting Intention		
Communist party	71	41
Socialist party	61	31
Majority	62	30
Abstain	21	15

NOTE: The entries are percentages of the stated respondent category who followed the campaign "every day or almost."

SOURCE: For 1974, Blumler, Cayrol, Thoveron, *La télévision*; for 1978, unpublished Louis Harris France poll, conducted by the author.

TABLE 5–3
Most Important Media, May 1974 and March 1978
(in percentages)

Medium	May 1974	March 1978
Television	63	47
Radio	10	32
Newspapers and magazines	13	39
Conversations	8	18
Meetings	4	4
Leaflets	1	5
Posters	1	5
Opinion polls	—	6
None, no opinion	—	22
Total	100	

Note: In 1974 respondents were asked which single medium had been most important in helping them decide how to vote; thus, the responses add to 100 percent. In 1978 they were asked which media they considered most useful; since multiple responses were permitted, this column adds to more than 100 percent. The item "opinion polls" and the response "none" did not appear until 1978.

Source: For 1974, Blumler, Cayrol, Thoveron, *La télévision*; for 1978, unpublished Louis Harris France poll, conducted by the author.

campaigning vehicles such as meetings, leaflets, and posters. The results are enlightening: television was considered by far the most important medium (see Table 5–3).

In 1974, a similar survey was taken; although the wording of the questions was slightly different, it is obvious that the overall distribution of responses was essentially the same. According to Monica Charlot, "In the 1974 French presidential elections the role of broadcasting was undoubtedly greater than in any previous French election."[4] Since 1974 broadcasting has become ever more important, to the point where the audiovisual media now dominate electoral campaigns in France. Nevertheless, the press still has a conspicuous number of followers: newspapers were mentioned by 39 percent of the respondents in 1978, far more than conversations or the traditional campaign media, which seem to have played a very limited role indeed.

---

[4] Monica Charlot, "The Language of Television Campaigning," in Howard R. Penniman, ed., *France at the Polls: The Presidential Election of 1974* (Washington, D.C.: American Enterprise Institute, 1975), p. 227.

These broad findings—the dominance of the audiovisual media, above all television, and the solid rating of the press—must be qualified and interpreted in the light of the sociopolitical composition of the French electorate. Television's margin over the press varies from one subgroup to another (see Table 5-4). The breakdown by sex, for example, shows that, although among women television is clearly ahead of the press, among men the two are roughly even. Clear differences also show up between the tastes of various occupational classes. Thus, among the well-to-do, who are also the best educated, the press ranks highest; in the middle classes radio maintains a good position, while in the lower classes, the electronic media are clearly ahead of the press. Finally, the importance of the press increases as the level of interest in politics rises and as party preference moves toward the left; the greater a voter's tendency to vote for the Communist party or for a group of the extreme left the more he tends to prefer the printed media to the electronic media.

These findings are similar to those concerning voters' interest in electoral campaigns. On the one hand, a high level of education coupled with an equally high civic education and socially prestigious occupation (all of which certainly favor political socialization) go along with an interest in politics and attention to sophisticated media. On the other hand, it is also true that the militant political culture of the revolutionary and Communist left has always regarded newspapers, books, and the print media in general as privileged vehicles for ideas, while media like television have been considered superficial and relatively futile. This belief has certainly been accentuated in France by the existence of a state monopoly over television, which has continually served the interests of the government. Thus, within an electorate for which television is the great cross-class, catchall medium, appealing to both sexes and every age, the printed media retain two strongholds: one among the socially privileged, the other among groups that are ideologically influenced by the militant culture of the left and the extreme left.

The Press in France

Since the middle of the 1950s the total circulation of the French daily press (national and regional) has hovered around 11.5 million copies, despite the increase in the active population and the relative democratization of higher education.[5] This stability suggests that,

---

[5] For a general overview of the French press see Alfred Grosser, "The Role of the Press, Radio and Television in French Political Life," in Penniman, ed., *France at the Polls*, pp. 207-226.

TABLE 5–4

MEDIA PREFERENCES IN VARIOUS SOCIAL AND POLITICAL GROUPS,
MARCH 1978

(in percentages)

Group	Television	Radio	Newspapers and Magazines
Sex			
Men	47	33	44
Women	47	30	33
Age Group			
18–24	45	32	36
25–34	41	34	33
35–49	48	38	43
50–64	51	26	40
65 and over	47	27	38
Occupation			
Industrialists, executives and upper management, professionals, merchants	49	32	51
Middle management and technicians	44	38	47
White-collar workers	46	42	42
Shopkeepers and craftsmen	47	22	34
Blue-collar workers	46	32	34
Agricultural workers and farmers	49	23	31
Retired and inactive	50	29	38
Interest in Politics			
Great interest in politics	41	33	51
Some interest in politics	56	35	45
Very little interest in politics	45	33	34
No interest in politics	33	21	19
Voting Intentions			
Extreme-left	36	29	57
Communist party	38	32	47
Socialist party	47	29	39
Majority	52	33	37
Abstain	41	30	27

NOTE: The survey question was: "Which media did you consider most useful in helping you decide how to vote?"
SOURCE: Unpublished Louis Harris France poll, conducted by the author.

relatively speaking, newspaper readership is undergoing a slight decline. A distinction must be drawn, however, between trends affecting the "national" press published in Paris and those affecting the provincial newspapers.

The Parisian press, in particular, is in the midst of a crisis that was embryonic until the beginning of the 1960s and has become increasingly apparent since. The causes of this crisis are many, but the most important is certainly competition from the broadcast media. This began with the transistor radio at the end of the 1950s and became more serious with the wide distribution of television in the mid-1960s. Newspapers lost their preeminence among the public's sources of information somewhat later than in the United States, England, and West Germany, but just as suddenly. Moreover, in France, newspaper owners and editors had not given much thought to the threat that faced them and were not able to adapt their product to the new market conditions.

Beyond this structural problem, there were other factors that aggravated the situation. First of all, weak management. The new directors of the French daily press after the war were mostly people who had been in the Resistance movement in 1944–1945. Their businesses prospered in the immediate postwar years 1945–1950, then entered a period of stability. On the whole these men failed to understand that the press had become an industry which required good management guided by market research on a strictly business basis. It was only very late, too late in most cases, that French newspaper publishers learned even the basic rules of bookkeeping and marketing.

These weaknesses in management were compounded by the rigidity of the labor unions and the problems of modernizing newspapers. All of the printers in Paris are members of the Fédération française des travailleurs du livre, a labor union affiliated with the Confédération générale du travail (CGT), and their control is pervasive. The printers' union has managed to arrogate to itself exorbitant privileges, such as complete control over hiring for the Paris newspapers: the newspapers do not hire their printing staff directly but must ask the labor union to provide them with qualified workers. In addition, the union has managed to impose norms concerning the number of workers needed, their salary, and their work rhythm which, even in the 1960s, were no longer consonant with modern printing technology. Finally, making the newspaper industry commercially viable meant convincing a reluctant public to subscribe to newspapers, rather than buying them one issue at a time, and—

even more important—revamping the cumbersome and very expensive distribution network.

The consequences of the newspapers' failure to modernize have been drastic. The political party press has practically disappeared; only the Communist party newspaper, *L'Humanité*, has survived, thanks to the financial success of the party's ideologically tame monthly for children, *Pif*. Another consequence has been consolidation: the thirty newspapers published in Paris at the end of the war had dwindled to ten in 1970. Furthermore, the circulation of the newspapers published in Paris has become concentrated in the Paris region. All of the Paris daily papers have seen their circulation drop conspicuously since 1960, with the exception of such quality newspapers as *Le Monde*, which has increased its readership, and *La Croix*, which has held is own (see Table 5–5).

Nevertheless, some bold entrepreneurs have recently tried to take advantage of the low costs of offset printing and the lowered demands of the printers' union (somewhat sobered by the crisis in the industry) to launch new daily papers. One such was the *Quotidien de Paris*, started in 1974 by a group of people who had worked for the defunct *Combat*. This new daily did not attract a large enough readership to last much beyond the March 1978 elections and finally folded in June of the same year. In addition, extreme-left groups have managed to put out daily newspapers in the last few years, notably, the libertarian extreme-left with *Libération* (which manages to survive thanks to low salaries and very cautious management), the Trotskyists (Ligue Communiste Révolutionnaire) with *Rouge*, and the Maoists, represented by two newspapers, *L'Humanité Rouge* and *Le Quotidien du Peuple*. These last three regularly operate at a loss. Finally, there is the daily *Le Matin*, an experiment started in 1977 by Claude Perdriel, director of the weekly *Nouvel Observateur*. Politically, *Le Matin* is sympathetic to the Socialist party, and although it has managed to win over several tens of thousands of readers, it still has not achieved commercial viability.

The other major event in the daily newspaper world was the acquisition of the *Figaro*, the newspaper of the liberal bourgeoisie, and of a share of *France-Soir*, the mass-circulation, general information daily, by Robert Hersant. Hersant was a Majority deputy up until 1978 (he lost his seat in the March elections) and is the head of an important provincial newspaper group equipped with modern printing technology and electronic facsimile systems. He also owns various magazines and is known for his authoritarian management methods. A kind of French Citizen Kane, Hersant is thought to have

TABLE 5–5

COPIES PRINTED AND CIRCULATION OF THE MAIN DAILY NEWSPAPERS
AND WEEKLY MAGAZINES

Title	Copies Printed	Circulation 1977–1978
Main Parisian Newspapers		
France-Soir	736,049	530,276
Le Monde	545,670	428,857
Le Parisien Libéré	486,743	359,112
Le Figaro	407,364	327,158
L'Aurore	370,614	289,291
L'Humanité	198,714	151,387
La Croix	129,272	121,925
Le Matin	150,000	104,743
Les Echos	66,036	51,116
Libération	50,781	29,600
Le Quotidien de Paris	35,000	15,000
Rouge	25,000	8,000
Main Provincial Newspapers		
Ouest-France	735,680	662,805
Le Progrès	445,695	390,475
Sud-Ouest	412,497	368,327
La Voix du Nord	402,951	375,266
Le Dauphiné Libéré	368,528	325,743
La Nouvelle République du Centre Ouest	299,465	274,193
La Dépêche du Midi	285,064	253,809
L'Est Républicain	278,548	254,623
La Montagne	276,374	251,222
Nice-Matin	268,882	238,685
Le Républicain Lorrain	224,047	211,106
Les Dernières Nouvelles d'Alsace	222,317	206,727
Midi Libre	207,696	186,114
Le Provençal	206,166	181,801
Main Weekly News Magazines		
Paris-Match	723,500	563,896
L'Express	651,590	537,726
Le Nouvel Observateur	425,987	342,322
Le Point	327,251	250,398

SOURCE: Official figures released by the "Office de justification de la diffusion," published regularly in the monthly Presse Actualité.

privileged relations with the political powers and is seen as a disturbing figure by leftist public opinion and by the press in general. As owner and editor of *Le Figaro*, he has certainly made this newspaper more politically committed, more pugnacious, and more hostile to the left than any of the great editors who preceded him.

In the provinces the situation is quite different. For one thing, newspapers are smaller and management tends to exercise tighter control. For another, the printers' union has been less powerful than in Paris, and the modernization of printing plants has been much more rapid and thorough. Furthermore, the provincial press does not have to compete for local advertising either with the Paris press or with radio and television since there is no regional or local broadcasting in France. Since they provide services ranging from local cinema programs to community news that are not available elsewhere, they are in no way threatened by the national media. As a result, the larger regional papers are better off than their Parisian counterparts and have been able to keep their circulation stable.

This relative calm follows on a period of consolidation which benefited the best established newspapers in each region. The marginal papers, those that were not able to attract a sufficiently large or loyal readership, one after another folded, were sold, or were absorbed by their more resilient competitors. Real press empires were created, each large regional newspaper tending to acquire a monopoly within its area. The publisher of the leading newspaper (who in most cases is also the editor) became one of the public figures who carried most weight in the social, cultural, and political life of each region, alongside the mayor of the largest city and the prefect (the highest government official of the department) and ahead of the bishop. This is the case of the owners of newspapers like *Ouest-France* in the west, *La Dépêche du Midi* and *Sud-Ouest* in the southwest, *Le Provençal* in the south and Mediterranean regions, *L'Est Républicain* and *Le Républicain Lorrain*, which are partly owned by the same publisher, in the east, *Les Dernières Nouvelles d'Alsace*, *La Voix du Nord*, *Midi Libre*, and so on.

The publishers of these newspapers have well-defined political opinions,[6] and the papers themselves have definite political sympathies—leftist in some cases, more often centrist. Their monopolistic

---

[6] For example, Gaston Defferre, publisher of *Le Provençal*, is the mayor of Marseille and president of the Socialist group in the National Assembly, and Jean Michel Baylet, publisher of *La Dépêche du Midi*, was elected to the Assembly on the Leftist Radical ticket in March 1978. I have already mentioned the case of Robert Hersant who owns the provincial newspaper group that includes such newspapers as *Nord-Matin*, *Paris-Normandie*, and *Centre-Presse*.

position, however, has led them, in order not to lose part of their readership, to keep side-taking and politicizing to a minimum, at least in reporting the news. Today the political press is more or less confined to the national weeklies printed in Paris. Foremost among these are the news magazines on the American model: first *L'Express*, which is sympathetic to the Majority and in particular to its reformist Giscardian branch, then *Le Nouvel Observateur*, which is sympathetic to the left, specifically to the Socialists. The newest weekly news magazine, *Le Point* (founded in 1972 by the Hachette publishing group), claims to be politically neutral but sometimes displays a preference for the Majority. Finally, there is *Paris-Match*, which is clearly right-wing.

The Press and the Campaign

During the 1978 campaign, the large regional dailies displayed their usual political sympathies—*Le Provençal* and *La Dépêche du Midi* for the non-Communist left, *Le Progrès, Sud-Ouest, La Voix du Nord, L'Est Républicain, Le Républicain Lorrain*, and *Les Dernières Nouvelles d'Alsace* for the Majority. They expressed them, however, with great discretion, especially in regions where the Majority and the opposition were evenly matched and papers ran the risk of alienating half their readers by taking too strong a stand.[7] In addition, given that the left was expected to win, centrist newspapers were concerned not to start off in the bad graces of a possible leftist Government.

On the other hand, it is clear that the Parisian press was even more politicized than usual. Most discreet were *La Croix*, sympathetic to the Majority in its editorials but balanced in its news reporting, and *Le Quotidien de Paris*, which leaned towards the Socialist party. Of course the party newspapers were the most open and decided in stating their opinions. They finished off the electoral campaign, as is their wont, with "appeals to the people": thus *L'Humanité* stated, "Voting for the Communist party on Sunday will create the necessary conditions to beat the right, force the Socialist party leaders to the necessary negotiations, and promote in unity and order a policy that will change for the better the lives of the majority of the French people."[8] *Rouge* wrote: "By voting for the

---

[7] After the elections the Socialist leaders of Marseille were for the first time brought before the local Socialist party branch to engage in "self-criticism"—specifically, to account for what was deemed an excessively tepid attitude toward the left on the part of *Le Provençal* during the electoral campaign.

[8] *L'Humanité*, March 10, 1978.

candidates of the Ligue Communiste Révolutionnaire you will be saying 'yes' to worker unity and 'yes' to socialism." [9] And *Le Quotidien du Peuple:* "Neither a rightist bourgeoisie nor a leftist one. For the struggles of tomorrow, in order to advance towards socialism, let us construct a large revolutionary force. Support the Workers' and Peasants' Union for Proletarian Democracy." [10]

Le Matin, though not affiliated with a political party, minced no words: "The most effective slogan would thus seem to be 'twenty years is enough!' Sweep away what exists in order to do something else. What? We will see. Anything would be better than what we have." [11] It also demanded a reconciliation between the Communist party and the Socialist party for the second ballot, pleading that "an understanding must be reached—this is necessary for the success of the left's policy even more than for its victory at the polls." [12] Still in favor of the left, but infinitely more cautious, *Le Monde,* the authoritative afternoon newspaper and a fixture of French intellectual life, ran a long editorial penned by its editor, Jacques Fauvet, entitled "Risks":

> Paradoxically, at a time when everything is being called into question, suddenly all doubts give way to certainty. . . . 'Twenty years is enough'? The slogan is simplistic and only half true. The men and the policies, after all, have changed since 1958. Mr. Valéry Giscard d'Estaing is not Georges Pompidou, who, in turn, was not General de Gaulle. Furthermore, we are dealing with legislative elections and not presidential ones. 'Five years is enough' would be more accurate and appropriate. Change is risky? Continuity can be risky too. [13]

Finally, *Libération,* while it printed articles favorable to the extreme-left and the Front Autogestionnaire, openly supported the "green" candidates, the Ecologists.

The Majority, of course, was backed by the newspaper of the business world, *Les Echos,* as well as by the mass-circulation *Parisien Libéré* and by *France-Soir,* which has supported every Government in power since 1945 (except the brief Mendès-France Government of 1954–1955) and in 1978 was more emphatically behind the

---

[9] *Rouge,* March 10, 1978.

[10] *Le Quotidien du Peuple,* March 11, 1978.

[11] *Le Matin,* January 23, 1978.

[12] Ibid., March 10, 1978.

[13] *Le Monde,* March 10, 1978.

Majority than ever. What was new on the scene was the empassioned tone adopted by *L'Aurore* and *Le Figaro* in defending the Majority against the threat from the left. What was at stake as they saw it was not the mere alternation of rival parties in power, a normal occurrence in a liberal democracy, but civilization threatened by the barbarians. Three samples of their prose and arguments make this clear. José Van den Esch, the editorial writer for *L'Aurore*, wrote:

> There is no doubt that in the course of this campaign, François Mitterrand has managed to make the public believe that the bureaucracy of his socialism could have a heart! But not one state in the world built on Marxism or inspired by its doctrine has evolved without terrible police oppression. Not one! Will we have to undergo it too?[14]

Jean d'Ormesson, chief editor of *Le Figaro*, wrote just before the first round:

> Sunday the destiny of France will be in the balance— your destiny and your children's, the destiny of your hopes and memories. Defend them. Think hard. Remain confident. Take courage. Do not bury all that. Do not run, deaf and blind, towards collective suicide.[15]

Finally, Max Clos, editor of *Le Figaro*, explained:

> François Mitterrand is reassuring to the French people, with his smooth voice and his warm humanism. Apparently they do not see, or do not want to see, that the real power inexorably lurking in the Socialists' shadow is the Communist party. . . . It is up to us to prevent the French nation from falling into another world, unknown and dangerous. We can do this by voting. Beginning with the first ballot, vote for the Majority. If you do not, if the left wins, it will all be out of our hands—probably forever.[16]

The news magazines also took sides. *Paris-Match* came out clearly for the Majority, *L'Express* less clearly so. In its last issue before the first ballot, *L'Express* ran editorials by Raymond Aron and Jean-François Revel, both in favor of the Majority, and a third, signed by Olivier Todd, that was hostile to the Communists but

---

[14] *L'Aurore*, March 11-12, 1978.
[15] *Le Figaro*, March 10, 1978.
[16] Ibid., March 11, 1978.

quite warm toward the Socialist party.[17] In *Le Point*, André Chambraud pleaded for a relaxation of political strife and an acceptance of the elementary rules of democratic alternation:

> Less individualistic than has been said, less preoccupied with epic battles, the French people are citizens of a democratic country. Once the verdict has been reached they will have to accept it loyally and without rancour.[18]

Jean Daniel, editor of *Le Nouvel Observateur*, reminded his readers of the magazine's position, saying:

> For a majority of the French people the only solution is to vote for the left, and for a majority of the left there is no solution other than a united left. . . . The more weight the Socialists have, the better they will be able to impose their antitotalitarian principles.[19]

But aside from taking positions, the newspapers and magazines had to inform their readers of the events of the campaign. This they did without much originality. Their campaign coverage can be studied under six headings.

(1) Statements released by and interviews with the national or regional leaders of the main political parties. Very few newspapers neglected these, though most of them devoted whole editorials or interviews only to the leaders of the four most important parties. The numerous secondary, marginal, and new parties got short shrift; the campaign as seen by the press was dominated by what Michel Jobert called the "gang of four."

(2) Speeches made by the major leaders on the radio or television or at campaign meetings. The press systematically reprinted the leaders' speeches, of which the most important—those announcing major policy stands, for example—were first broadcast live. All of the leaders felt that the broadcast media guaranteed them more effective access to a greater number of voters than the press alone.

(3) The party platforms. Here again, only the platforms of the four dominant parties received careful comparative analysis from most papers, and only important newspapers scrutinized the platforms in their entirety.[20] Specialized publications—on sports, animals, the

---

[17] *L'Express*, March 16, 1978.
[18] *Le Point*, March 6, 1978.
[19] *Le Nouvel Observateur*, March 11, 1978.
[20] See, for example, *Le Monde*, March 10 and 11, 1978.

cinema, the elderly, and so on—tended to confine their attention to proposals in their areas of particular interest.

(4) Studies of key districts. Many papers used detailed reporting of developments in particular districts as an indirect way of expressing their political preferences.[21] Some, such as *Le Quotidien de Paris*, published opinion polls conducted in the districts they covered.

(5) Campaign announcements paid for by political parties or by groups supporting a particular party. These were first used in France in 1967 but did not become common until 1978. The most sought-after vehicle for such advertisements was *Le Monde*, which is considered the opinion leaders' newspaper par excellence. *Le Monde* published numerous appeals from groups, including full-page spreads paid for by the UDF announcing the most important television debates in which UDF leaders would take part.

(6) Opinion polls. The publication of the national voting-intention surveys set the pace for the campaign. One could almost say that the polls were the dominant feature of the preelection period, and in this the press lived up to its task of stimulating interest in the election. The papers carrying polls regularly and the pollsters associated with them were: *L'Aurore*, Publimétrie; *Le Matin*, Louis Harris France; *Le Figaro*, SOFRES; *Le Point*, IFOP; and *L'Express*, Louis Harris France. To these must be added the polls by Démoscopie carried in *Le Quotidien de Paris* and by Public in *Paris-Match*. These polls provided a constant barometer of opinion in the last few months before the elections. The pollsters also published surveys on the issues (for example a "compass" by SOFRES in *Le Nouvel Observateur* or IFOP's monthly "barometer" in *France-Soir*). Voting-intention surveys from selected electoral districts were also published (IFOP's in the weekly magazine *Valeurs Actuelles* or the Lyon newspaper *Le Progrès* and Public's in *Paris-Match* or *Le Quotidien de Paris*). The newspapers which did not conduct their own polls often printed the results of several, *Le Monde* leading the way; in addition, both radio and television often cited the polls at some length.

Another innovation in 1978 was the practice of publishing at regular intervals projections of the final distribution of seats in the National Assembly based on voting-intention data. *L'Aurore*, *Le Point*, *L'Express*, and *Le Matin* all issued such projections, which

---

[21] An article on the constituency in which François Mitterrand was running, published by *L'Aurore* on January 11, 1978, was entitled: "J. M. Basset, Mitterrand's opponent, points to the disastrous balance-sheet of the Deputy of the Nièvre." In presenting the "complete" list of candidates on January 5, 1978, *Le Figaro* "omitted" the name of Florence d'Harcourt (who was eventually elected) from the list running in the constituency of its director, Robert Hersant.

were reprinted and commented upon by other papers and magazines. Except for one forecast by Public published in *Paris-Match* whose validity was questioned by several experts, all of these projections named the Union of the Left the winner. A few days before the voting, the big question seemed to be the one asked by *Le Point* as early as January 23: "Can the Majority still win the elections?" In fact, a crucial fraction of the potential Socialist electorate (who, for the most part, had voted for the Socialist party in the cantonal elections of 1976 and the municipal elections of 1977) would switch to Giscard's UDF in the last few days of the campaign.[22]

Even if the polls had registered this change they could not have revealed it to the public since a law passed on July 19, 1977, prohibited the publication of voting-intention polls during the week preceding the first ballot as well as between the two rounds. The intention of the Majority (the left had opposed this law) had been to curb the possible influence of opinion polls in the final phase of electoral campaigns. All of the pollsters and most of the newspapers had protested unsuccessfully against this measure, which they held to be an attack on the freedom of speech and access to information. Some observers thought that foreign newspapers might poll in France during the prohibited period, but none of the French pollsters would settle for this arrangement. Front-page news throughout the campaign, the opinion polls disappeared for the last two weeks, then reappeared in the election post-mortems. The left, disillusioned by the outcome, bitterly accused the polls of having failed.

Broadcasting in France

By law, the French state has a monopoly on broadcasting. As far as television is concerned, this monopoly is very strictly applied: no private television broadcasting occurs on French territory. A state-controlled television broadcasting company, Radiodiffusion Télévision Française, was created in 1945, and in 1964 it became the Office de Radiodiffusion Télévision Française, generally known as ORTF. From 1964 until just after Giscard d'Estaing's election as president of France, the ORTF was in charge of the three French television networks. A law of August 7, 1974, dissolved the ORTF and created three separate state-controlled companies, which now compete with one another: TF 1 (Télévision Française 1), A 2 (Antenne 2), and FR 3 (France Régions 3). A rule book drawn up by the authorities

---

[22] On this point see the postelection SOFRES poll printed in *Le Nouvel Observateur*, April 23, 1978.

fixes the mutual obligations of the state and the television companies, on the understanding that the companies will be entirely free of political pressure from the Government. It is well known, however, that in this domain practice is not the same as theory; there has always been some confusion in France between state monopoly and control by the Government in power. The television companies are financed in two ways. TF 1 and A 2 receive half their funds from an annual tax paid by all television owners and the other half from advertising, while FR 3, which is not allowed to broadcast advertisements, is exclusively financed by the television tax.

Theoretically, the state monopoly on radio broadcasting is just as strict, and after 1975 the government cracked down on the movement for local and "independent" radio. In practice, however, the situation is fluid, as long as it benefits the French state. Up until 1974 the state-controlled radio was part of the ORTF, but on August 7, 1974, it became an independent state-controlled company under the name Radio France; the links between the directors of the radio stations and members of the Government are informal but permanent, much like those mentioned for television. Radio France manages various radio networks: France Inter, which has a mass audience; France-Culture and France-Musique, which aim at more specialized audiences; and local networks in the large cities, which broadcast nonstop music and some local news.

Alongside the state radio stations and competing with them are the *périphérique* stations, so called because they do not broadcast from French territory but from neighboring countries. These stations are privately owned commercial companies supported by advertising; it is worth pointing out, however, that the French state through the state-controlled company SOFIRAD (Société Financière de Radio-Diffusion) has a share in them, often a controlling interest. It also controls their publicity management and lends them technical support, beginning with the cables that link the Paris studios to the *périphérique* antennas. Thus, despite court decisions ruling otherwise, the French state violates its own monopoly.

The main peripheral radio stations are Europe no. 1 and RTL (previously Radio Luxembourg), which, together with the state radio, France Inter, attract 75 to 80 percent of the radio audience, followed by Radio Monte Carlo (about 12 percent) and Sud Radio. Their ties with the Government are such that they can act neither as opposition nor as totally independent stations. Nevertheless, their approach is freer than that of the state radio stations and their political commentaries are sometimes more uninhibited.

Nonofficial Broadcasting in the 1978 Campaign

Radio and television stations are required by law to make time available to the political parties, free of charge, during the official campaign. This is considered part of their duty to the public. Of course, before the onset of the official campaign all of the radio and television networks, both public and private, make a considerable effort to cover the race.

Radio. From January on, the campaign invaded the radio networks, starting, of course, with the news programs. As in the press, the "gang of four" dominated the campaign coverage. All of the radio stations handled the campaign in much the same way. Essentially they relied on interviews with or debates between political leaders, keeping to a minimum the effort required from their journalists in the way of gathering information or analyzing the proceedings. Most of the air time was actually used by politicians.

France Inter, for example, put most of its effort into a nine-part program from 7 to 8 A.M. entitled "Petits déjeuners politiques," during which a political leader was interviewed live by the editorial staff of the station. It also held live debates three times a week from 7:15 to 8 P.M. with two to four representatives of the political parties discussing specific issues—national defense, nationalizations, public education, inflation, unemployment, and so on. The first of these debates, on January 12, and the last, on February 17, brought together representatives of the four main parties; others pitted Alain Peyrefitte of the RPR against the Socialist Pierre Mauroy (February 3) and Jean Lecanuet of the UDF against the Communist Roland Leroy (February 6). France Inter also devoted its daily morning program, "Parlons clair," from 7:45 to 7:55 A.M., to interviewing someone connected with the electoral campaign, and politicians were invited every day to the midday news program "Inter-Midi." France Inter—unlike its competitors, the peripheral radio stations—included the representatives of marginal political movements among the participants in its campaign programs, especially these last two. Finally, on the program "Le téléphone sonne" a guest politician or local union spokesman answered questions phoned in by the public.

Europe no. 1 organized its campaign coverage around live debates broadcast between 7 and 8 P.M. Representatives of the four main political parties participated, and the topics were the major campaign issues, defense, education, economic policy, foreign affairs, social policy, institutions, and freedom. On a few occasions just two leaders debated and the topic was French politics in general; thus, on February 20 Georges Marchais confronted Alain Peyrefitte.[23] On "Clubs de la presse," meanwhile, broadcast live between 7 and 8 P.M. (sometimes 8:30), a political leader answered questions from well-known print and broadcast journalists. In addition, Europe no. 1 organized a series of programs called "Studio volant" on board an airplane that flew from one city to another. This program, broadcast between 7:15 and 8 P.M., pitted the main local candidates in fifteen different districts against each other. Also on Europe no. 1, "La Ville Europe no. 1" evoked life in a small provincial town, Paray-le-Monial, throughout the campaign. And in a series of four one-hour programs broadcast at 10 A.M., George Marchais, Jacques Chirac, François Mitterrand, and Raymond Barre addressed a primarily female audience.

On RTL two radio journals—"Journal inattendu," scheduled between 1 and 2 P.M. on Saturdays, and "Le Journal de Jacques Paoli," weekdays at 6 P.M.—invited a variety of politicians to act as guest editors. RTL also mounted special programs such as "Gros plan, spécial éléctions," broadcast at 8:30 A.M., and "Débats régionaux," a series of hour-long debates between regional leaders of the left and the Majority broadcast at 8 P.M. between February 27 and March 10.

The only radio station that did not organize debates was Radio Monte Carlo, which stuck with feature programs. On "Les grands leaders face aux journalistes," a series of six programs from 7 to 7:40 P.M., politicians were interviewed in their home towns, while on "Les grands leaders répondent aux auditeurs," another series of six programs, candidates answered questions that had been telephoned in and recorded. On "RMC Choc," which lasted only eight minutes and was broadcast at 1:15 P.M., two candidates whose opinions were different responded to the same question. Finally, Radio Monte Carlo broadcast profiles of districts considered electoral "hot spots."

The peripheral radio stations, as we have seen, gave very little coverage to the minor parties, but they were careful to balance their coverage of the Majority and the left. The debates on Europe no. 1 featured thirteen representatives of the Majority and an equal number from the left, "Clubs de la presse" had four Majority candidates and four from the left (as well as a representative of the employers' association and a labor union spokesman), while "Studio volant" reflected the make-up of the electoral districts it visited, featuring fifteen Socialists, fourteen Communists, fifteen UDF candidates,

---

[23] The Marchais-Peyrefitte debate was organized by both Europe no. 1 and Antenne 2 and was broadcast simultaneously on both radio and television.

TABLE 5–6

France Inter's Guest Speakers, by Political Tendency

Program	Majority	Oppo-sition	Various Right[a]	Various Left[b]	Other[c]
"Petits déjeuners politiques"	6	3	—	—	—
"Parlons clair"	13	10	4	2	5
"Inter-midi"	21	13	5	5	2
"Débats de France Inter"	21	19	—	—	1
"Le téléphone sonne"	9	8	2	2	2
Total	70	53	11	9	10

[a] Mostly representatives of the business world and the extreme-right.
[b] Mostly representatives of labor unions and the extreme-left.
[c] For example, Michel Jobert (Mouvement des Démocrates), Yvan Charpentié (Confédération Générale des Cadres), Jean-Claude Delarue (Ecologie 78), and André Bergeron (Force Ouvrière).
SOURCE: Documents made available by France Inter.

eleven RPR candidates, and one member of the Front Autogestionnaire. Three members of the Majority and three representatives of the left appeared on Radio Monte Carlo in "Les grands leaders face aux journalistes" and also in "Les grands leaders répondent aux auditeurs." On the other hand, France Inter, the only station along with RTL to give any coverage to the marginal groups, showed a certain favoritism towards the Majority, as may be seen in Table 5–6.

Television. Between February 9 and 11, Louis Harris France questioned a national sample on their preferences in campaign programs on television.[24] The results, in percentages, were as follows:

Speeches	4
Interviews	22
Debates (two participants)	42
Round tables (four to five participants)	17
None of these	7
No opinion	8
Total	100

Beginning early in January, TF 1 and A 2 broadcast political interviews and debates regularly either at peak spectator hours in the

[24] Louis Harris France, *Télérama*, n. 1468 (March 4, 1978).

evening ("L'évènement" on TF 1 and "Cartes sur table" on A 2) or at midday ("Les invités du journal de 13 heures" on TF 1 and "Samedi et demi" on A 2). The political leaders invited to appear prepared themselves with great care. These broadcasts were popular and much quoted and commented upon by the press.

Like the press and radio, television focused on the four major parties. TF 1 invited seven representatives of the Majority to appear on its evening programs and an equal number from the left, while A 2 invited eight speakers from the Majority and only six from the opposition.

The president's speeches have not been included in this count, although he addressed the nation several times on the state radio and television networks, perhaps with decisive effect. In one of these speeches (delivered at 7 P.M. on January 27 at Verdun-sur-le-Doubs and broadcast live) Giscard plainly stated his support for the Majority, "the right choice for France." Long excerpts of this speech were rebroadcast later in the evening. The president also held a televised press conference on February 9, and his final speech was broadcast on Saturday, March 11, after the official campaign had ended, which meant that the party leaders had no opportunity to reply.

In addition, various ministers and Majority candidates were invited to appear on FR 3 shows not directly connected with the electoral campaign; Jean-Jacques Beucler, for example, appeared on a program about ex-servicemen on January 16, Christian Gerondeau on one discussing highway safety on February 2, and Robert Galley on one about French cooperation with Africa on February 16. In other words, the Majority was quite clearly favored by the television networks.

Thanks to some unpublished polls carried out by SOFRES, we now know the size and audience for some of these programs. In particular, the data show that not all of the viewers were partisans of the candidates participating (see Table 5–7). This is one of the great strengths of television during an electoral campaign: while the other media tend to reach only people who already agree with their message (the problem of "selective exposure"), television attracts a broad spectrum of viewers.

As the table shows, even interviews with a single candidate were watched by significant numbers of his opponents. His supporters predominated, of course, but it is important to notice that a fairly large segment of each partisan group listened to the arguments set forth by other leaders, in interviews as well as debates. Potential Communist voters watched television the most, especially when Georges

165

TABLE 5–7
AUDIENCE FOR EVENING CAMPAIGN COVERAGE ON TELEVISION, FEBRUARY 1978

Participants	Network	Date	Audience[a]				
			All respondents	PCF	PS	UDF	RPR
Debates							
Defferre (PS)—							
Bonnet (UDF)	A2	Feb. 6	12	14	14	8	16
Rocard (PS)—							
Fourcade (UDF)	TF1	Feb. 7	17	19	18	16	19
Servan-Schreiber (UDF)—							
Leroy (PCF)	TF1	Feb. 14	19	25	18	20	19
Guéna (RPR)—							
Fabre (MRG)	TF1	Feb. 16	21	24	20	19	24
Marchais (PCF)—							
Peyrefitte (RPR)	A2	Feb. 20	38	51	37	35	45
Kanapa (PCF)—							
Lecanuet (UDF)	TF1	Feb. 23	12	16	9	13	12
Interviews							
Chirac (RPR)	A2	Feb. 8	20	14	15	22	43
Barre (UDF[b])	A2	Feb. 13	27	18	25	34	40
Mitterrand (PS)	A2	Feb. 15	26	33	32	22	24
Barre (UDF)	TF1	Feb. 21	21	11	16	28	37
Poniatowski (UDF)	A2	Feb. 22	12	8	9	16	20

[a] Percentages of all respondents or of the stated party subgroup who watched either "from beginning to end" or "only part" of the program.
[b] The prime minister was linked to the UDF but was not formally a member.
SOURCE: Unpublished SOFRES poll, made available to the author.

Marchais, who has become a real television star, was appearing. But about one-fifth of each partisan group watched the debates regardless of who was participating. Equally interesting is the great success of the Marchais-Peyrefitte "match," which was certainly one of the high points of the campaign for the television audience.

Television counteracts to some extent the voter's selective exposure to the media and to issues and points of view. This does not mean, however, that viewers belonging to a given group are easily won over by spokesmen for other groups (see Table 5–8). The response to the Marchais-Peyrefitte debate makes this clear: although 36 per-

TABLE 5–8
Most Convincing Contenders in the Television Debates

Most Convincing Contender	Percentage of all Respondents	Percentage of Party Group			
		PCF	PS	UDF	RPR
Defferre (PS)	43	67	68	15	6
Bonnet (UDF)	30	6	5	65	72
Rocard (PS)	38	50	66	12	9
Fourcade (UDF)	24	4	13	44	48
Kanapa (PCF)	30	80	38	3	15
Lecanuet (UDF)	35	5	23	70	46
Servan-Schreiber (UDF)	24	6	10	61	10
Leroy (PCF)	41	78	61	12	14
Guéna (RPR)	21	6	7	35	54
Fabre (MRG)	48	61	69	31	11
Marchais (PCF)	36	91	49	6	8
Peyrefitte (RPR)	36	3	15	70	67

NOTE: Some respondents answered that the adversaries were equally convincing or that neither was convincing; thus the pairs of figures for each debate do not add to 100 percent.
SOURCE: Unpublished SOFRES poll, made available to the author.

cent of the spectators thought Marchais the more convincing and just as many chose Peyrefitte, the different partisan groups actually expressed very set but opposite opinions. Also, there is always a small group who are displeased by the performance of their own party's spokesman. Furthermore, the "centrist" phenomenon manifests itself in a rather unexpected way (at least quantitatively) in some of the debates. For example, almost as many UDF voters named Robert Fabre, theoretically their opponent, the most convincing contender, as named their Gaullist ally, Yves Guéna. Meanwhile, RPR voters very clearly refused to choose between a Communist and Jean-Jacques Servan-Schreiber, expressing dislike for both, whereas at least in theory the president of the Radical party was their ally in the struggle against the Communists.

Broadcasting in the Official Campaign

In accordance with the law, the three television networks, TF 1, A 2, and FR 3, and the state radio network, France Inter, broadcast official party propaganda during the two weeks preceding the first round of the election and during the week between the two rounds every evening (except weekends) for half an hour at peak audience time (8:35 P.M.). The regulations governing these broadcasts give equal time to the Majority and to the opposition (two hours each), the allocation of time within these two camps being a function of the parliamentary strength of the various political groups. Those not represented in the current Assembly are entitled to two seven-minute broadcasts each in the two weeks preceding the first ballot and a five-minute broadcast in the week between the two rounds, as long as they are running candidates in at least seventy-five districts: in 1978 eleven such minor groups qualified.[25]

In each half-hour program representatives of various political parties spoke for three to ten minutes. All of these programs were simultaneously broadcast by France Inter and by all three television networks, leaving television audiences, at least, no choice but to watch campaign broadcasts during this slot. Eighty-one percent of a survey sample expressed dissatisfaction with this arrangement,[26] but it is clearly a powerful way of inducing the public to watch the official campaign. Even those not interested in politics, if they are in the habit of watching television, will tend to watch election broadcasts while waiting for the evening programs to come on. Since the parties are not allowed to make use of any filmed material (a rule intended to deny the wealthier parties an unfair advantage) these programs are little more than radio broadcasts taped in a television studio.

In the past, most parties chose to fill their portions of these programs with speeches from their leaders. This approach is rapidly losing favor since according to the party experts it is not popular with the public. Now the tendency is to show discussions—between the leaders of the party, between rank-and-file party members (the RPR used this formula before the first ballot), between political leaders and friendly journalists (the usual choice of the Communist party), or

---

[25] The eleven minor groups were: Ecologie 78, Front Autogestionnaire, Lutte Ouvrière, Ligue Communiste Révolutionnaire, Union Ouvrière et Paysanne pour la Démocratie Prolétarienne, Démocratie Chrétienne, Action Républicaine Indépendante et Libérale, Centre National des Indépendants et Paysans, Mouvement des Démocrates, Parti des Forces Nouvelles, Rassemblement des Usagers des Services Publics, des Contribuables et des Groupements de Défense.

[26] Louis Harris France, *Télérama*, n. 1468 (March 4, 1978).

between party leaders or militants and independent journalists brought in as interviewers for these special programs (also used by the RPR).

These programs were, on the whole, quite dreary. Each was aimed at a specific category of voter, beginning with workers and moving on to women, the young, and so on. The audience level was quite high because of the time the programs were broadcast and because of the lack of choice mentioned earlier. According to the SOFRES polls, anywhere from 32 to 40 percent of the electorate watched at least parts of the official campaign broadcasts. The youngest voters seem to have been the least interested. On February 27, according to SOFRES, 26 percent of the voters in the eighteen to twenty-four age group watched the campaign program as compared with 31 percent for the twenty-five to thirty-four year olds, 33 percent for the thirty-five to forty-nine age bracket, 43 percent for the fifty to sixty-four age bracket, and 53 percent for the voters sixty-five and over. On the other hand, audience selectivity as a function of partisan interests was less pronounced for the official campaign programs than for those organized by the television networks themselves—which is the advantage of denying the viewer the right to choose the program he prefers.

Conclusion

Despite the presence of the most sophisticated media, then, French campaigning techniques tend to be old-fashioned, and the absence of commercial television keeps the confrontation within bounds. What remains to be decided is whether the French mass media adequately inform the electorate. Radio and television, the regional newspapers, and at times even the Parisian dailies tend to be self-effacing, neglecting their role as analysts and commentators and leaving the political parties to set the agenda. It cannot be said that the media entirely fulfill their responsibility to a democratic electorate by merely giving space to the campaign and providing a forum for debate, even if they do this with more flair and technical ability than the media in most Western democracies. The French media are very efficient at providing what Elihu Katz calls "platforms" for the political parties' arguments, but in so doing they seem to have forgotten their role as "windows" onto social and political reality.[27] Of course, by simply making

---

[27] Elihu Katz, "Platforms and Windows: Broadcasting's Role in Election Campaigns," in Dennis McQuail, ed., *Sociology of Mass Communications* (London and Baltimore: Penguin Books, 1972), pp. 353-371.

169

themselves available to the politicians, the media protect themselves against the charge of bias, but they also neglect the opportunity they possess to broaden the political debate.

6

Women in Politics in France

Monica Charlot

Women were latecomers to politics in France despite the fact that France was among the first countries to adopt universal suffrage for men, on March 2, 1848. Under the Third Republic, from 1870 to 1939, an active minority crusaded for the vote for women, and between the world wars the Chamber of Deputies gave it lukewarm support, but the Senate remained obdurately opposed. It was only in 1944 that General de Gaulle extended the franchise to all women over twenty-one.

It is probably significant that the decree granting female suffrage was not preceded by a vote in Parliament or by a referendum; it was not the result of pressure from the women's groups or from the elite. Officially a government decision, it was made by General de Gaulle himself—whether as a tribute to the role of women in the Resistance or simply a sign that times were changing and there was no going back to the prewar order of things, there is no telling. In any case, women were given the same rights as men: they could vote at twenty-one and stand for election to the National Assembly at twenty-three, to the Senate at thirty-five. In 1974 the qualifying age for voting was lowered to eighteen for both sexes.

Voting Behavior

In the interwar parliamentary debates a number of arguments were advanced against the vote for women. These arguments have been repeated over the years to explain women's political attitudes, so it is perhaps of interest to look at them more closely and translate them into questions about women's voting behavior today. First, there was the notion that women lacked political maturity and were on the whole indifferent to politics. This meant that they were unworthy of the vote, for if they obtained it they would not use it. Is it true, then, we may ask, that women today do not in fact use their right to vote? Second, it was claimed, especially by radicals, that women in France were so religious, such convinced, practicing Catholics, that they would simply vote as their priests commanded, and this implied hostility to the left. And we may ask, does religion play a fundamental part in women's voting behavior? Does it cause them to vote for the right more often than men?

Next came the argument that woman's very nature made her unable to play any part in politics. Not only was she incapable of assuming responsibilities, but her emotional nature drew her to extremist groups and causes. To what extent, then, do women today waste their votes on minor parties? Finally, the very stability of the social structure, it was claimed, was linked to the subordination of women. If they were encouraged to make claims on society, for instance by voting, the family would disintegrate, the number of children would decrease rapidly, and male authority within the family would cease to be the norm. Were this not so, women would simply vote as their husbands or fathers told them to and women's suffrage would in fact create a "family vote." Does an enfranchised wife today simply mean an extra vote in her husband's pocket?

Women today make up 52 percent of the electorate. They have outnumbered men as prospective voters ever since they obtained the right to vote. It is therefore all the more important to know to what extent the stereotypes of the interwar years are founded.

Participation. First, are women less interested in politics than men and do they vote less often than their male counterparts?

In 1953 when a French polling institute tried to measure men and women's interest in politics, it was clear that a sizable proportion of men (almost a third) and a clear majority of women (60 percent) were not interested at all.[1] Only a third of male voters and a mere 13 percent of women voters declared that they had any real interest in politics. It was thus difficult to claim that only women were apathetic. Twenty-five years later things had changed considerably. Not only had the number of men and women interested in politics increased, but the gap between the sexes had narrowed (see Table 6–1).[2] The

---

[1] *Sondages*, no. 2 (1954), p. 52.

[2] Unpublished IFOP Election Survey, carried out for the author February 13-20, 1978, and funded by the DGRST (Délégation Générale à la Recherche Scientifique et Technique).

TABLE 6–1

INTEREST IN POLITICS, BY SEX, 1953 AND 1978

(in percentages; difference in percentage points)

	1953			1978		
Interest in Politics	Men	Women	Differ- ence	Men	Women	Differ- ence
Very interested ⎫ Fairly interested ⎭	36	13	−23	49	31	−18
A little interested	36	27	− 9	37	48.5	+11.5
Not at all interested	28	60	+32	13	19.5	+ 6.5

NOTE: The survey question was, "Are you interested in politics?"
SOURCE: Adapted from IFOP Opinion Polls.

most striking change was the decline in the proportion of both men and women showing no interest at all in politics. For men the figure had fallen from 28 to 13 percent. For women the change was even more spectacular, the figure falling by two-thirds, from 60 percent to 19.5. With the trend so clear, it seems only realistic to believe that time will put the sexes on a par with one another sooner or later. It is already plain that the charge of immaturity as witnessed by lack of interest can no longer be applied to women. They have served their apprenticeship, and it is clear that cultural heritage, not basic incompetence, accounted for the lack of interest women showed.

The turnout of women at election times reinforces this picture. Jean Stoetzel estimated that 24 percent of women as against 17 percent of men did not vote[3] in the legislative elections of 1951—a gap of seven percentage points. Since 1951 no national study of differential turnout by sex has been undertaken, and opinion polls have been shown to be of dubious value in estimating abstention. For the 1978 election the only serious study is a monograph concerning the town of Vienne in Isère carried out by Claude Leleu.[4] It shows that in Vienne turnout among women was very marginally lower than among men: on the first ballot in 1978 abstention was 2.2 points higher among women than among men (18.9 as against 16.7). If this were the national figure it would, of course, confirm that women's interest in politics had increased: the gap would have closed from 7 to 2.2

[3] Jean Stoetzel, "Voting Behaviour in France," *British Journal of Sociology*, vol. 6, no. 2 (June 1955).
[4] *Le Monde*, April 1, 1978.

TABLE 6–2

RELIGIOUS PRACTICE OF MEN AND WOMEN, BY PARTY PREFERENCE, 1978

(in percentages)

| | Party | | | | Total |
Attendance at Mass	RPR	UDF	PS-MRG	PCF	Sample
Men					
Every Sunday	19.9	17.7	2.7	2.7	10.9
Once or twice a month	4.2	10.1	4.8	1.3	4.5
Occasionally	28.1	23.5	15.6	6.9	18.0
Rarely	28.0	27.0	38.2	15.4	28.4
Never	19.8	21.6	38.0	73.7	37.9
Women					
Every Sunday	22.1	29.7	5.8	2.9	16.4
Once or twice a month	12.1	8.6	3.4	1.7	6.7
Occasionally	23.4	23.8	22.9	16.0	23.6
Rarely	28.9	23.7	26.9	23.0	25.6
Never	13.5	12.5	41.0	53.3	27.0

SOURCE: Unpublished IFOP Opinion Polls.

percentage points. On the second ballot the difference in participation between men and women in Vienne was a mere 1.4 points, 16.8 percent as against 15.4. In other words, one of the effects of the second ballot was to mobilize women. In such a situation even if the rate of turnout is slightly lower among women the number of women actually voting is higher than the number of men.

We can therefore say that women do indeed use their right to vote. But do they make their own choices or does the Church tell them how to vote?

Religion and Voting Behavior. If one wishes to ascertain the part played by religion in voting behavior, a straightforward survey question such as "Are you a Catholic?" is of little use, for 77.9 percent of all male voters and 86.8 percent of all female voters in France reply in the affirmative. We have therefore tried to probe a little further by taking attendance at mass—which is compulsory, according to present-day Roman Catholic doctrine—as an indicator (see Table 6–2).[5]

When this variable is correlated with voting behavior, we find that the major difference lies not between the sexes but between the

[5] Cf. footnote 2.

parties. The Communist party draws the majority of both its male and its female voters from among those who never go to mass. On the whole, the more one goes to mass the less likely one is to vote for the left. For the Majority parties the pattern is less clear. Neither the RPR nor the UDF draws the major part of its support from regular churchgoers. This is not surprising when one notes that practicing Catholics only amounted to 10.9 percent of male voters and 16.4 percent of female voters in 1978, as against 29 percent of men and 52 percent of women in 1952.[6]

Within the electorate there are in fact two clear subcultures. The first consists of those who go to mass every Sunday. Here the left-wing parties are clearly underrepresented, and men reject both Communist and Socialist parties, while women reject communism more strongly than socialism. Among the regular mass-goers, men favor the RPR (+2.2 points) more than the women, who prefer the UDF to the RPR (+7.6 points). In this subgroup women outnumber men by over three to two. The second subculture is that of voters who never go to mass. Here the most striking fact is the overrepresentation of Communist voters. Within the PCF non-mass-going men and women are both twice as numerous as they are in the electorate as a whole. Over half of the party's women voters and almost three-quarters of its men voters do not go to mass. It would seem that within these two "extreme" subcultures the voting behavior of men and women is similarly oriented. Going to mass every Sunday constitutes a sort of bulwark against communism and to a slightly lesser degree against socialism, while complete rejection of mass-going is linked to a high level of Communist voting.

As for the specific question of whether or not women follow their priests' advice—if indeed priests give any—we can only underline again the similarity of behavior between the sexes. Women are more inclined to be practicing Catholics than men, but practicing men behave similarly to practicing women, so if the Church does dictate a political line, it is followed more or less to the same extent by the faithful whatever their sex. It must be added that since Vatican II the influence of the clergy in France can scarcely be accused of having favored exclusively the right-wing parties. Certainly the French clergy of the 1970s is far from devoid of left-wing firebrands.

Conservatism. In fact, women do vote more to the right than men, though their devoutness does not necessarily explain their conservative voting. If we look at six elections since the war—1946, 1951,

---

[6] *Sondages*, no. 4 (1952), p. 14.

TABLE 6-3
INTENDED VOTE FOR THE RIGHT, BY SEX, 1946–1978
(in percentages; difference in percentage points)

Year	Men	Women	Difference
1946	35	47	+12
1951	42	53	+11
1962	50	63	+13
1967	47	56	+ 9
1973	49	59	+10
1978	40	47	+ 7

SOURCE: Adapted from IFOP Election Surveys.

1962, 1967, 1973, and 1978—we can see that the gap is real (see Table 6-3). On the other hand, the 1978 figure is the lowest ever; it may be that the gap is closing. It is also obvious that right-wing voting cannot be claimed to be a simple reflex. In two elections out of the six (1946 and 1978) fewer than half the women voting supported right-wing candidates. On the other hand, in 1962 more than three women out of five did so. The right-wing vote is not stationary, nor does it steadily rise or fall over time. Although they may be broadly speaking more conservative, women, like men, weigh the alternatives and consider the issues of the day.

So far we have only examined the major left-right division. If we look now at a more detailed breakdown of voting intentions by party and sex, we can see that over the four months preceding the 1978 election and after the rift within the left there was a certain amount of change within the electorate (see Table 6-4). The distribution of the sexes in the different parties changed more within the Socialist party and the RPR than in the two other parties. The RPR ceased to be a male stronghold; indeed, the postelection survey reported in Table 6-4 shows that the majority of its supporters were women. As for the Socialist party, which had previously had a clearly male-oriented image, the sexes were probably running even by the time the election took place. The Communist party on the other hand continued to attract more men than women, the gap between the sexes increasing as the election drew nearer. Changes in the UDF are more difficult to appreciate since the party was only formed a matter of weeks before the election; still, if we add the 1977 voting-intention figures for the CDS and the PR (the two major components of the UDF), the overall loss of five points would seem to have come

TABLE 6–4

VOTING INTENTIONS, BY SEX, DECEMBER 1977 AND APRIL 1978

(in percentages)

Party	Men	Women	Total Sample
PCF			
December 1977	22	20	21
April 1978	24	19	21
PS and MRG			
December 1977	29	24	27
April 1978	25	25	25
UDF[a]			
December 1977	23	30	26
April 1978	19	22	21
RPR			
December 1977	22	20	21
April 1978	20	24	22

[a] For December 1977, the figures are the sums of the figures for the CDS and the DR, which merged (with others) to form the UDF a few weeks before the elections.

SOURCE: Adapted from SOFRES and Louis Harris Opinion Polls published in *Le Nouvel Observateur*, April 24, 1978, and *Le Matin*, December 5, 1977.

from women more than men. When it actually came to voting, women voted in 1978 more for the Socialist party and the RPR than for the UDF or the Communist party.

Were they attracted more than men by the minor parties, by the ecologists for instance or the women's movement, Choisir? Not significantly so. The proportion of women intending to vote for the four major parties varied little over the six months preceding the election, whereas the number of men switching to the minor parties reached 8 percent (see Table 6–5). In the end a slightly greater proportion of men than of women "wasted" their votes.

Male Dominance? Last but not least, women are said to model their attitudes—and their votes—on those of their male counterparts. Duverger claimed in 1955, "While women have, legally, ceased to be minors, they still have the mentality of minors in many fields, and particularly in politics they usually accept paternalism on the part of men. The man—husband, fiancé, lover, or myth—is the mediator

TABLE 6–5

PERCENTAGE OF MEN AND WOMEN VOTING FOR THE MAJOR PARTIES

Sex	December 1977	April 1978
Men	96	88
Women	89	90

SOURCE: Adapted from *Le Matin*, December 5, 1977.

between them and the political world."[7] Data showing that couples tend to vote the same way are immediately interpreted as evidence that women copy their menfolk. As Lazarsfeld put it when speaking of husbands and wives in *The People's Choice,* "The almost perfect agreement between husband and wife comes about as a result of male dominance in political situations."[8]

In January 1978 for the first time in France, IFOP studied the voting intentions of 456 couples.[9] Only one-third (31 percent) were in perfect agreement. For a couple to be classified as in perfect agreement they had to fulfill three conditions: first, husband and wife intended to vote for the same party; second, the husband stated correctly the party his wife intended to vote for; and third, the wife stated correctly the party her husband intended to vote for. Perfect agreement was twice as frequent on the left (20 percent) as on the right (10 percent). If we look simply at couples both of whom supported the same party, though each without knowing how the other intended to vote, the figure reaches 41 percent. There is greater agreement among couples voting for the left (27 percent) than among those voting for the Majority (13 percent). Identity of view is most frequent among Socialist voters (19 percent), followed by Communist voters (8 percent). The three Majority parties make up the remaining 13 percent, with 6 percent for the RPR, 5 percent for the PR, and 2 percent for the centrists. In 1 percent of the couples surveyed, both partners intended to vote for the Ecologists.

If we leave aside those couples in which neither partner was sure of his or her vote (13 percent of the sample) we find divergent opinions among 46 percent of the couples interviewed. In just under a third of these couples husband and wife voted for different parties

---

[7] Maurice Duverger, *The Political Role of Women* (Paris: UNESCO, 1955), p. 129.
[8] Paul Lazarsfeld, *The People's Choice* (New York: Columbia University Press, 1968), p. 141.
[9] IFOP survey, carried out for *Le Point*, January 11-18, 1978.

on the same side—in 6 percent of the cases both partners voted for opposition parties, in 7 percent for parties of the Majority. In just over a third of the diverging couples one partner was undecided, and women were twice as likely to be undecided (12 percent) as men (6 percent). In 8 percent of the couples who disagreed, one partner had decided to vote for the Ecologists. Here the sexes divided evenly, with 6 percent of the men and 6 percent of the women supporting this group.

How many couples diverged so strongly that one voted for the left, the other for the right? Only 9 percent, with men making up the left-wing element in just over half of the cases (5 percent). This may seem very little—but it must be remembered that in France the cleavages between the Communist party and the Socialist party and between the RPR and the PR are almost as deeply felt as the differences between right and left. So there are real divergences among almost a quarter of all the couples (13 percent voting for different parties on the same side, 9 percent voting for parties on opposite sides, of the left/right divide).

This shows clearly that women's political behavior does not simply reflect that of their husbands. Other indicators point in the same direction. For instance, only 58 percent of the husbands stated their wives' votes correctly, and only 61 percent of the wives knew how their husbands had voted. Here it is particularly interesting to note that the husbands' major errors concerned the PR: only 43 percent of those women whose husbands thought they had voted PR did in fact vote for the president's party. Prediction was most accurate for husbands who believed their wives had voted Communist, but even here 27 percent of them were wrong, as were a third of those who thought their wives had voted RPR (33 percent) or PS (31 percent). Not only do husbands not seem to command the voting preferences of their wives, in many cases they simply do not know how their wives are in fact behaving.

Husbands themselves do not seem to share the prejudices of political scientists. The number of husbands who answered "yes" to the question, "Do you have any influence on the way your partner votes?" was only 20 percent—admittedly higher than the 7 percent of women who believed they had influenced their husbands or the 16 percent of wives who thought that their husbands had in fact influenced their voting behavior. It should be noted, too, that 86 percent of the husbands and 88 percent of the wives declared that they did not wish to influence their partner's vote. A majority (51 percent of husbands, 52 percent of wives) did not even think it important for husbands and wives to have the same political opinions, and an overwhelming majority (96 percent husbands, 89 percent wives) declared that their political opinions had not changed when they had married. Thus, however we look at the problem, we are a far cry from the simplistic model in which the man is mediator between the woman and the political world, at least in the husband-wife relationship.

Women in Political Elites

Women in the Party Hierarchies. In no party do women constitute anywhere near the majority of active members. Even the Communist party only claims 200,000 women members out of a total membership of 611,000; still this is a considerable improvement on the 18 percent women PCF members in 1951. At best women represent a third of the grass-roots support for political parties. It is not therefore surprising that they play a small part within the party hierarchies. On the other hand, the various parties have very different attitudes towards women.

As Table 6–6 shows, some parties are willing to give women responsibilities at the national level but reluctant to admit them to the very highest posts. This is the case for the Communist party and for the Radicals. In neither was there a woman in the inner circle in 1977. The president's party, similarly, gives much greater representation to women on the executive committee, with its 307 members, than in the small leader's bureau where power really lies. The

TABLE 6–6
WOMEN IN LEADERSHIP POSITIONS WITHIN THE PARTIES, 1977

Party	Executive Committee		Office of the Executive Committee		Office of the Leader	
	No.	%	No.	%	No.	%
PCF	23	18.3	2	9.5	0	0
PS	18	13.7	4	14.8	3	17.6
MRG	11	9.2	2	4.5	0	0
PR	71	23.1	3	12.0	2	8.3
CDS	34	9.7	8	7.9	3	7.5
RPR	32	13.3	4	12.5	3	18.7

SOURCE: Adapted from Le Matin, December 12, 1977.

Socialist party and the RPR, inversely, increase the representation of women at the highest level; in the Socialist party they represent over 17 percent, in the RPR over 18 percent. Within the RPR it is well known that Marie France Garraud, for instance, often played a decisive role in decision making and was listened to attentively by Jacques Chirac over the 1974–1979 period.

Although party membership figures are not very reliable and breakdowns by sex are difficult to come by, it is obvious that at all levels (with the possible exception of the executive level in the PR) women are not represented on party committees in proportion to their strength within the movement.

Representation in the National Assembly: A Historical Outline. Two different electoral systems have been used for the National Assembly since women received the vote: between 1945 and 1956 a proportional representation, party-list system was used, with the department as the electoral district; then in 1958 the single-member majority system with two ballots was adopted. This latter system is still in effect. As Table 6–7 shows, the number of seats in the Assembly has constantly varied; for this reason the percentages of women deputies as well as the numbers have been given in the table.

Under the earlier system women candidates were seldom given safe positions and very rarely the privilege of leading lists, but they

TABLE 6–7

WOMEN IN THE NATIONAL ASSEMBLY, 1945–1978

Election	Number of Women	Total Number of Seats	Percentage of Women
Oct. 1945	32	586	5.5
June 1946	28	586	4.8
Nov. 1946	38	627	6.1
1951	22	625	3.5
1956	19	595	3.2
1958	8	552	1.4
1962	8	482	1.6
1967	10	487	2.0
1968	9	417	2.1
1973	8	490	1.6
1978	18	491	3.7

SOURCE: Compiled by the author.

TABLE 6–8

FEMALE PCF DEPUTIES, 1945–1978

	Female PCF Deputies	
	---	---
Election	Number	Percentage of all women deputies
First Period		
October 1945	17	53.1
June 1946	17	60.7
November 1946	26	68.4
1951	15	68.1
1956	15	78.9
Second Period		
1958	0	0.0
1962	3	37.5
1967	4	40.0
1968	2	22.2
1973	3	37.5
1978	12	66.6

NOTE: During the "first period" a proportional representation, party-list electoral system was used, during the "second period" a single-member-majority system.
SOURCE: Compiled by the author.

did manage to receive middling positions often enough to win a certain number of seats.

One of the effects of the change in the election law that went into effect in 1958 was to reduce drastically the number of women candidates nominated by the parties. The Communist party, for instance, presented only 27 women candidates in 1958, as against 107 in 1946; the MRP 11 as against 71; the UNR 5. Thus the first election of the Fifth Republic was much less favorable to women than the first Assembly election of the Fourth Republic.

If women voters tend to support the right, women deputies are paradoxically associated with the left—especially the Communist party (see Table 6–8). Like the UDF and the RPR, the PCF selects its candidates at the national level, and women are included as a matter of party policy.

Local Elections, 1977. The local elections of April 1977 constituted if not a breakthrough for women at least a step forward at the local level, since the number of women municipal councillors almost

TABLE 6–9

Women in Local Government, 1977

	Municipal Councillors		Mayors	
	Number	Percentage	Number	Percentage
Feb. 1977	20,684	4.4	671	1.8
April 1977	38,304	8.3	1,018	2.8

Source: Compiled by the author.

doubled (see Table 6–9). The percentage of women mayors also increased, from 1.8 percent to 2.8 percent, although 80 percent of the communes that elected women mayors had fewer than 5,000 inhabitants. Nevertheless, for the first time four towns of over 30,000 inhabitants—Athis-Mons, Noisy-le-Grand, Bagnolet, and Dreux—chose women mayors, the first three members of the Communist party and the fourth a Socialist.

Candidates and Deputies, 1978 General Election. In 1978 the only major party to nominate a sizable number of women candidates was the Communist party: 13.6 percent of its candidates were women. The Socialist party gave them only 5.4 percent of its nominations, despite the prominence of women in the Socialist movement, while for the Gaullist party the figure was a mere 2.7 percent (see Table 6–10). The results were consistent with the pattern of nominations. The Communist party gave seven safe seats to women candidates—seats held by Communists for the last ten, twenty, or thirty years and from which the sitting member was retiring. Six of them were elected, as were six women in more marginal seats. Women now make up 13.9 percent of the Communist parliamentary group. In no other group do they represent even 2 percent.

None of the parties, of course, was totally without women candidates—there is no men's party, as it were—though some, particularly among the minor parties, were more male-oriented than others. It would not be particularly revealing, however, to look at the proportion of women candidates among the handful of royalists, Christians for a New World, French of Good Sense, or supporters of the Movement of Taxpayers and Users of Public Services. The deposit, which a candidate forfeits if he does not obtain 5 percent of the votes, is low in France—1,000 francs—and does not act, as it is intended to, as a deterrent to those who want to air their views

TABLE 6-10

WOMEN DEPUTIES AND CANDIDATES FOR
NATIONAL ASSEMBLY, BY PARTY, 1978

Party	At Dissolution No.	At Dissolution %	Candidates No.	Candidates %	After 1978 Election No.	After 1978 Election %
PCF	3	4.1	64	13.6	12	13.9
PS	0	0.0	24	5.4	1	0.9
MRG	1	7.7	4	3.1	0	0.0
CDS	0	0.0	5	4.5 } UDF 2		1.5
PR	1	1.6	10	4.8 }		
RPR	2	1.1	11	2.7	3	1.9
Other	1	—	—	—	1	—
Total	8	1.6	108	2.5	19	3.7

SOURCE: Compiled by the author.

or seek a few days' limelight. On the other hand, the most active of the minor parties deserve to be mentioned because they had an impact greater than their electoral results might lead one to suppose. Table 6–11 includes all of the minor parties that ran at least twenty female candidates.

The party that espoused the women's cause most vigorously was the women's party, Choisir (Choose). All the candidates were women, and they did not do very well—a paltry 32,650 votes all told. Even in the districts where they did best (Bordeaux, the nineteenth arrondissement in Paris, St. Germain-en-Laye, and Versailles-South),

TABLE 6-11

MINOR PARTY WOMEN CANDIDATES, 1978

Party[a]	Women Candidates Number	Women Candidates Percentage
Choisir	43	100.0
Ecologistes	54	27.1
Front Autogestionnaire	53	24.2
Front National	23	14.4
Ligue Communiste	27	15.1
Lutte Ouvrière	191	40.6

[a] Includes any movement that ran twenty or more women candidates in 1978.
SOURCE: Compiled by the author.

Choisir candidates polled fewer than 2,000 votes. Even Gisèle Halimi, the party's leader, lost her deposit, although her 4.3 percent of the vote was easily the party's best showing. If we look briefly at the professional backgrounds of Choisir's candidates we find, as might have been expected, that they were not exactly representative of women in the population as a whole. Seven of them, 16 percent of the list, were "without a profession." Of the remaining thirty-six, almost two-thirds, twenty-three, were executives or professionals (including four doctors and three lawyers). The candidate with the humblest profession was the one sales-girl. There were no factory workers and no civil servants other than teachers or nurses.

Lutte Ouvrière, the Trotskyist movement led by Arlette Laguiller, the first woman to run for president of the republic (in 1974 she won 600,000 votes), fared little better than Choisir. Arlette Laguiller herself did manage to save her deposit, scoring just over 5 percent in her constituency in the Puy de Dôme. Broadly speaking the movement did best in rural areas, such as the Morbihan or the Vosges, and the sex of the candidate was not of major importance for the result. But in any case, none of the minor groups came anywhere near electing a candidate, man or woman.

Women's Role in Government. Government members in France are not required either by law or by tradition to be members of Parliament. Thus, Léon Blum was able to include three women in his Government in 1936, almost ten years before women obtained the right to vote. All junior ministers, they were Irène Joliot Curie, a scientist and Nobel prize winner, Suzanne Lacorre, and Cécile Brunschwig, holding office respectively at the Ministries of Scientific Research, Childhood, and Education. Throughout the Fourth Republic remarkably few women held any Government post. Germaine Poinso-Chapuis was minister of health in 1947, but no other woman was given the title of minister until well into the Fifth Republic, when Simone Veil became minister of health in 1974. She was joined in 1978 by Alice Saunier Séité, minister of the universities— which brought the total to three women ministers in over twenty years.

Throughout the Fourth Republic prime ministers did not even feel the need to have a token woman in some lower governmental post. In 1946 Georges Bidault took Andrée Vienot into his Government as undersecretary of state for youth and sports, and Léon Blum kept her on in his December Government. He did not, however, increase the number of women, and neither René Pleven, who succeeded Blum after the election of 1951, nor Guy Mollet after the election of 1956 gave any woman a post in his Government.

The early years of the Fifth Republic were very similar. Michel Debré gave a post to Néfissa Sid Cara from Algeria, but his successor, Georges Pompidou, had a womanless Government. In 1968 and 1969 Marie Madeleine Dienesch sat in the Governments of Maurice Couve de Murville and Jacques Chaban-Delmas, dealing first with social affairs, then with health. She continued under Pierre Messmer and was eventually joined by Suzanne Ploux who came to the Ministry of Education.

Since 1974 President Giscard d'Estaing has greatly encouraged the inclusion of women in the Government. The first Government during his presidency under Jacques Chirac included four women: Simone Veil, minister of health; Françoise Giroud, secretary of state for women's affairs; Hélène Dorlhac, secretary of state for prisons; and Anne Lesur, secretary of state for infant schooling. When Parliament was dissolved in 1978 there were six women and thirty-four men in the Government. Of the six women only one had been in office since the Chirac Government, Simone Veil, the popular minister of health and social security. Another woman had joined her in the highest spheres of government, Alice Saunier Séité, minister of the universities, and four women served as secretaries of state: Hélène Missoffe at the Ministry of Health and Social Security, and Christiane Scrivener, Monique Pelletier, and Nicole Pasquier, in charge of consumers, prisons, and women's employment respectively. Of the six women in the Government only two (33 percent) ran for Parliament in 1978, whereas thirty-one of the thirty-four men in the Government (91 percent) did so. It could be that this is a sign of a real difference in outlook between men and women who reach the highest levels of government—that the women are reluctant both to call into play their popularity and to see the opposition towards them crystallize. If it is, then what appeared to be a step forward may well have been a step back. The attitude of President Giscard d'Estaing would confirm this interpretation: it seems significant that he asked Simone Veil to wind up the UDF campaign on television despite the fact that she herself was not running, and that he reinstated Alice Saunier Séité as minister of the universities after she was defeated on the first ballot in Metz. Recent appointments, too, confirm a certain attitude toward the problems men are most willing to entrust to women. Over the last ten years the only two fields where women have reigned supreme are health and education, both of which are considered technical rather than political.

New Alternatives for Women

A Specific Appeal. The attitudes towards women adopted in the party manifestos are of special interest at a time when women's changing work patterns and their changing vision of their own status in society have made them more conscious of their political strength. All the major parties, in generous but singularly vague terms, insisted on an egalitarian approach—very much along the lines of the preamble to the Constitution of 1946, ratified again in 1958, which declares that in France "the law guarantees to women, in all fields, rights equal to those of men." The Common Program of the left quoted this passage and specified that equality would be ensured "at work, in society at large, and within the family," adding that "each man, each woman has the right to respect for his or her life, physical integrity, and personality." But the Blois Program issued by Raymond Barre and his Government was not to be outdone: the Government of the morrow, if the Majority were returned to power, would do away with all "the obstacles women encounter in their professional lives such as discrimination in the nature of the work offered, insufficient training, and ill-adapted conditions and hours of work." Thus for the woman at work the path would be singularly smoothed whoever won. And that was not all. Equality before the law would be brought to women. Legal texts, many going back to the frankly phallocratic Napoleonic code, would be rewritten. Only the RPR in its *Proposals for France* declared that "certain rights are little short of being fully recognized— the equality between men and women for instance."

On closer inspection, however, even the parties that readily admitted the existence of sex discrimination proved to make very few concrete promises. The few they made, moreover, were designed to extend to the weak sex the help and protection of their male counterparts. The left erased from the 1972 version of its Common Program the phrase the "responsibilities of women who are both workers and mothers," but it continued to promise retirement age at fifty-five for women and sixty for men (even though women live on average seven years longer than men) and longer vacations for the young and for women. The categories of women for whom the parties showed most concern were widows and the divorced—women deprived of male support.

The basic orientation toward male and female roles was as clear on the left as on the right. The Common Program stressed that group child care facilities had to be developed to free women of "an important part of their domestic duties," while the Blois Program promised the mother real social status and full recognition of her function "as educator of her children." The Republican party was even more explicit: "the mother in her home does the washing, the cleaning, and the cooking. But she is ignored in the records of public accounts." At no time in any manifesto was the notion that the husband and father might be equally responsible for daily tasks even implied.

Although the manifestos paid lip service to equality at work, the parties' attitude towards the work of women was ambivalent to say the least. The Blois Program promised that women would be "given the right to choose reduced hours of work" in order to assume the double role of worker and homemaker. As for the Republican party, it asked: "Where is freedom, where is happiness, if the mother is obliged to work out of financial necessity?" Do fathers, one wonders, work for the love of it?

The manifestos reflected a sort of double-think: In principle all the parties favored equality between the sexes. At the same time, they completely accepted, even sought to reinforce, the traditional role of the wife and mother, the housewife as a sort of welfare agent in in society. Women themselves were less gullible than the parties seemed to believe. When SOFRES in December 1977 asked: "Which of the following organizations in your opinion best defends the interests of women?" the left-wing parties were cited by 7 percent of the women respondents and the parties of the Majority by 4 percent, but both were far behind the recently created civil service department for women (32 percent) and the women's liberation movements (22 percent).

In what may well be looked back on as an era of increasing equality, the parties' insensitivity to sex discrimination is surprising. Perhaps the major explanation lies in the fact that the important cleavages on this issue are within the parties rather than between them. Nonetheless the parties have never paid as much attention to women in their election manifestos as they did in 1978. This sudden interest is obviously not linked to the right to vote, which women have had for the last thirty-four years, nor is it linked to the left-right balance of power. It is women themselves—though as yet a minority of them—who have begun to realize that the power of the ballot box can be used to change their status in society.

The Angry Young Women. So far two different types of activity have developed. On the one hand, groups on the women's liberation movement model have sought to express the aspirations of women as a distinct subsection of the community. The best example of this during the 1978 election was the creation of the women's party, Choisir. On the other hand women have increasingly sought a more equal distribution of power and responsibility between the sexes within the traditional parties.

Did the election help these groups improve their position? Choisir produced a platform, a collective effort coordinated by Gisèle Halimi, a barrister, Andrée Michel, a sociologist, and Geneviève Pastre, a poetess, in the form of a 358-page book published in March 1978. It was a sort of Common Program for women, setting forth long-term objectives. On each of the topics it addressed (in chapters headed "The Family: To What End?," "Working Women: Proles Twice Over," and so on), the manifesto outlined the existing situation, then illustrated it with statistics, opinion poll findings, and personal experiences, and finally proposed concrete measures to be taken. Choisir was far from an electoral success, but many of its proposals will no doubt be taken up by the traditional parties, which in itself is no small measure of achievement.

Within all the major parties the voices of women were heard more clearly than before, both during the campaign and after the election. A spokesman for the Elysée claimed that women's participation in politics was "one of the fields in which the president of the republic [was] in favor of progress,"[10] but the party itself lagged behind. The president might insist on women ministers, but his lieutenants did not choose women candidates.

For the women's subsection of the RPR Noëlle Dewavrin, assisted by Odile Proust and Régine Noulin, produced a brochure entitled "A Project for Women." It included a family charter, a charter for independent working women, and a proposal concerning the professional activities of the young. *La Lettre de la Nation*, the Gaullist daily newsletter, declared in an editorial in October 1977 that if there were so few candidates it was because Gaullist women were less disciplined activists than their Communist counterparts.[11] But despite Noëlle Dewavrin's insistence the women's group failed to convince Jacques Chirac of the importance of nominating women in greater numbers or in seats where they stood a real chance of winning. At the Gaullist Women's National Day in January when Christiane Papon complained of the derisory number of women candidates, Chirac explained that although women were as competent, intelligent, and devoted to the cause as men, "no risk could be taken" when the

[10] Pierre Hunt, Elysée spokesman, March 1, 1978.
[11] *La Lettre de la Nation*, October 21, 1977.

stakes were so high. It is not surprising, when the leader himself credits the myth that women candidates necessarily lose votes, that requests for "temporary quotas" or national minimums of women candidates are ineffectual.

Under direct pressure from women activists at the party conference, the Socialist party amended its constitution in June 1977. Article 6 was changed to institute a minimum female quota of 10 percent at all levels in the party from the Executive Committee to the grass roots, the quota to be revised at each party conference so as to take into account the proportion of women in the party. Article 46 also indicated that at all elections the 10 percent quota must be respected on every list. The problem is most acute at general elections, where competition is keenest. In 1978 no quota was enforced, but the party did decide to break its sacrosanct law that candidates always be selected locally; the party executive reserved the right to nominate directly a certain number of candidates. But when it is a question of sharing out important political posts, old reflexes come quickly into play.

The results of the election, as we have seen, were hardly likely to satisfy women Socialist activists. In the months following the election they indicated clearly that the present state of affairs could not be allowed to continue, and they moved to create a new faction within the party. The group is led by three women whose ages range from thirty-two to sixty-two: Françoise Gaspard, a member of the office of the party executive and mayoress of Dreux; Cécile Goldet, a gynecologist and member of the party executive; and Edith Lhuilier, a lecturer in political economy in Paris. To establish itself formally as a faction, the group must capture 5 percent of the votes at the party conference due to be held in 1979. If it does, it will become the third faction, the first being the Mitterrand faction and the second the left-wing CERES. Even then it will have a long way to go before it realizes its ambition of seeing women represented fairly among the Socialist candidates at a general election.

One of the Communist party's first publicity stunts after the 1978 election was to introduce its twelve women deputies to the press. As we have seen, the Communist party's performance in this area, although derisory, was brilliant compared with the other parties'. On April 27 Georges Marchais defined five major objectives for the party, one of which was "improving the condition of women and the young." Here was one party where relations between the sexes seemed harmonious. Then on June 9 in a forceful letter to *Le Monde* five grass-roots PCF activists—Michèle Guenon, Annie Mejean,

Juliette Nicolas, Peggy-Inès Sultan, and Nicole Edith Thevenin—claimed that the party executive was doing nothing to advance the women's struggle within the Communist movement.[12] In the *Nouvelles Littéraires* of the same week Christine Buci-Glucksmann, one of the leaders of discontent within the party, denounced the deep-rooted attitudes that, she said, resulted in repressive sexism and forced even the most militant women back into their homes. The party executive was not long in replying. Georges Marchais publicly attacked the women's groups on June 10, claiming that they would "make men in general bear the brunt of the legitimate struggle of women against inequality." Madeleine Vincent, an orthodox member of the Executive Bureau, declared: "Women's groups are not organized to promote unity. . . . Their only function is agitation directed against men in general, not against the government and big business. Their reasoning, disguised as revolutionary discourse, entirely by-passes the real questions of social class." [13]

The hatchet had been unearthed, and the party will not soon bury it. If the 1978 election changed little as far as the representation of women is concerned, it may well bring in its wake fundamental changes in the condition of women, for the parties will adopt reforms if only to divorce the moderate many from the militant few.

---

[12] *Le Monde,* June 10, 1978.
[13] *Le Monde,* June 11, 1978.

7

Patterns of Partisanship in Post-Gaullist France

Jeane J. Kirkpatrick

Changing Patterns

A decade after Charles de Gaulle retired for the last time to Colombey-les-deux-églises his Constitution remains the framework through which French politics is conducted, but the substance and the style of political competition are again in flux. In the 1978 elections both the participants and the patterns of interaction showed signs of significant change. Each of the four major parties that contested the 1978 elections claimed to be, in some sense, new. Although it was a direct descendant of the UDR, the Gaullist Rally for the Republic had assumed a new name and shape in December 1976. Its principal partner and rival in the Majority, the UDF, was the newest aggregate of all—having come into being just in time for the 1978 elections—although its component center and right groups had been around at least since World War II. The Socialist party too was both old and new. Though a legitimate offspring of the SFIO, the new Socialist party was born only in July 1969 when it was constituted out of the Federation of the Left (the FGDS, which itself had been formed from the union of the SFIO and selected leftist Radicals) and the political clubs gathered into the CIR (Convention des Institutions Républicaines). Only the French Communist party approached the election of March 1978 with its name and its organizational structure intact, yet some (though by no means all) observers believed that of all the major groups the PCF had undergone the most important transformation—from the most frankly Stalinist party in a non-Communist nation to one that embraced the Eurocommunist label and claimed to have cast off subservience to the Soviet Union, to have abandoned the dictatorship of the proletariat, and to have committed itself to respecting the institutions and requirements of representative democracy. Each of the major blocs that contested the 1978 elections had roots in both the Fourth and the Fifth Republics, but each could claim to have transformed itself—a fact that testified both to the impressive stability of France's political institutions and to their adaptive capacities.

These capacities for survival and adaptation could also be discerned in the shifting pattern of political competition. The 1978 legislative elections constituted another indication that the Gaullist phase of French political life is ending and that a new pattern of politics is taking shape. Political competition during the period of Gaullist ascendency featured bipolar contests between one coalition dominated by a Gaullist party and a second coalition into which were gathered all significant elements of the left, among which the Communist party was most powerful. This pattern has rested on an electoral system that encourages but does not require bipolar competition[1] and a Constitution that permits but does not ensure presidential dominance. It took shape in response to the towering political presence of Charles de Gaulle, who, especially after 1962, progressively polarized political groups and politicians into those who were for him and those who were not. Its minimal requisites would appear to have been second-ballot alliances oriented to the two poles of a hypothetical left-right spectrum rather than a fragmented pattern or a system of alliances that pits a center against the ends. Through 1973, Gaullists dominated one of the two coalitions and also the system as a whole, while the Communists were the strongest group in the coalition of the left. However, it is not clear whether the Gaullist pattern of bipolar competition requires that the two most "extreme" parties dominate their respective ends of the ideological spectrum and France's political agenda, functioning as magnets powerful enough to attract the other political groups away from the center. Whether bipolar competition can be maintained if the Socialists and the UDF become France's two leading political parties remains to be seen.

The fact that the pattern of interaction characteristic of the Gaullist period was maintained in the first elections following the

---

[1] The electoral system of the Fifth Republic goes further than any previous electoral system in encouraging bipolar competition. It not only organizes competition on the basis of single-member districts, but it discourages splinter parties and frivolous candidacies by its requirement that a party poll at least 12.5 percent of the first-ballot vote to be eligible for participation in the second ballot. The runoff provision in the presidential election (restricting to two the number of second-ballot candidates) obviously reinforces the system's bipolarizing tendencies and can be expected to do so as long as the president is powerful.

resignation of Charles de Gaulle in 1969 encouraged observers to believe that the existing version of two-bloc competition had become a permanent feature of French politics. This interpretation was reinforced by the tendency, ever present among political analysts, to overestimate the impact of formal and legal factors on entrenched habits of political behavior. But the presidential election of 1974, in which no Gaullist candidate survived the first ballot, led some to conclude that the Gaullist era was past.[2] The legislative elections of March 1978 provided fresh evidence of the demise of this phase of French politics; for although only two blocs contested the second ballot in March 1978 (as compared with three groups in the 1973 legislative elections), important and probably irreversible processes of decomposition afflicted each of the two coalitions. Three interrelated aspects of depolarization could be observed in the 1978 legislative elections: the breakdown of the Union of the Left, the reconstruction of the center, and the end of the Gaullist domination of the Majority. Subsequent events have clarified what the March elections established: that in France today there exist not two, but four political groups of nearly equal size, each of which has a distinctive orientation and clientele, and each of which has distinctive roots in the French political tradition.

In this chapter I propose to summarize some salient characteristics of the four groups whose leaders, composition, and goals shaped the events of 1978 and promise to influence the pattern of French politics in the decade to come. Throughout, I take special cognizance of those factors which seem most likely to destabilize the political patterns of the Fifth Republic.

The Unmaking of an Alliance

For many observers, the great surprise of the 1978 elections was, of course, that the left, which had been so widely expected to win, did not. The dissolution of the Union of the Left was one explanation, but that in turn must be explained by reference to the character of its component parts.

Understanding the relations between the Socialist and Communist parties in 1978 requires confronting the difficulties and ambiguities

---

[2] Nicholas Denis, "Du 5 mai 1946 au 19 mai 1974" [from May 5, 1946, to May 19, 1974], *Revue française de science politique*, vol. 24, no. 5 (October 1974), pp. 893-910. The theme of this article is the remarkable stability of French voting patterns in the post-World War II period. The author concludes that as of 1965, "la parenthèse de l'époque gaullienne semble donc bien s'être fermée" (p. 904).

present in the notion of a Union of the Left. Even in the land of their origin, the concepts "right" and "left" contribute more to the obfuscation than to the clarification of contemporary political conflict. The notion that the PS and the PCF belong to the same left end of a unidimensional political spectrum suggests that there is an essential affinity between them and invites one to underestimate the barriers to their collaboration. It is useful therefore to remind oneself, in considering the Union of the Left in the 1978 elections, that through most of their histories the French Socialist and Communist parties have been related to one another by open and often bitter disagreement and rivalry; and, further, to recall that instead of being unusual, such nonfraternal feelings are the norm for relations between Socialist and Communist parties elsewhere—in places whose political cultures and traditions are as disparate as those of Scandinavia, Spain, the United Kingdom, and the Federal German Republic. The reason, of course, is that the politics of the twentieth century have not been unidimensional and that, though parties of the hypothetical left share some (but by no means all) economic views, they have also disagreed about the desirable form of government, about the rights and duties of citizens, and about the relations between state and society.

From the time the French Communist party was founded out of a split in the old Socialist party (SFIO) at Tours in 1920, periods of alliance between the French Socialist and Communist parties have been relatively rare and brief; the first was the period of the Popular Front (1934–1936), the second that of *"tripartisme"* following World War II (1944–1947), and both experiences left the Socialists with a bitter aftertaste. Socialists feared and disliked the PCF for its subordination of national objectives to Soviet policy, for its autocratic structure and suppression of internal dissent, and for its lack of attachment to political democracy and republican institutions.[3]

The PCF reciprocated this low regard, rejecting the Socialists as reformers who had betrayed their commitment to revolution in favor of class collaboration and compromise with a corrupt, capitalist society, opportunists who zigged left during elections and zagged right to govern. Collaboration between these two adversaries came into being in the Fifth Republic only after de Gaulle had preempted

---

[3] See, for example, Daniel Ligou, *Histoire du socialisme en France, 1871-1961* [History of socialism in France, 1871-1961] (Paris: Presses Universitaires de France, 1962); Georges Lefranc, *Histoire du front populaire* [History of the Popular Front], 2d. ed. (Paris: Payot, 1974). Note that the Nazi-Soviet Pact of August 1939 was only the last of a number of acute strains on prewar collaboration that included the PCF's defense of the Soviet role in the Spanish Civil War and also of the Stalinist purge trials.

the national agenda, forcing others to respond to his plans, his initiatives, and his personality; after the early elections had demonstrated that electoral alliances were a precondition for political survival; and after a limited experiment with electoral collaboration in 1962 had proved successful.[4] The gains of both Communist and Socialist parties in 1967 in their first national effort at second-ballot collaboration suggested that a policy of alliances could stop the process of attrition that had afflicted the left throughout the Fifth Republic.[5] The eventual result was the pact of June 1972 in which the two parties agreed on a Common Program.

Born out of declining electoral fortunes, frustration, and ambition, nurtured on ambiguity, the Union of the Left which was so widely expected to win in 1978 was a precarious, incomplete alliance based on a limited number of shared perspectives reflected in the Common Program and a mutual desire to win elections.[6] The success of this promising if uneasy alliance required (1) that the Socialist leaders and a substantial portion of the Socialist rank and file be willing to collaborate with the PCF despite continuing ambivalence about its ultimate objectives, (2) that the Communist party at least appear to respect the rules, rights, and institutions of political democracy, (3) that both parties tolerate a platform that contained compromises and ambiguity, and (4) that the PCF be willing to let François Mitterrand and the Socialist party take the starring roles in all public performances of the Union of the Left.[7]

The evolution of relations between the Socialist and Communist parties in the period preceding the legislative elections of March 1978 illuminated certain characteristics of each. It clarified the extent to which the PCF remains, in some very fundamental ways, a party not like the others. And it confirmed that, its rhetoric and fantasies not withstanding, the French Socialist party remains, at its base and in its dominant leadership, what it always has been: a social demo-

---

[4] The limited collaboration of 1962 yielded the PCF thirty-one new deputies (raising their total from ten to forty-one) and the Socialists twenty-five new seats (up from forty to sixty-five).

[5] Note that the popular vote of both parties increased much less than their parliamentary representation and that, in terms of seats, the PCF again gained more than the PS.

[6] On the negotiation of the Common Program see Pierre Guidoin, *Histoire du nouveau parti socialiste* [History of the new Socialist party] (Téma-éditions, 1973); and Jean Poperen, *L'unité de la gauche, 1965-1973* [The unity of the left, 1965-1973] (Paris: Fayard, 1975).

[7] But note that the PCF did not actually agree to the proposition that the leader of the united left should be a Socialist until the death of Georges Pompidou made presidential elections imminent.

cratic party committed to social and economic reform within the context of political democracy.

The PCF. There has always been a degree of ambiguity about the goals of the French Communist party. Like other Communist parties it has invoked the symbols of "bourgeois" democracy and participated in its processes while calling for the system's replacement by something more "progressive"; it has sought political power in the electoral arena but also through other means; and it has affirmed democracy while functioning internally as an autocracy. This ambiguity was heightened when the PCF leadership embraced Eurocommunism, formally abandoning the dictatorship of the proletariat, declaring its independence from the Soviet Union, and promising to respect and preserve universal suffrage and political competition. Each of these steps seemed to reduce the distinctiveness of the Communist party. Yet the events of 1977–1978 clearly demonstrate that, though it has surely changed in some respects, the PCF is far from having become a conventional democratic political party.[8]

The lessons of 1978 may be summarized as follows: (1) *The Communist party still seeks a radical transformation of French society and politics.* In their polemics against the Socialists, the PCF leaders repeatedly affirmed the necessity of dismantling capitalist society in order to achieve democracy. In the debate on the extent of nationalization, they emphasized as a first priority the transformation of the structure and control of the economy. The Common Program signed in 1972 called for extending the public sector without dramatically affecting the autonomy of a sizable remaining private sector. However, the extensions demanded by the PCF in 1977 were designed not only to expand the public sector but also to reduce the private sector to a minimum through the progressive extension of state ownership; ultimately they looked to state control of the entire economy.

---

[8] A good discussion of these changes is: André Laurens and Thierry Pfister, *Les nouveaux communistes aux portes du pouvoir* [The new Communists at the gates of power] (Paris: Stock, 1973). Several accounts of the PCF's venture into Eurocommunism are available in English including: Annie Kriegal, *Eurocommunism: A New Kind of Communism?* (Stanford, Calif.: The Hoover Institute, 1978); Ronald Tiersky, "French Communism, Eurocommunism and Soviet Power," in Rudolf L. Tokes, ed., *Eurocommunism and Détente* (New York: New York University Press, 1978), pp. 138-203; Bernard E. Brown, "The Common Program in France," in Bernard E. Brown, ed., *Eurocommunism and Eurosocialism: The Left Confronts Modernity* (New York: Cyrco Press, 1979), pp. 14-66; Jean-François Revel, *The Totalitarian Temptation* (New York: Doubleday, 1977); Roy Godson and Stephen Haseler, *Eurocommunism: Implications for East and West* (New York: St. Martin's Press, 1978).

The party's commitment to transforming the economy and the society was also reflected in its plans for wages, taxes, indemnification, and the governance of industry. Its plan for running the nationalized industries (carefully keyed to the PCF's own skills and resources) proposed to vest control in directors selected through unions within each industry. It sounded enough like *autogestion* to win some support from the CFDT, but it would also enable the PCF, working through the CGT, to take control of the nationalized industries even though Socialists would control the Government. With control of work places, the party would be able to transform the society without "smashing the state." The bases of bourgeois democracy could thus be destroyed without violence.[9] If economic and social institutions could be penetrated and organized from the base up, then the institutions supporting pluralistic democracy and the existing political regime would be undermined, and the PCF could win and exercise effective leadership and hegemony over the society's evolution without resorting to such heavy-handed devices as the dictatorship of the proletariat or the outright suppression of opposition.

(2) The PCF had little interest in the victory of a left it did not control. The PCF's attack on the Socialists, launched in 1974,[10] intensified in the fall of 1977 and continued to the eve of the March elections. It made sense not as a tactic for winning an election, but as part of a more comprehensive contest for control of the left in French politics and for influence over the nation's political agenda. The success of the Union of the Left required that the Socialists *appear* to be the dominant partner and the Communists subordinate. But there is an important difference between the appearance and the fact of leadership. The conviction that their party was the most powerful political force on the left doubtless had made it easier for the PCF leaders to assume a subordinate position in public arenas, especially since they profited handsomely from the united left strategy. The PCF's claim to being the strongest party on the left rested on two decades of electoral performance, its formidable organizational skills, its control of France's largest labor confederation and of half

---

[9] This point was emphasized by Georges Marchais in his "secret speech" of June 1972 and in his speech to the twenty-second congress of the PCF. These speeches are discussed in Brown, *Eurocommunism and Eurosocialism*, pp. 43-45 and pp. 48-49.

[10] See Jean-François Bizot, *Au parti des socialistes* [On the Socialist party] (Paris: Grasset, 1975).

a hundred of France's largest cities.[11] As of June 1972 when the Common Program was signed, the PCF had outpolled the Socialists in every national election for two and a half decades, including in 1968 when Prime Minister Pompidou had managed to associate the Communist party with the disorders of May and when the Socialist resurgence had already begun. However, evidence of PCF stagnation and Socialist growth had been present even in 1967.

In no election of the Fifth Republic had the PCF done as well as it had in the Fourth Republic, while the Socialists had already surpassed their 1951, 1956, and 1958 levels. Furthermore, after 1967, polling data pointed to other problems for the PCF and suggested that the Socialists had greater growth potential. While public opinion grew more favorable to the Socialists, it remained skeptical of the PCF and that party's favorite programs. In 1972 only 12 percent of voters believed a united left could best assure economic growth and only 15 percent thought it most capable of assuring social progress while 20 percent and 24 percent respectively believed a coalition of the non-Communist left and center could deal successfully with these matters. Once the Common Program was signed, polls also revealed that the Common Program was more popular among Communists than any other group including Socialists: 75 percent of the Communist voters as compared with 42 percent of the Socialists said the Common Program's commitment to nationalizing certain industries would make them more certain to vote for the united left.[12]

The first important electoral challenge to PCF dominance of the united left came with the legislative elections of March 1973 in which the PS registered its first great leap forward (from 16.5 to 21.7 percent of first-ballot votes, thanks in large part to its absorption of most of the left Radicals), while the PCF failed to match the PS or its own 1967 showing. François Mitterrand's near miss in the 1974 presidential election illustrated a united left's potential for victory without further public embarrassment to the PCF. However, a series of by-elections in 1974 confirmed a continuing Communist decline and Socialist surge. It was then that the PCF began its attacks on the PS, which continue to the present.

---

[11] Jean Montaldo, *Les Communistes* [The Communists] (Paris: Albin Michel, 1979).

[12] See especially IFOP polls reported in Jean Charlot, ed., *Quand la Gauche Peut Gagner: les élections législatives des 4-11 mars 1973* [When the left might have won, the legislative elections of March 4-11, 1973] (Paris: Editions Alain Moreau, 1973), Table 1.05, p. 25; Table 1.17, p. 33; and Table 1.18, p. 34. See also Jérôme Jaffré, Chapter 2, in this volume.

Despite these attacks on the Socialists and despite the PCF's efforts to shake its Stalinist legacy and image, public opinion polls continued to reflect Socialist growth unmatched by corresponding Communist gains. In the period from December 1972 to August 1977 the percentage of adults expressing the intention to vote for the Socialist party and its Radical allies rose from 22 percent to 28 percent, while the PCF support level declined from 21 percent to 19 percent.[13] The PCF's inability to expand its electoral support, already present in the Fourth Republic, continued despite the leftward trend of French public opinion and despite the PCF's embrace of Eurocommunism.[14] As Ronald Tiersky noted, "Neither détente, nor the Socialist Party decline in the 1960s, nor the PCF's doctrinal innovations, nor autonomy from the Soviet party, nor even severe unemployment and general economic recession had increased the Communist electorate."[15]

Votes are, of course, only one indicator of one type of political power. The Communist party's financial resources[16] and legendary organizational skills are still unmatched on the French political scene. Because of its capacity to translate electoral penetration into enduring political strength—a skill repeatedly demonstrated in the CGT and in Communist controlled municipalities—each electoral victory offered the PCF an opportunity to organize an area.[17] Through skillful use of the organizational weapon the PCF could hope to extend its social control even if the Government were headed by Socialists. Its 1977 demands to expand the nationalized sector beyond that originally provided in the Common Program and its demands concerning the governance of these nationalized industries were alike designed to open new opportunities for PCF organization.

---

[13] The figures for 1972 were published in *France Soir* and are reproduced in Charlot, *Quand la Gauche*, p. 43. Those for 1977 were first published in *Le Point* and are reproduced in *Sondages*, no. 1 (1978), p. 8.

[14] Only one development brightened the Communists' electoral prospects. This was the party's success in the municipal elections of March 1977—a success mostly due to the use of a single, combined list of PCF-PS candidates.

[15] Tiersky, in Tokes, *Eurocommunism and Détente*, p. 180.

[16] See Jean Montaldo's new book, *La France Communiste* [Communist France] (Paris: Albin Michel, 1978), an excerpt of which is reprinted in *L'Express*, January 16-22, 1978, pp. 60-66.

[17] The municipal elections of 1977 (in which the PCF demanded and won the Socialist leadership's agreement to run a single unified slate) resulted in broad PCF gains (504 more PCF mayors), giving the PCF a large new terrain to organize and leaving it with mayors in 7 cities of over 100,000 inhabitants (as compared with 4 before the elections), mayors in 72 cities of 30,000 to 100,000, and a share of the power in many other cities large and small. The PCF's role in the municipal governments of France is the subject of Montaldo's new book, *La France Communiste*.

As the Lavaus point out in Chapter 4, no one knows for certain why the PCF suddenly escalated the price of its collaboration, or why Marchais sought to embarrass Mitterrand and the alliance with the PCF's inflated estimates of the Common Program's cost, or why Marchais withheld assent to a policy of second-ballot *désistement* until the chance for victory had virtually eluded the parties of the left, or whether he expected and desired a rupture, or whether he thought the Socialist leadership would capitulate.[18] But whatever the motives, unremitting criticism and demands made clear that the PCF was willing to assist the Socialist leaders in taking power only if it could commit a Government of the left to a scheme that would ensure PCF control of a greatly enlarged public sector. In exchange for helping the PS take control of the Government, the PCF demanded the economy. By pressing their demands to the point of rupturing the Union of the Left, the PCF leaders indicated (as they had before) that winning elections was not their highest priority. In refusing the proferred bargain, François Mitterrand and other Socialist leaders proved that winning an election and organizing the Government was not their highest value either.[19]

Whatever the PCF leaders expected when they clung to their escalated demands in the spring of 1978, what they got was their now conventional 20 percent of the vote—and credit for having spoiled the chances of the left. In the electoral arena the party's standing continued to stagnate. One commentator noted:

> The French Communist Party was France's first party during the time of Maurice Thorez. During Waldeck Rochet's time as leader it was France's second party and the first party of the left. Under George Marchais it has become the second party of the left and third party of France.[20]

(3) The PCF demonstrated in the period before the 1978 elections that it is still capable of sharp and unexpected shifts in policy. Almost no one expected that in the period before the legislative elections the PCF would make important new demands and press these to the point

---

[18] Annie Kriegel tells us that the Communists calculated that the Socialists would probably give in but not go as far as breaking the alliance. Annie Kriegel, *Eurocommunism,* p. 118.

[19] Montaldo argues that the PCF strategy is not founded on *putschisme* of the sort practiced by Cunhal and the Portuguese Communist party or on the prospect of electoral victory, but resembles that described by Togliatti for the Italian Communist party: "To penetrate as deeply as possible the foundations of civil society." According to Montaldo, this "amounts to conquering the state in successive stages." *L'Express,* January 16-22, 1978, p. 62.

[20] Jean-François Revel, *L'Express,* March 13-19, 1978, p. 43; author's translation.

of rupture. Virtually no one expected that Marchais would withhold until the very last minute his assent to an agreement on second-ballot withdrawal in favor of whichever candidate of the left ran first. This type of second-ballot cooperation, practiced in 1967 and 1973 and in various local elections, had enabled both parties to increase their numbers in the National Assembly. By making unanticipated demands and attacks and by waiting till election eve before agreeing to second-ballot cooperation, the PCF leaders demonstrated the unique tactical flexibility of a hierarchical, centralized party. They demonstrated, too, that no evolution which had occurred in the name of Eurocommunism had inhibited the leadership's power for swift, decisive action or diminished its control of a disciplined party.

(4) *Despite its Eurocommunist posture, the PCF remained unacceptable to a substantial number of voters who were willing to support other candidates of the left.* In 1978 as in the past, when the second-ballot candidate was a Socialist or Leftist Radical, he received a vote equal to the combined first-ballot total of the Communists, the Socialists, and the MRG. But where the candidate of the left was a Communist, he lost approximately 10 percent of those who had voted for other left candidates on the first ballot. Nicholas Denis summed up this pattern: "In 146 districts where the left was represented on the second ballot by a Communist, the left polled 249,351 votes less on March 19 than March 13; but in the 264 districts where the left was represented by a Socialist, MRG or other left candidate, it gained 243,962 votes."[21]

This pattern, which has reappeared in each legislative election in which the parties of the left have collaborated on the second ballot, testifies to the distrust and fear that the PCF continues to inspire not only among voters of the right and center, but also among an electorally significant part of the non-Communist left. The table presented by Jérôme Jaffré in Chapter 2 reflects the steady decline of popular regard for the PCF in the year preceding the election. Another national opinion study, conducted between the first and second ballots, confirmed that 43 percent of the French electorate would have liked a Government of the left without Communist participation, 57 percent believed that Government by a "united left" (PCF-PS-MRG) would not prove able to govern, and 44 percent believed the PCF might

---

[21] Nicholas Denis, "Les élections législatives de mars 1978 en métropole" [The legislative elections of March 1978 in metropolitan France], *Revue française de science politique* (December 1978), pp. 977-1005, p. 1001. Jérôme Jaffré discusses this pattern in Chapter 2, pp. 73-75, in this volume.

attempt to come to power illegally.[22] This continued distrust, which constitutes an invisible barrier to a victory of the left, was not assuaged by Marchais's intransigent conduct before the election.[23]

(5) *The electoral stagnation of the PCF does not reflect an inability to attract new supporters.* The "ecological fallacy" warns against drawing inferences about individual behavior from findings concerning aggregates.[24] From the fact that the PCF is regularly supported by about 20 percent of French voters it is tempting—but mistaken—to assume that the same 20 percent turn out again and again to vote for the PCF. As Jaffré emphasized in Chapter 2, there are strong fluctuations among the Communist party's supporters.[25] In 1978 the PCF was especially successful in attracting young voters. Depending on the poll consulted, the PCF attracted between one-quarter and one-fifth of the votes of people eighteen to twenty-four, and voters under thirty-five comprised two-fifths of its entire electorate. In 1978 the PCF's appeal was strongest among young workers, who were substantially more likely to support it than the Socialist party.

The strong relationship between age and voting Communist persists in all socioeconomic groups. If the PCF is able to retain the loyalties of younger persons as they grow older and to continue to attract new voters at roughly the present level, then its electoral future should be much rosier than its recent past. However, the fact that the party continues to draw most heavily from a shrinking sector of the population—blue-collar workers—bodes less well. The Socialists attracted approximately 27.4 percent of blue-collar workers, to the PCF's 31.6 percent; however, the PS was much more appealing than the PCF to white-collar workers and professionals, both of which categories are increasing more rapidly than the blue-collar workers.

The Socialists. Of the new Socialist party which forged the Union of the Left, negotiated and signed a Common Program with the PCF, and collaborated with it in the legislative and municipal elections, Raymond Aron wrote: "The Socialist party exists in its present form

---

[22] Louis Harris Institute, reported in *L'Express*, March 20-26, 1978, pp. 46-47.

[23] The fact that 41 percent of the voters considered Marchais principally responsible for the defeat of the left is another indicator of his lack of credibility. Ibid.

[24] See W. Phillips Shavely, "Ecological Inference: The Use of Aggregate Data to Study Individuals," *American Political Science Review*, December 1969.

[25] See Jaffré, Chapter 2, pp. 59-60, in this volume.

only by and for cooperation with the Communist party."[26] Repudiating the centrist and anti-Communist policies of the SFIO, the new Socialist party took a sharp leftward turn, describing itself as Socialist rather than social democratic. The significance of these policies for the elections of 1978 and later may be less clear than it seems at first.

(1) *Founding the new Socialist party.* Three aspects of the transition from the SFIO to the PS deserve special note. First, there is the fact that the Socialist reformation occurred at a moment when the dynamics of Gaullist politics had greatly weakened the center. With a significant portion of the center absorbed by the Majority, the Communists constituted the only large bloc of voters with whom the Socialists might make an alliance that would have some hope of winning elections.

Second, the founding of the new Socialist party coincided not only with the adoption of a policy of alliance with the PCF but also with the accession to the leadership of François Mitterrand, a man with long experience in centrist politics and Governments, no genuine Marxist leanings, a deep-seated distrust of the Communist party, a commitment to "bourgeois liberties,"[27] and a powerful desire to be president of France.

Third, the Socialist reformation occurred after the onset of a long-term leftward trend in French politics which had been only briefly interrupted by the backlash after the events of May 1968. Soon after its birth the new Socialist party was attracting new supporters, new adherents, and new militants. Many of the militants who entered the new Socialist party after 1968 viewed the Communist party as less menacing and a Union of the Left as less problematic than had the cadres of the SFIO.[28]

(2) *Socialist perspectives.* The "new" Socialist party of 1978 was much less ideologically homogeneous than the SFIO had been. Not only were more points of view present among its militants and leaders but the ideological distance separating these points of view

---

[26] *L'Express*, January 16-22, 1978, p. 33.

[27] See François Mitterrand's own books, especially *La rose au poing* [The rose in the fist] (Paris: Flammarion, 1973) and *Ma part de vérité* [My truth] (Paris: Fayard, 1969).

[28] Roland Cayrol, "L'univers politique des militants socialistes: une enquête sur les orientations, courants et tendances du parti socialiste" [The political world of the Socialist militant: an inquiry into outlooks, factors, and tendencies in the Socialist party], *Revue française de science politique*, vol. 25, no. 1 (February 1975), pp. 23-52. This reports and analyzes a survey conducted at a party congress in June 1973. The militants' attitudes supported the policy of alliance with the Communists.

was greater. By 1977 the new Socialist elite had grouped itself into several factions in which personal rivalries reinforced programmatic and ideological differences. The most important of these were CERES (Centre d'études, de recherches, et d'éducation socialistes), which was and is the most resolutely leftist faction, supporting extended nationalization, a leftist strategy, and *autogestion* [29] and opposing continued French membership in the EEC and the Atlantic Alliance; a second faction, grouped around Michel Rocard, which expressed a more libertarian conception of *autogestion*, rejected large-scale centralized bureaucratic organization of social and economic life in favor of a more egalitarian, more libertarian, more participatory society and contained persons with strong Christian identifications; and third, the leadership faction headed by François Mitterrand, which was and is the least clearly defined and the most influential. In addition, there were still people in the Socialist party who clung to the attitudes of the SFIO—including its distaste for Communists and its commitment to Europe and the Atlantic Alliance. The new Socialist party had its center of gravity definitely to the left of the SFIO's and was definitively committed to a policy of alliance with the PCF. But the events of 1977 and 1978 made it clearer than ever that the Common Program and the Union of the Left depended on the PCF as well as the PS.

As it approached the election, then, the Socialist party featured cadres who, though divided among themselves, nonetheless held views that differed from those of many of the Socialists' rank and file supporters. These differences between elite and rank and file were especially marked with regard to the Communist party, the Union of the Left, and the Common Program. The existence of leadership factions with divergent views on many policies and of followers who were suspicious of the Communists and unenthusiastic about nationalization was a powerful constraint on the Socialist leaders, limiting their room for maneuver in the long negotiations with the PCF.

Successive public opinion surveys carried out between 1973, "when the left might have won," [30] and 1978 revealed that the growing popularity of the Socialist party derived less from a new wave of

[29] Jean-Pierre Cot, struggling with how best to convey the full meaning of *autogestion* in English, asserted, "Basically, autogestion is a revolt against the abuses of hierarchy, an aspiration to power at the lowest possible level: the plant, the street, the consumer's association, the university, or the classroom." He proposes "workers' control" as probably the closest equivalent, but notes that it is misleading in being implicitly limited to the factory. Jean-Pierre Cot, "Autogestion and Modernity in France," in Brown, ed., *Eurocommunism and Eurosocialism*, p. 70.

[30] The title of a well-known study of that election, Charlot, *Quand la Gauche.*

conversions to socialism than from the voters' growing dissatisfaction with the Majority. The polls also confirmed continuing distrust of the Communist party and the decline of radicalism.[31] Although a good many observers attributed the Socialists' new popularity to the leftward turn the party had taken under François Mitterrand's leadership, public opinion data indicate, rather, that the PS had become the catchall party of the period and was attracting a diverse new following that included a large part of the floating vote, known as the *marais* in France, that large group of independent voters, devoid of partisan and ideological commitments, who float from one party or surge movement to the next.[32]

(3) *Social composition.* The popular following of the new Socialist party was both socially and ideologically heterogeneous. Its most notable characteristics in 1978 were, first, its broad socioeconomic continuity since the mid-fifties. In 1978, as in 1956, the Socialist party drew supporters from all major sectors in the population, but blue-collar workers comprised the largest single portion of its voters, with white-collar employees the second most numerous group.[33]

A second impressive characteristic was the extent to which the PS had come to resemble in its structure the whole of French society, and the extent to which its evolution had paralleled that of the French population: the proportion of youth had increased with the increasing numbers of young voters in the population and in the electorate; the proportion of blue-collar voters had declined alongside the decline in the total population, and so forth. The Socialist rank and file was less male in 1978 than in 1956, more Catholic,[34] and more evenly distributed geographically.[35]

---

[31] Socialist growth is supported not only by public opinion polls but also by the results of cantonal elections. See, inter alia, Jérôme Jaffré and Jean-Luc Parodi, "La poussée et le reflux de la gauche (1973-1978) [The gains and losses of the left, 1973-1978], *Revue française de science politique*, vol. 28, no. 6 (December 1978), p. 1006-1017.

[32] In his study of the 1973 elections, Jean Charlot noted that the Socialist party grew most in districts controlled by the Majority. Charlot, *Quand la Gauche*, p. 104.

[33] In 1978 somewhat more blue-collar workers supported the Communists than the Socialist party (31.6 percent for the PCF, 27.4 percent for the PS), but support for the Socialists was much stronger among white-collar employees (16.1 percent supporting the PCF, 29.8 percent the PS). *Sondages*, no. 1, 1978, p. 22.

[34] A study of delegates to the 1973 PS congress reported that 37 percent of the delegates described themselves as Catholic. Roland Cayrol, "Les militants du parti socialiste: Contribution à une sociologie" [Towards a sociology of Socialist militants], *Projet*, vol. 88 (September-October 1974), pp. 929-940.

[35] Underlying this overall geographical change were both losses in some former strongholds and gains in areas where the PS had been weak. (See Jaffré, Chapter 2, pp. 59-60, in this volume.)

Of all the major political blocs contesting the 1978 elections the Socialists most closely mirrored the composition of the whole population. The deviations give the PS its distinctive flavor: The slight underrepresentation of management and professionals and the slight overrepresentation of blue- and white-collar workers provide the demographic foundations of the Socialists' collectivist, egalitarian socioeconomic policies. Most numerous were voters under thirty-five (among whom the PS was the strongest party), white-collar employees (especially teachers and civil servants), and blue-collar workers (among whom the PS attracted very nearly as much support as did the PCF). The diversity of the party's appeal is most clearly reflected, however, in the fact that during the period preceding the 1978 elections the Socialist party attracted nearly one-fourth of the people in every major social category: agricultural, commercial, professional, and retired as well as blue- and white-collar.[36] No other political group attracted so much support from such diverse groups. The Socialist party of 1978 had won support in the strongholds of all the other parties, attracting rural and commercial support that might have gone Gaullist or Giscardian, and working-class support that had once gone in larger proportions to the Communist party; and at the same time it had retained its uniquely strong position among white-collar workers.

The Socialist electorate's diverse socioeconomic structure was paralleled by a comparable ideological diversity. Over one-third of its supporters had doubts concerning the Union of the Left, distrusted the Communist party, and doubted the viability of any alliance with the Communists.[37] The Common Program, especially its provisions for nationalization, aroused no greater confidence.[38] The social and ideological heterogeneity of the Socialist party was the source of both its strength and its weakness, making it an effec-

---

[36] *L'Express* combined the findings of three polls, each of which was based on a sample of 1,000, to provide a larger base for studying the composition of the various support groups. That analysis yields the following findings concerning the appeal of the Socialist party and the MRG: agricultural sector, including farm workers, 23 percent; small shopkeepers and artisans, 24 percent; liberal professions and managers, 24 percent; employees and middle-level managers, 31 percent; blue-collar workers, 32 percent; retired and unemployed, 24 percent. *L'Express*, March 13-19, 1978, p. 49.

[37] The poll done by *L'Express* between the two ballots revealed that 39 percent of those who supported the Socialists favored their abandoning the Union of the Left in favor of rapprochement with the center. *L'Express*, March 20-26, 1978, p. 47.

[38] One widely circulated, hostile treatment is Frederic Deloffre, *Guide pratique du Programme commun* [Practical guide to the Common Program] (Paris: Pauvert, 1977).

TABLE 7-1

SOCIAL CHARACTERISTICS OF THE PCF AND PS ELECTORATES,
1956 AND 1978
(in percentages)

Category	PCF		PS		Whole Population, 1978
	1956	1978	1956	1978	1978
Liberal professions, management, owners of businesses	10[a]	7	10[a]	13	16
White-collar workers	17	18	23	24	21
Blue-collar workers	49	52	39	31	30
Farmers and farm workers	5	2	8	8	8
Retired	19	20	20	24	25

NOTE: There are certain differences in the manner of reporting between these two years. The most important of these is the inclusion of the MRG in the 1978 data for the Socialist party. Had the Radicals been included in the 1956 data for the Socialists, the percentages of professionals, farmers, and self-employed persons would have been higher.

[a] For 1956 this category includes the self-employed, who comprised 7 percent of both the PCF and the PS electorates.

SOURCE: Sondages, no. 4 (1960), p. 18 and no. 1 (1978).

tive magnet for discontented voters who wanted change and setting limits on its adoption of a truly "socialist" program that would transform the economic and social structure of France.

(4) Internal contradictions. Those who perceive ideas and programs as a manifestation of underlying social forces see the Socialist party's broad base as "explaining" its ideological heterogeneity. They give special emphasis to the PS's white-collar following as the basis of its attachment to bourgeois society, its hesitation concerning widespread nationalization, and other manifestations of "class collaboration." Whether the class composition of a political movement "causes" its ideological orientation or vice versa, it remains the case that the Socialist party drew (and draws) significant support from all sectors of society and that it is especially attractive to the salaried middle class, from which about one-fourth of its rank and file and most of its leadership are drawn.[39] The stable composition of

---

[39] A recent study noted that teachers comprised 13 percent of the members of the PS, 25 percent of its militants, 45 percent of its board of directors, and 40 percent of its deputies. Patrick Hardouin, "Les Caractéristiques Sociologiques du Parti Socialiste" [The sociological characteristics of the Socialist party], Revue française de science politique, vol. 28, no. 2 (April 1978), pp. 220-256.

the Socialist party's support group, its continuing strength among teachers, professors, civil servants, and blue-collar workers, testifies to the presence in French society of support for a non-Communist left, more egalitarian than the center but no less devoted to "bourgeois" democracy and its associated personal liberties. This conjunction of attitudes—with or without an admixture of Marxist doctrine—has defined the social democratic orientation in contemporary politics[40] and creates an enduring tension between the "reformist" and "revolutionary" tendencies of democratic socialism.

The problem of finding the right orientation between these ideological poles is dealt with again and again but never finally resolved. During the Fourth Republic, as during the Third, the SFIO followed a policy of alliance with the center (except for the brief periods of the Popular Front and *tripartisme*). But the evolution of the debate between the parties of the left in 1977 and 1978 made it less clear than ever what kind of ideological space existed between social democracy and the PCF. Ironically, every new attack by the PCF left the identity of the dominant leadership of the Socialist party a bit more clearly defined. The PCF's demand for a progressive extension of nationalization confirmed the dominant Socialist leadership's commitment to a mixed economy in which substantial public and private sectors would coexist and compete. The PCF's demands concerning the governance of the newly nationalized industries clarified and confirmed their suspicion of their ally. The PCF's military policy, which called for a neutralist defense strategy oriented to all fronts (*tous azimuts*), clarified the Socialist leadership's preference for the Atlantic Alliance, and the PCF's European policy contrasted with the Socialists' sentiment in favor of the EEC and Europe. Meanwhile the PCF's refusal to agree in advance of the first ballot to a policy of mutual withdrawals on the second ballot and Mitterrand's assurances that the Socialists remained committed to electoral cooperation clarified the extent to which it was the PCF that had shattered the Union of the Left and the PS that had eagerly attempted to maintain it.[41]

---

[40] This orientation was described with special clarity by François Mitterrand in his book *Ma part de vérité*.

[41] A Louis Harris study at the time of the rupture showed that 28 percent of the voters blamed Marchais for the rupture of the left's negotiations and alliance, as compared with 8 percent who blamed Fabre and 11 percent who held Mitterrand responsible. However, only 5 percent of Communist voters blamed Marchais, as compared with 37 percent of Socialist voters. On the other hand, 8 percent of Socialist voters and 33 percent of Communist voters thought Mitterrand was responsible for the rupture. *L'Express*, October 3-9, 1977, pp. 40-42.

Nonetheless, although François Mitterrand would eventually blame Marchais and the PCF for the left's defeat, he never wavered in his offer of second-ballot collaboration or, even after the election, in his view that a united left should be the cornerstone of Socialist policy. Should the centrifugal force of the Gaullist years be replaced by centripetal pulls, the PS would face severe internal debate and probable schisms over any effort to reorient the party's alliances toward the center, for centrism remains as unacceptable to important segments of the Socialist party as a Union of the Left was to most of the leaders of the SFIO through most of its history. Alone, the Socialist party can never hope to become what François Mitterrand insists it is: a party of Government and not of permanent opposition. The events of 1978 demonstrated that in an alliance with the Communist party, the Socialist party is utterly vulnerable to shifts in Communist policy. But the ideological predisposition of some of the Socialist leadership suggests that the party could not move to a centrist strategy without suffering serious defections.

The Majority

Right and Left Again. The notion of a left-right spectrum, which is of limited use in clarifying relations between the Communist and Socialist parties, is an even less useful conceptual tool for uncovering the character and relations of the groups on the so-called right. It is generally understood by students of French politics that in France the symbols of the left enjoy much greater prestige than those of the right. This mystique (explored several decades ago by Raymond Aron in *Opium of the Intellectuals*)[42] has long since created a situation in which parties vie for symbolic identification with the left. No significant political group in France describes itself as right, a term with many negative connotations. Parties are only termed right by others, by their opponents and by political observers with a habit of arranging political forces on a left-right spectrum. No alliance would term itself "a union of the right" or propose a common program of the right. The parties that others call right or place on the right side of the hypothetical political spectrum call themselves "national" or "center" parties and adopt names such as Popular Republicans (PR) or Rally for the Republic (RPR) or Independents (CNI) or Independent Republicans (RI) or the Popular Republican Movement (MRP) or Center Democrats; they give their alliances

---

[42] Raymond Aron, *Opium of the Intellectuals* (New York: Norton, 1962).

names such as Union for French Democracy (UDF) or Union for a Democratic Republic (UDR) or Union for the Fifth Republic. There is more involved here than subterfuge. At stake is a way of conceptualizing politics which rejects any identification with the historic French right. That historic right was antirepublican, antidemocratic, and antimodern. There are no legitimate offspring of that right in the mainstream of contemporary French politics. The Gaullist party (RPR) and the Giscardian party (UDF) are thoroughly committed to republican institutions, popular sovereignty, individual liberty, and modernization.

Similarities within the Majority. The Independents, Republicans, Radicals, Reformists, and Gaullists who comprise the Majority that sustains the presidency of Valéry Giscard d'Estaing and the cabinet of Raymond Barre are divided by neither socioeconomic composition nor religion nor commitment to republican institutions. All seek economic growth, modernization, and a rising standard of living and rely largely on technology, education, and planning, a large private sector, and a mixed economy to achieve these goals. The various groups and tendencies present in the Gaullist and UDF blocs share an attachment to French society as it exists and a desire to preserve its characteristic institutions—representative democracy, the limited state, a mixed economy, a skill-based allocation of roles—in roughly their present form and to honor the associated values, including individualism, liberty, private property, and popular sovereignty. While Gaullists and Giscardians are too thoroughly modern in spirit to oppose change, neither desires to transform or fundamentally alter French society in the fashion discussed by the contemporary Socialist party and its sometime ally, the PCF.

This desire to preserve French society and culture serves as the basis for common political action between the Gaullists and the Giscardians. Although these groups differ in their priorities and emphasis, they do not find it too difficult to unite to combat a major challenge from groups who seek political power in order to transform the society. Because they have collaborated repeatedly during the Fifth Republic and because their supporters have similar socioeconomic characteristics, some observers suggest that there are four major political blocs in contemporary French politics but only three electorates: the Communist, the Socialist, and the center-right.

It is true that the UDF and the RPR are similar in social composition. Both draw more heavily than the Socialists or Communists from among professionals, owners of businesses, farmers, Christians, and the retired. Both are relatively unattractive to workers, especially blue-collar industrial workers. Neither is as attractive to persons under fifty as to those over it. Each, however, has a historic geographical base. The Gaullists are especially strong in Paris, the North, the West, and the Southwest, and the UDF substantially stronger than the RPR in the Mediterranean region, the Southeast, the East, and some areas around Paris. It is ideology and tradition that mainly distinguish these groups from one another. Furthermore, the tradition in which each is rooted is strong and may be expected to persist.

Differences within the Majority. In fact, the differences between the Gaullist and Giscardian blocs are not trivial, nor are they limited to the personal rivalries of their leaders, though the bad personal relations between President Giscard d'Estaing and his erstwhile colleague and supporter, Gaullist leader Jacques Chirac, exacerbate ideological and programmatic disagreements. To the contrary, persistent differences between Gaullist and "center" perspectives is one major source of the transformation of the pattern of political competition that is under way. These ideological differences are both real and limited. For one group, the RPR, General de Gaulle is the transcendental point of reference, with his vision of a France that is proud, powerful, and above all "independent" in the world, and his Constitution, which blends traditional antinomies to include authority and democracy, the nation and the individual. For the parties and leaders of what was traditionally called the center and center-right, Charles de Gaulle had less magic, his Constitution had less appeal, and his vision of France in the world seemed (and still seems) unrealistic and unattractive.

The Gaullist vision. At the core of the Gaullist vision of France is nationalism—not the megalomanic nationalism of a Hitler that expresses itself in racism and war, but a conception of history that sees peoples rather than classes as creative historical actors, a conception that celebrates the national character and emphasizes the distinctive identity and destiny of France, a conception expressed in Charles de Gaulle's conviction that France can only be herself when she is great. The essence of Gaullism, Edmond Michelet insists, is just this: a conception of French identity and grandeur that is in the first place spiritual, but which will eventually be realized and concretized in the world.[43] Gaullism is, I believe, the purest expression of nation-

---

[43] Edmond Michelet, *Le Gaullisme: passionante aventure* [The adventure of Gaullism] (Paris: Fayard, 1962), p. 141.

alism in the contemporary Western world. Its founder said, "That enterprise which after 1940 was called Gaullism [is] nothing other than the contemporary form of the spirit of France, once more aroused, moving toward a degree of splendor, power and influence that corresponds to its human vocation."[44] From this nationalism flows a conception of domestic policy that emphasizes economic modernization, social unification, and national independence, along with an ideological orientation that is resolutely anti-Communist.

Gaullists are anti-Communist because their world view is very nearly antithetical to that of Marxism-Leninism. As against the Communists' materialistic conception of history, Gaullists see human events as shaped by spiritual factors among which national character is preeminent. Nations rather than classes are historical actors; history's outcome is uncertain rather than predetermined and is influenced more by will and morale than by historical laws or economic forces. National unity rather than class war is the natural and desirable condition of a people. The national interest rather than internationalism should be the orienting principle in the world. A powerful sense of the antithetical relations between communism and Gaullism spurred Chirac's vigorous, vocal anticommunism during the 1978 election campaign (as it did Pompidou's equally explicit anticommunism in 1968). It also fueled his offensive against the Socialists for seeming to acquiesce in the visions and values of the PCF.

But class struggle, revolution, and proletarian internationalism are not the only targets of France's Gaullist tradition. Gaullism is also at odds with the tradition of parliamentary supremacy and the regime of parties that existed in the Third and Fourth Republics. With their founder, Gaullists reproach France's traditional political parties with fracturing rather than representing the national will and disdain their pedestrian conception of France's purposes and role. It is the Communists whom they perceive as their ultimate antagonists, but there is also righteous disapproval of the traditional bourgeois parties.

The UDF perspective. As against the grand conceptions of Gaullists and Communists, the political orientations of the Radicals, the Reformists, and the Independents seem mundane. The parties of the UDF see politics not in terms of class struggle nor as the expression of the nation's spirit but as the effort of individuals to find

---

[44] Charles de Gaulle, Press conference, Elysée Palace, September 9, 1968, quoted in Jean Charlot, *Le Gaullisme* [Gaullism] (Paris: Librairie Armand Colin, 1970), p. 182.

workable solutions to common problems. For the Gaullists and Communists alike a "movement" is perceived as the appropriate institutional embodiment of their purposes; for the parties of the UDF interest groups and associations, local notables, and loose electoral alliances will do. Like the Gaullists, the parties of the UDF support modernization, growth, and technology in the economic sphere, but they are less concerned with the fact that these make France strong than with the fact that they enable Frenchmen to live better.

The emergence in 1978 of the UDF as a political entity as large as the Gaullist RPR rested on various factors. But the most important of these factors was the existence of a strong political tradition of which the UDF is the contemporary institutional expression. That tradition emphasizes individual liberty, private property, and parliamentary supremacy and welcomes international collaboration with democratic Europe and the Atlantic Alliance. These were the attitudes characteristic of most middle-class parties during the Third and Fourth Republics. They were present in the various Radical parties, in the Moderates, the Independents, and the MRP parties, which collectively constituted the backbone of the "regime of parties" for which Charles de Gaulle and his lieutenants had such disdain. These are the parties that gave politics under the Third and Fourth Republics their defining characteristics, among which were multipartyism, coalition Government, ministerial instability, executive impotence, legislative supremacy, and that combination of strong pressure groups and weak institutions that was described in such terms as *immobilisme* and *incivisme*. But these were also the parties that acted through the same governmental structures to construct the economic and political institutions of "Europe" (the most important of which is the Common Market), who undertook the modernization of the French economy, who developed the foundation and the framework of France's extraordinary economic growth, who constructed the modern French welfare state, expanded its public sector, and devised imaginative institutions for the governance of nationalized industries. Less important than the fact that these groups have a record of impressive successes and failures is the fact that the parties of the center and right speak for one of the enduring orientations that have shaped French politics in the democratic era.

The persistence of the center. The center's assumptions, attitudes, and values concerning the individual, the society, the state, and the world have found expression throughout the twentieth century. Most of the parties embodying these attitudes have been afflicted with a tendency to schism and with the other organizational weaknesses common in democratic institutions in Latin nations. But that does not mean the orientations they embody are also weak. The persistence of these political views and values in the absence of strong institutionalization indicates that we are dealing here with attitudes that have deep roots in the political culture. Their characteristic institutional weaknesses leave these parties uniquely vulnerable to surge movements and other sudden shifts in the political scene. So far, however, the center-right has repeatedly proved more durable than expected: groups split, names change, but parties recreate themselves around the orientation. The strength of this orientation can be seen in the record of the center-right parties after the appearance of a Gaullist movement.

In 1951, when the first Gaullist party (the RPF) attracted 21.6 percent of the votes cast, the combined votes of the Moderates (14.1), the MRP (12.6), and the Radicals (RGR, 10 percent) was 36.7 percent. In 1958, when the new Gaullist party (the UNR) had made its appearance to support its leader's governmental policies, the Gaullists won 20.4 percent of the votes cast, compared with a total of 22 percent for the Moderates, 11 percent for the MRP, and 7.3 percent for the Radicals (for a total of 40 percent). In 1962, after the political effects of de Gaulle's policies and Constitution had been felt, the Gaullists polled 31.9 percent of the vote, as against 30 percent for the Moderates (9.6), RIs (4.4), MRP (8.9), and Radicals (7.5). In 1967, when a national alliance between Communists, Socialists, and Leftist Radicals speeded the bipolarization of electoral competition, the identifiable center was reduced to 13.4 percent of the votes cast, and in 1968 this total dropped to 10.3 percent, but soon afterward, in the presidential election of 1969, centrist Alain Poher polled 23.4 percent of the votes cast, running second to Georges Pompidou, outstripping the Communist candidate Jacques Duclos and denying the left a place in the runoff.

In 1973 the non-Gaullist parties of the right and center were again decimated, more than ever the victims of bipolarization. Of that election Jean Charlot wrote, "the Radicals, in fact, have lost all political autonomy,"[45] and the reformists "proved incapable of profiting from the erosion of the Majority by capturing some of the votes the Majority lost."[46] The allied Democratic Center group did no better. But one year later, in 1974, Valéry Giscard d'Estaing, a Gaullist fellow traveller with a frank affection for the center, mounted

---

[45] Charlot, *Quand la Gauche,* p. 90.
[46] Ibid, p. 104.

a presidential campaign that eliminated the Gaullist candidate, Jacques Chaban Delmas, on the first ballot and rallied mainly voters who were non-left and non-Gaullist.

Differences in conception and style between the Gaullists and the UDF are most acute in regard to the Constitution and foreign policy. Because the parties of the UDF would profit by a return to proportional representation, and because in any case they see France as comprising diverse interests which should be reflected in a representative government, they support the adoption of a new electoral law that would provide for proportional representation. They are not deterred in this by the supposedly negative effects of proportional representation: they do not regard multipartyism as an unmitigated evil; neither do they see the "regime of the parties" of the Fourth Republic as an abomination. Since they tend to perceive government as a necessary evil, they are not much bothered by the possibility that an altered electoral law might lead France back to weak coalition government. Gaullists, on the other hand, are loyal to the institutions of the Fifth Republic precisely because they delivered France from the embarrassment of weak, unstable government based on "coalitions of fragments," and they correctly perceive the single-member district as an important foundation of the Gaullist pattern of politics.

In foreign policy, the traditional parties' interest in strengthening the institutions of the EEC and the bonds of an Atlantic Alliance conflict sharply with the Gaullist abhorrence of supranational bodies and their distaste for participation in alliances that could conceivably restrict the national sovereignty.

In the months before the 1978 elections, three clear-cut political facts testified to the end of the Gaullists' dominance of the Majority but also to their continued importance to it. First, despite his long participation in the cabinets of Charles de Gaulle and Georges Pompidou, France's president, Valéry Giscard d'Estaing, was a man who had always insisted on maintaining a separate identity, who had long since made known his commitment to "enlarging" the Majority to include other parties of a reconstructed center and his desire to see an end of bipolar politics. Second, France's prime minister, Raymond Barre, was not a Gaullist. And third, the policies of the president and the Barre Government depended on Gaullist deputies for Majority support in the Chamber of Deputies.

When, in the weeks preceding the elections, Giscard pulled together the remnants of the Reformists, the Independents, and those Radicals outside the Union of the Left, he recreated a vehicle for the expression of that aspect of the political tradition that had

216

dominated the Third and Fourth Republics. The success of the UDF should have come as no surprise since successive public opinion polls had reflected the steady appeal of its constituent parties.

The success of UDF candidates in the 1978 legislative elections and in the cantonal elections a year later proved definitively that the Gaullist era had not finally extirpated this centrist orientation in French politics and suggested that the bipolarization of the previous elections had not reflected a permanent restructuring of partisanship in the French electorate. But the RPR's showing provided equally persuasive testimony to the continuing power of the Gaullist vision. Clearly Gaullism still had a solid appeal after the passing of de Gaulle and his intimates and the emergence of an alternative on the center-right.

A Concluding Comment

This book and the above analysis testify to the existence in contemporary France of four major political orientations. Others exist (including tiny but persistent *gauchiste* and hard-right factions), but only the Communists, Socialists, Giscardians, and Gaullists have large followings within the electorate and a demonstrated capacity to persist. Relations within and among these parties may be expected to shape French political outcomes in the foreseeable future. Several quite different scenarios can be constructed concerning the relations among these parties: (1) the Union of the Left may be reconstructed and reinforced, (2) disagreement between the UDF and the RPR may split the Majority and deprive Giscard of a parliamentary majority, (3) the RPR, the PS, and/or the UDF may be splintered by internal disagreements, and (4) all or significant parts of the UDF and the PS may form a new coalition of the type common in the Fourth Republic.

In assessing these evolving possibilities it is important to bear in mind the distinctive political orientations represented by each of the major groups and also the fact that no one of them has a monopoly —or near monopoly—on the loyalties of any significant social class. Blue-collar workers are almost equally divided between Communists and Socialists, and a substantial minority are Gaullists. White-collar workers are similarly divided among Socialists, Communists, Gaullists, and Giscardians. So are professionals and farmers. This distribution of voters means, first, that no economic class recognizes any one of the major political parties as its spokesman and, second, that all groups have a chance (though not an equal chance) of recruiting support from all classes. This is another way of saying that the political alignments in French politics do not reflect economic divisions in any simple or automatic fashion. Neither do they reflect religious divisions as reliably as in the past. In the period before 1978 the Socialists had increasing success in attracting support from Catholic and Protestant voters. Furthermore, some of both these types of Christians are now found in the ranks of the Socialist militants. Religious affiliations and especially religious practice remain the most reliable single social predictor of left-right voting in France: most practicing Christians vote for either the UDF or the RPR, most Socialists and virtually all Communists are strictly secular in perspective. But the correlations between right and left politics and Christian identifications are not as high as in the past.[47]

In social composition, the Socialists and Communists resemble one another most closely and compete most actively for the support of the working class and intellectuals, while the UDF and the RPR draw support mainly from the middle-class professional and entrepreneurial categories. But there is competition for the support of all groups, and this competition bridges the conventional left-right categories. It is very important for the style and substance of political competition in France that all parties compete for the support of all kinds of people and that social, cultural, and economic cleavages are not automatically or wholly reflected in and reinforced by political alignments. The layered conflicts that have characterized and complicated French political life are slowly yielding to changed circumstances. This does not necessarily augur a less fractionalized politics, but it might foreshadow cleavages that are less profound and complex. On the other hand, it seems quite likely that the weakening of the social bases of political cleavages constitutes a new source of volatility in an already volatile electorate.[48]

Whether the characteristic institutions of the Fifth Republic persist or succumb will depend on the emerging pattern of political alignments. A regime dominated by a strong president who exercises leadership over policy requires a reliable parliamentary majority. And a reliable parliamentary majority requires a majority coalition of at least two of the four major political blocs. It also requires that each of those groups be sufficiently cohesive and disciplined that it

---

[47] *Le Monde*'s analysis of the religious factor in the 1978 elections began with the assertion, "Less and less, Christians form a specific and homogeneous group." *Le Monde*, March 7, 1978.

[48] The importance of sudden shifts and of surge parties in French electoral politics is well known. At the moment the Socialists would appear to be profiting from the shifting loyalties of voters.

can hold together in the face of temptations and difficulties. The absence of such cohesion and discipline within the groups or of a stable alliance between two groups would effectively transform the French political system.

As I write, personal rivalries and political disagreements disturb relations within and between the RPR and the UDF; the depth and intensity of factionalism inside the Socialist party increases as François Mitterrand's capacity to dominate the party declines; signs multiply that the PCF has made another turn that will create serious new problems for the possibilities of a Union of the Left; and recently published polls document a widespread longing among the rank and file of both the UDF and the PS for an alliance between these two parties in preference to the existing pattern of alliances.[49] None of these developments would seriously affect the fundamental ideological orientations but any one could definitively disrupt the pattern of politics of the Fifth Republic.

---

[49] "Voters Looking for Radical Realignment among Parties," *Washington Post,* May 26, 1979, pp. A-19 and A-20.

APPENDIX A

French Ballots, 1978

The ballots used in the first round of the 1978 legislative election in the sixth district in Paris are reproduced on the following pages. Registered voters received all eleven ballots in the mail shortly before the election in a packet also containing a one-page campaign statement from each candidate. At the polls, where more ballots were available, the voter placed his candidate's ballot in a special envelope provided only at the polling place and dropped it into the ballot box.

These ballots illustrate the variety and ambiguity of the party labels used in French elections. Only three of the eleven bear a single, straightforward label that the Ministry of the Interior adopted in essentially the same form in the official election returns—namely, Communist, Socialist, and Ecologist ("Paris Ecologie 78"). The ballot of the winner, Maurice Couve de Murville, identifies him as the RPR incumbent, his alternate as a PR member, and his candidacy as "For the Union of the Majority"; in the official returns for the first ballot his votes were entered in the RPR column. The remaining seven ballots all bear labels that require interpretation to fit under one of the headings used in the official returns (see Appendix B).

This fact accounts for the minor discrepancies one encounters between reports of the outcome of any legislative election in France. The parliamentary groups joined by the winners establish a clear set of affiliations for them, but it is not necessarily the same as the set derived from their election labels; some deputies surprise observers by joining parliamentary groups one would not have predicted from their identifications as candidates. And for the losing candidates, one has no choice but to wrestle with the election labels, which are diverse enough to make it virtually impossible even for two experts to agree on the categories to use or the placement of every candidate within them.

The actual size of the ballots reproduced here is 10.5 × 15 centimeters.

Yvette Saintier

**30 ans, technicienne supérieure à E.D.F.
responsable parisienne du P.C.F.**

Charles Nouhailletas, suppléant
38 ans, agent de conduite à la S.N.C.F.

parti communiste français

PARTI SOCIALISTE

Jean-Pierre LESAGE
Candidat titulaire

Frédéric SAINT-GEOURS
Candidat suppléant

ÉLECTIONS LÉGISLATIVES

6ᵉ CIRCONSCRIPTION DE PARIS

PARIS ECOLOGIE 78

Albina du BOISROUVRAY
CANDIDATE

Christian HUGLO
SUPPLEANT

ÉLECTIONS LÉGISLATIVES DES 12 ET 19 MARS 1978

6ₑ Circonscription de Paris - 8ₑ Arrondissement

POUR L'UNION DE LA MAJORITÉ

Maurice COUVE de MURVILLE
Député sortant
R.P.R.

Suppléant :

Marcel NORMAND
Avocat à la cour
P.R.

POUR LE
PRESIDENT DE LA REPUBLIQUE

Elections législatives des
12 et 19 Mars 1978
6ᵉᵐᵉ Circonscription de Paris

Candidat :

Bernard **PLASAIT**

Suppléante :

MADAME P. VACHON

DEMOCRATIE CHRETIENNE

jacques sylvain
BRUNAUD
CANDIDAT

alain
JEZEQUEL
SUPPLEANT

ELECTIONS LEGISLATIVES MARS 1978

UNION DE LA DROITE
PARTI DES FORCES NOUVELLES

Paris - 6ème Circonscription

Jean-François FERRER

Suppléant:

François-Xavier BAEHR

ELECTIONS LEGISLATIVES
6ᵉ CIRCONSCRIPTION DE PARIS
12 MARS 1978

CANDIDAT

MICHEL BAYVET

SUPPLEANT
Elizabeth Harismendy

FRONT NATIONAL

CANDIDAT

CONTRIBUABLES

présenté par le **R.U.C.**

Henri JANNES

Polytechnicien
Ingénieur général des Télécommunications (E R)
Ancien Expert près la Commission des Finances du Sénat
Président du R.U.C.

Suppléant :

FERDINAND FERRAND

Courtier assermenté près le Tribunal de Commerce de Paris

ELECTIONS LEGISLATIVES DE MARS 1978

6ᵉ circonscription de Paris

Raymond HALLARD

ouvrier métallurgiste, 29 ans

candidat présenté par

LUTTE OUVRIÈRE

Suppléant :

Marcel PEYTIER

médecin, 33 ans

6e circonscription de Paris

Ligue communiste révolutionnaire

Pour le socialisme,
le pouvoir aux travailleurs

Laure Laufer
caissière

Suppléant : Pascal Buhot
employé PPT

Section française de la IVe Internationale

APPENDIX B

French National Assembly Election Results, 1973 and 1978

Compiled by Richard M. Scammon

The tables that follow have been compiled from the official election returns published by the French Ministry of Interior under the title *Les Elections Législatives de 1978*. The party labels conform to the ministry's usage.* The abbreviations used are as follows:

UDR   Union des Démocrates pour la République, Union of Democrats for the Republic

CDS   Centre des Démocrates Sociaux, Social Democratic Center

RPR   Rassemblement pour la République, Rally for the Republic

UDF   Union pour la Démocratie Française, Union for French Democracy

CDP   Centre Démocratie et Progrès, Center for Democracy and Progress

---

*EDITOR'S NOTE: Elsewhere in this book the term Majority refers to the broad center-right coalition comprising the UDF, the RPR, and lesser parties and independent candidates, which was opposed by the left coalition of Communists, Socialists, and Leftist Radicals. In this appendix, the heading Majority covers only some of the candidates and smaller parties that are generally part of the center-right coalition. See also Appendix A.

NATIONAL ASSEMBLY ELECTIONS, 1973 AND 1978: FIRST-BALLOT VOTE TOTALS, BY PARTY, METROPOLITAN FRANCE

Party	Popular Vote
March 1973	
Registered voters	29,901,822
Votes cast	24,289,285
Valid votes	23,751,213
Extreme-left	778,195
Communist	5,085,108
Socialist	4,559,241
Other left	668,100
UDR	5,684,396
Independent Republican	1,656,191
CDP	883,961
Other Majority	784,735
Reformist	2,979,781
Other right	671,505
March 1978	
Registered voters	34,394,378
Votes cast	28,656,845
Valid votes	28,098,113
Extreme-left	919,054
Communist	5,791,525
Socialist	6,412,240
Leftist Radical	606,675
Center-left	808,577
Majority	884,480
CDS	1,402,018
Republican	3,028,810
RPR	6,303,611
Other[a]	1,941,123

The candidates endorsed by the UDF before the first ballot won a total of 5,738,938 votes.[b]

[a] Moderates, 545,576; Ecologists, 611,210; other, 784,337.
[b] Ministry of the Interior footnote.

NATIONAL ASSEMBLY ELECTIONS, 1973 AND 1978: SEATS WON, BY PARTY, METROPOLITAN FRANCE

Party	Seats
March 1973	
UDR	178
Independent Republican	52
CDP	20
Reformist	28
Socialist	91
Communist	73
Other[a]	31
Total	473
March 1978	
RPR	144
Republican	65
CDS	32
Majority	16
Center-left	10
Leftist Radical	10
Socialist	102
Communist	86
Other	9
Total	474

[a] Includes 12 "other left."

Distribution of Seats in the National Assembly after the 1978 Elections, by Parliamentary Group

Parliamentary Group	Metropolitan France	Overseas Departments[a]	Overseas Territories[b]	Total Seats[c]
Rally for the Republic (RPR)	145	6	3	154
Union for French Democracy (UDF)	119	2	2	123
Socialist	112	2	1	115
Communist	86	—	—	86
Independent	12	1	—	13
Total	474	11	6	491

[a] The "Départements d'outre mer" include Guadeloupe (3 seats), Martinique (3), Réunion (3), French Guiana (1), and Saint-Pierre-et-Miquelon (1).

[b] The "Territoires d'outre mer" include New Caledonia and the New Hebrides (2 seats), French Polynesia (2), Mayotte (1), and Wallis and Futuna (1).

[c] Totals include associated members as follows: RPR 11, UDF 15, Socialists 12. All 86 members of the Communist group belong to the PCF.

NATIONAL ASSEMBLY ELECTIONS, 1978: FIRST-BALLOT RETURNS FOR METROPOLITAN FRANCE, BY DEPARTMENT

Department		Total	Extreme Left	Communist	Socialist	Leftist Radical	Center Left	Majority	CDS	PR	RPR	Other[a]
Metropolitan France	Total	28,098,113	919,054	5,791,525	6,412,240	606,675	808,577	884,480	1,402,018	3,028,810	6,303,611	1,941,123
	% of vote		3.3	20.6	22.8	2.2	2.9	3.1	5.0	10.8	22.4	6.9
Ain	Total	197,419	7,237	32,695	31,704	16,151	—	2,934	14,499	53,752	27,043	11,404
	% of vote		3.7	16.6	16.1	8.2		1.5	7.3	27.2	13.7	5.8
	Seats	3								2	1	
Aisne	Total	299,724	10,318	86,073	71,704	767	38,300	10,455	—	14,531	64,666	2,910
	% of vote		3.4	28.7	23.9	.3	12.8	3.5		4.8	21.6	1.0
	Seats	5		2	2		1					
Allier	Total	218,944	4,955	67,900	45,048	—	41,894	—	—	—	39,903	19,244
	% of vote		2.3	31.0	20.6		19.1				18.2	8.8
	Seats	4		2			1				1	
Alpes-de-Haute-Provence	Total	67,540	1,169	17,160	8,907	8,123	2,901	9,921	—	4,236	11,242	3,881
	% of vote		1.7	25.4	13.2	12.0	4.3	14.7		6.3	16.6	5.7
	Seats	2		1		1						
Alpes (Hautes-)	Total	57,976	1,149	11,789	5,159	8,105	—	—	15,186	11,230	3,783	1,575
	% of vote		2.0	20.3	8.9	14.0			26.2	19.4	6.5	2.7
	Seats	2				1			1			
Alpes-Maritimes	Total	460,536	9,572	92,414	61,608	2,678	—	1,252	23,026	81,473	114,923	73,590
	% of vote		2.1	20.1	13.4	.6		.3	5.0	17.7	25.0	16.0
	Seats	6							1	3	2	
Ardèche	Total	155,762	2,748	30,001	34,672	—	—	—	10,161	45,719	20,019	12,442
	% of vote		1.8	19.3	22.3				6.5	29.4	12.9	8.0
	Seats	3								2	1	

Ardennes	157,420	5,566	39,945	41,192	—	—	987	—	18,616	47,107	4,007
% of vote		3.5	25.4	26.2			.6		11.8	29.9	2.5
Seats	3		2							1	
Ariège	84,263	2,042	21,480	31,237	3,041	—	—	—	6,564	19,569	330
% of vote		2.4	25.5	37.1	3.6				7.8	23.2	.4
Seats	2			2						1	
Aube	150,403	5,154	29,015	36,603	—	14,685	18,136	—	10,574	31,963	4,273
% of vote		3.4	19.3	24.3		9.8	12.1		7.0	21.3	2.8
Seats	3						1		1	1	
Aude	167,349	3,329	43,456	53,112	3,252	—	—	6,051	13,198	38,203	6,748
% of vote		2.0	26.0	31.7	1.9			3.6	7.9	22.8	4.0
Seats	3			3							
Aveyron	170,071	5,287	19,161	25,685	32,897	—	1,511	27,388	30,276	26,802	1,064
% of vote		3.1	11.3	15.1	19.3		.9	16.1	17.8	15.8	.6
Seats	3			1	1			1		1	
Bouches-du-Rhône	765,461	19,733	245,947	171,902	10,009	23,171	7,552	22,899	93,934	123,842	46,472
% of vote		2.6	32.1	22.5	1.3	3.0	1.0	3.0	12.3	16.2	6.1
Seats	11		7	2					1	1	
Calvados	308,319	9,421	40,471	75,459	2,020	31,611	—	7,086	72,271	28,014	41,966
% of vote		3.1	13.1	24.5	.7	10.3		2.3	23.4	9.1	13.6
Seats	5			1		1			1	1	1
Cantal	98,903	2,687	13,928	23,494	—	—	—	—	—	57,058	1,736
% of vote		2.7	14.1	23.8						57.7	1.8
Seats	2									2	
Charente	195,319	5,503	43,493	44,125	9,642	—	1,845	—	6,750	70,914	13,047
% of vote		2.8	22.3	22.6	4.9		.9		3.5	36.3	6.7
Seats	3		1	1						1	

(Continued on next page)

233

Department	Total	Extreme Left	Communist	Socialist	Leftist Radical	Center Left	Majority	CDS	PR	RPR	Other[a]
Charente-Maritime	279,620	8,185	53,753	40,045	39,013	2,854	8,368	—	54,956	63,976	8,470
% of vote		2.9	19.2	14.3	14.0	1.0	3.0		19.7	22.9	3.0
Seats	5			2	1		1			1	
Cher	176,762	5,353	58,335	28,370	1,219	—	28,612	—	—	49,396	5,477
% of vote		3.0	33.0	16.1	.7		16.2			27.9	3.1
Seats	3		1				1			2	
Corrèze	156,456	2,672	43,684	29,396	743	—	—	—	—	66,751	13,210
% of vote		1.7	27.9	18.8	.5					42.7	8.4
Seats	3		1							2	
Corse-du-Sud	64,730	—	10,027	2,079	14,414	—	—	—	10,235	24,157	3,818
% of vote			15.5	3.2	22.3				15.8	37.3	5.9
Seats	2								1	1	
Corse (Haute-)	78,333	—	12,948	4,236	20,790	—	—	—	8,099	23,470	8,790
% of vote			16.5	5.4	26.5				10.3	30.0	11.2
Seats	2								1	1	
Côte-d'Or	233,013	7,234	32,870	48,578	18,743	—	25,186	—	21,245	67,199	11,958
% of vote		3.1	14.1	20.8	8.0		10.8		9.1	28.8	5.1
Seats	4			1			1		1	1	
Côtes-du-Nord	332,144	10,827	73,555	87,434	704	—	6,143	58,750	30,267	58,319	6,145
% of vote		3.3	22.1	26.3	.2		1.8	17.7	9.1	17.6	1.9
Seats	5		1	1				1	1	1	
Creuse	89,470	2,378	23,731	26,193	—	3,383	—	—	—	32,495	1,290
% of vote		2.7	26.5	29.3		3.8				36.3	1.4
Seats	2			1						1	

	Total	(1)	(2)	(3)	(4)	(5)	(6)	(7)	(8)	(9)	(10)
Dordogne	244,844	6,821	63,101	49,497	19,461	—	1,702	—	7,441	92,657	4,164
% of vote		2.8	25.8	20.2	7.9		.7		3.0	37.8	1.7
Seats	4		1	1	1					1	
Doubs	232,250	13,380	35,051	68,013	2,369	—	19,304	—	11,722	79,466	2,945
% of vote		5.8	15.1	29.3	1.0		8.3		5.0	34.2	1.3
Seats	3			1						2	
Drôme	198,912	3,418	35,786	61,871	—	10,783	3,587	11,480	18,740	36,844	16,403
% of vote		1.7	18.0	31.1		5.4	1.8	5.8	9.4	18.5	8.2
Seats	3			2						1	
Eure	241,394	8,243	50,089	42,148	14,775	5,752	2,977	20,431	36,332	50,860	9,787
% of vote		3.4	20.7	17.5	6.1	2.4	1.2	8.5	15.1	21.1	4.1
Seats	4			1				1	1	1	
Eure-et-Loir	188,054	7,121	30,101	39,616	13,577	4,923	—	14,865	46,212	27,811	3,828
% of vote		3.8	16.0	21.1	7.2	2.6		7.9	24.6	14.8	2.0
Seats	3			1					1	1	
Finistère	483,412	22,655	73,479	117,536	—	—	48,722	30,966	43,192	139,256	7,606
% of vote		4.7	15.2	24.3			10.1	6.4	9.1	28.8	1.6
Seats	8			2					1	5	
Gard	282,319	6,607	95,393	60,958	4,621	—	29,865	—	23,471	44,375	17,029
% of vote		2.3	33.8	21.6	1.6		10.6		8.3	15.7	6.0
Seats	4		2	1						1	
Garonne (Haute-)	409,490	10,895	77,989	126,941	11,908	12,162	3,659	—	67,642	56,961	41,333
% of vote		2.7	19.0	31.0	2.9	3.0	.9		16.5	13.9	10.1
Seats	6			6							
Gers	107,240	3,672	17,233	36,320	—	9,766	17,104	—	9,055	10,571	3,519
% of vote		3.4	16.1	33.9		9.1	15.9		8.4	9.9	3.3
Seats	2			2							

(Continued on next page)

Department	Total	Extreme Left	Communist	Socialist	Leftist Radical	Center Left	Majority	CDS	PR	RPR	Other[a]
Gironde	572,059	14,906	103,051	168,990	13,672	30,470	5,966	3,043	24,595	143,298	64,068
% of vote		2.6	18.0	29.5	2.4	5.3	1.0	.5	4.3	25.0	11.2
Seats	10			5	1					4	
Hérault	350,290	15,323	88,589	80,835	14,348	1,251	3,633	50,336	40,754	47,165	8,056
% of vote		4.4	25.3	23.1	4.1	.4	1.0	14.4	11.6	13.5	2.3
Seats	5		2	2					1		
Ille-et-Vilaine	389,031	16,055	36,613	97,172	4,781	11,697	9,940	47,763	28,082	126,502	10,426
% of vote		4.1	9.4	25.0	1.2	3.0	2.6	12.3	7.2	32.5	2.7
Seats	6							1	1	4	
Indre	147,466	4,412	38,982	31,932	—	—	—	—	20,076	40,084	11,980
% of vote		3.0	26.4	21.7					13.6	27.2	8.1
Seats	3								1	2	
Indre-et-Loire	252,976	9,208	36,369	64,097	8,318	—	28,549	—	36,734	49,647	20,054
% of vote		3.6	14.4	25.3	3.3		11.3		14.5	19.6	7.9
Seats	4						1		1	2	
Isère	426,149	7,394	100,223	110,826	990	9,152	12,962	10,477	82,958	59,458	31,709
% of vote		1.7	23.5	26.0	.2	2.1	3.0	2.5	19.5	14.0	7.4
Seats	7		1	4					2		
Jura	135,235	6,375	24,815	33,335	1,038	16,013	15,310	—	25,615	6,925	5,809
% of vote		4.7	18.3	24.6	.8	11.8	11.3		18.9	5.1	4.3
Seats	2					1			1		
Landes	180,531	2,766	30,249	58,061	9,142	—	—	49,026	—	24,956	6,331
% of vote		1.5	16.8	32.2	5.1			27.2		13.8	3.5
Seats	3			3							

Loir-et-Cher	166,593	7,625	29,807	43,040	—	—	33,604	23,256	—	27,365	1,896
% of vote		4.6	17.9	25.8	—	—	20.2	14.0	—	16.4	1.1
Seats	3						1	1		1	
Loire	370,918	12,582	76,712	62,134	17,681	15,438	—	37,205	44,130	68,942	36,094
% of vote		3.4	20.7	16.8	4.8	4.2	—	10.0	11.9	18.6	9.7
Seats	7		1	1	1	1		1	2	1	
Loire (Haute-)	124,437	2,146	10,988	35,957	—	827	—	37,639	30,472	3,465	2,943
% of vote		1.7	8.8	28.9	—	.7	—	30.2	24.5	2.8	2.4
Seats	2							1	1		
Loire-Atlantique	511,376	18,720	61,988	129,688	13,960	—	34,635	10,671	57,515	150,652	33,547
% of vote		3.7	12.1	25.4	2.7	—	6.8	2.1	11.2	29.5	6.5
Seats	8			3			1		1	3	
Loiret	269,567	8,186	55,134	53,603	4,027	—	500	11,927	34,009	79,205	22,976
% of vote		3.0	20.5	19.9	1.5	—	.2	4.4	12.6	29.4	8.5
Seats	4								1	3	
Lot	97,402	3,018	15,608	18,276	20,468	1,115	19,256	—	—	16,557	3,104
% of vote		3.1	16.0	18.8	21.0	1.1	19.8	—	—	17.0	3.2
Seats	2			1	1						
Lot-et-Garonne	172,944	3,345	40,217	44,256	1,317	20,484	1,750	—	4,026	27,045	30,504
% of vote		1.9	23.3	25.6	.8	11.8	1.0	—	2.3	15.6	17.6
Seats	3		1	2							
Lozère	46,149	1,409	3,885	6,754	—	—	1,301	—	26,115	1,149	5,536
% of vote		3.1	8.4	14.6	—	—	2.8	—	56.6	2.5	12.0
Seats	2								2		
Maine-et-Loire	338,562	12,681	34,426	78,908	1,714	29,064	11,945	12,105	6,477	96,731	54,511
% of vote		3.8	10.2	23.3	.5	8.6	3.5	3.6	1.9	28.6	16.1
Seats	6					1		1		3	1

(Continued on next page)

Department	Total	Extreme Left	Communist	Socialist	Leftist Radical	Center Left	Majority	CDS	PR	RPR	Other[a]
Manche	260,111	10,976	21,512	51,019	—	3,534	—	20,431	72,326	57,571	22,742
% of vote		4.2	8.3	19.6		1.4		7.9	27.8	22.1	8.7
Seats	5			1				1	1	2	
Marne	274,022	6,297	66,382	52,028	2,710	1,304	—	44,673	18,882	69,760	11,986
% of vote		2.3	24.2	19.0	1.0	.5		16.3	6.9	25.5	4.4
Seats	4		2	1				2		2	
Marne (Haute-)	115,099	3,463	23,525	23,810	3,666	3,836	—	4,138	16,820	34,522	1,319
% of vote		3.0	20.4	20.7	3.2	3.3		3.6	14.6	30.0	1.1
Seats	2			1					1	1	
Mayenne	153,042	6,599	9,325	43,087	—	—	—	—	55,504	36,827	1,700
% of vote		4.3	6.1	28.2					36.3	24.1	1.1
Seats	3								2	1	
Meurthe-et-Moselle	367,986	13,972	80,414	92,674	2,129	37,663	40,125	—	60,713	27,093	13,203
% of vote		3.8	21.9	25.2	.6	10.2	10.9		16.5	7.4	3.6
Seats	7		2	2		2			3		
Meuse	113,393	4,778	15,471	33,899	—	—	12,907	—	29,133	11,340	5,865
% of vote		4.2	13.6	29.9			11.4		25.7	10.0	5.2
Seats	2			1			1		1		
Morbihan	333,055	12,223	43,932	75,271	—	—	627	41,448	85,908	45,463	28,183
% of vote		3.7	13.2	22.6			.2	12.4	25.8	13.7	8.5
Seats	6			1				2	2	1	
Moselle	499,299	18,958	78,588	119,090	—	26,261	12,242	36,110	32,328	131,781	43,941
% of vote		3.8	15.7	23.9		5.3	2.5	7.2	6.5	26.4	8.8
Seats	8		1	1				1	1	4	

Nièvre	141,418	5,086	29,348	52,753	—	—	—	12,276	18,444	13,107	10,404
% of vote		3.6	20.8	37.3				8.7	13.0	9.3	7.4
Seats	3			3							
Nord	1,333,184	38,560	351,059	347,534	2,007	46,252	83,186	50,795	82,401	258,478	72,912
% of vote		2.9	26.3	26.1	.2	3.5	6.2	3.8	6.2	19.4	5.5
Seats	23		9	8			2			4	
Oise	325,727	10,598	77,867	62,902	9,233	6,951	12,299	12,522	17,391	93,969	21,995
% of vote		3.3	23.9	19.3	2.8	2.1	3.8	3.8	5.3	28.8	6.8
Seats	5		1	1				1		3	
Orne	164,911	6,264	16,733	38,220	—	8,208	—	13,584	18,506	53,962	9,434
% of vote		3.8	10.1	23.2		5.0		8.2	11.2	32.7	5.7
Seats	3							1	1	1	
Pas-de-Calais	788,346	23,339	236,063	234,510	13,734	21,645	3,787	45,424	33,981	157,738	18,125
% of vote		3.0	29.9	29.7	1.7	2.7	.5	5.8	4.3	20.0	2.3
Seats	14		5	8	1					3	
Puy-de-Dôme	312,680	16,121	52,463	95,318	4,044	11,642	13,412	—	81,038	31,508	7,134
% of vote		5.2	16.8	30.5	1.3	3.7	4.3		25.9	10.1	2.3
Seats	5			3					2	1	
Pyrénées-Atlantiques	312,376	5,029	40,886	90,039	1,632	—	—	30,223	5,813	123,335	15,419
% of vote		1.6	13.1	28.8	.5			9.7	1.9	39.5	4.9
Seats	4			1						3	
Pyrénées (Hautes-)	133,751	4,375	31,316	17,443	25,423	2,625	1,447	17,862	7,637	22,274	3,349
% of vote		3.3	23.4	13.0	19.0	2.0	1.1	13.4	5.7	16.7	2.5
Seats	2		1	1	1					1	
Pyrénées-Orientales	165,371	6,237	50,011	37,004	—	—	—	—	14,866	28,215	29,038
% of vote		3.8	30.2	22.4					9.0	17.1	17.6
Seats	2		1							1	1

(Continued on next page)

Department	Total	Extreme Left	Communist	Socialist	Leftist Radical	Center Left	Majority	CDS	PR	RPR	Other[a]
Rhin (Bas-)	445,194	9,827	29,280	79,788	2,943	—	6,820	69,925	7,310	166,602	72,699
% of vote		2.2	6.6	17.9	.7		1.5	15.7	1.6	37.4	16.3
Seats	8							3		4	1
Rhin (Haut-)	318,218	6,836	21,360	66,867	4,142	23,381	—	51,159	21,261	90,265	32,947
% of vote		2.1	6.7	21.0	1.3	7.3		16.1	6.7	28.4	10.4
Seats	5					1		1		3	
Rhône	654,372	29,646	112,002	156,737	7,639	30,902	42,778	27,696	63,209	125,597	58,166
% of vote		4.5	17.1	24.0	1.2	4.7	6.5	4.2	9.7	19.2	8.9
Seats	13		1	2		1	1	2	2	4	
Saône (Haute-)	130,471	3,575	15,737	30,920	13,631	—	—	31,727	18,277	14,290	2,314
% of vote		2.7	12.1	23.7	10.4			24.3	14.0	11.0	1.8
Seats	2							1	1		
Saône-et-Loire	303,131	6,653	56,236	70,638	24,375	14,997	600	—	11,093	85,186	33,353
% of vote		2.2	18.6	23.3	8.0	4.9	.2		3.7	28.1	11.0
Seats	5			2	1					1	1
Sarthe	275,589	12,515	57,418	60,523	—	—	—	17,489	27,223	91,925	8,496
% of vote		4.5	20.8	22.0				6.3	9.9	33.4	3.1
Seats	5		1						1	3	
Savoie	165,016	2,731	26,152	53,219	—	—	1,853	3,892	22,676	46,381	8,112
% of vote		1.7	15.8	32.3			1.1	2.4	13.7	28.1	4.9
Seats	3			2						1	
Savoie (Haute-)	222,972	4,001	30,577	46,462	812	—	—	21,825	78,392	17,288	23,615
% of vote		1.8	13.7	20.8	.4			9.8	35.2	7.8	10.6
Seats	3			1				1	2		
Paris	1,045,124	36,382	163,210	175,067	22,764	24,609	32,091	75,662	118,314	277,554	119,471
% of vote		3.5	15.6	16.8	2.2	2.4	3.1	7.2	11.3	26.6	11.4
Seats	31		3	1			2	2	3	20	

Seine-Maritime	630,140	22,083	177,782	127,444	12,919	32,756	2,265	21,215	58,569	147,498	27,609
% of vote		3.5	28.2	20.2	2.1	5.2	.4	3.4	9.3	23.4	4.4
Seats	10		4	1				1	1	3	
Seine-et-Marne	407,099	17,364	85,098	85,672	13,006	15,764	2,055	17,626	17,291	130,819	22,404
% of vote		4.3	20.9	21.0	3.2	3.9	.5	4.3	4.2	32.1	5.5
Seats	5		1	1				1	1	2	
Yvelines	549,383	23,631	97,070	97,504	24,089	19,547	3,201	7,087	75,885	157,725	43,644
% of vote		4.3	17.7	17.7	4.4	3.6	.6	1.3	13.8	28.7	7.9
Seats	8		1	1					2	5	
Sèvres (Deux-)	192,391	9,131	17,831	58,667	—	21,990	637	28,814	—	17,775	37,546
% of vote		4.7	9.3	30.5		11.4	.3	15.0		9.2	19.5
Seats	3			1				1			1
Somme	313,650	9,697	95,667	59,011	834	19,733	34,861	6,181	25,419	57,569	4,678
% of vote		3.1	30.5	18.8	.3	6.3	11.1	2.0	8.1	18.4	1.5
Seats	5		3	1			1			1	
Tarn	204,893	5,575	33,276	63,860	7,182	1,521	3,236	1,536	27,962	55,799	4,946
% of vote		2.7	16.2	31.2	3.5	.7	1.6	.7	13.6	27.2	2.4
Seats	3			2	1					1	
Tarn-et-Garonne	110,305	6,101	20,613	16,582	14,359	—	—	—	—	47,006	5,644
% of vote		5.5	18.7	15.0	13.0					42.6	5.1
Seats	2		1		1					1	
Var	357,746	7,102	85,913	73,823	—	20,575	22,900	—	74,507	41,347	31,579
% of vote		2.0	24.0	20.6		5.8	6.4		20.8	11.6	8.8
Seats	4		1	1					3	1	
Vaucluse	214,945	3,505	53,694	46,984	2,127	4,662	—	14,976	17,380	55,680	15,937
% of vote		1.6	25.0	21.9	1.0	2.2		7.0	8.1	25.9	7.4
Seats	3		1	1				1	1	1	

(Continued on next page)

241

Department	Total	Extreme Left	Communist	Socialist	Leftist Radical	Center Left	Majority	CDS	PR	RPR	Other[a]
Vendée	271,212	10,903	25,649	53,264	—	5,930	32,966	—	39,439	83,058	20,003
% of vote		4.0	9.5	19.6		2.2	12.2		14.5	30.6	7.4
Seats	4						1		1	2	
Vienne	205,377	7,006	34,182	59,759	—	771	2,444	22,959	29,702	44,424	4,130
% of vote		3.4	16.6	29.1		.4	1.2	11.2	14.5	21.6	2.0
Seats	3			1				1		1	
Vienne (Haute-)	212,500	8,631	71,803	56,674	—	—	—	7,877	24,747	41,961	807
% of vote		4.1	33.8	26.7				3.7	11.6	19.7	.4
Seats	3		3								
Vosges	218,473	7,235	27,822	63,241	958	6,685	—	4,204	36,475	65,890	5,963
% of vote		3.3	12.8	28.9	.4	3.1		1.9	16.7	30.2	2.7
Seats	4			1					1	2	
Yonne	172,042	6,874	36,453	35,851	—	—	—	1,063	33,245	42,738	15,818
% of vote		4.0	21.2	20.8				.6	19.3	24.8	9.2
Seats	3								1	1	1
Territoire de Belfort	64,744	2,659	8,187	24,397	8,155	—	15,480	—	—	10,851	3,170
% of vote		4.1	12.6	37.7	1.8		23.9			16.8	4.9
Seats	2			2							
Essonne	461,003	18,311	122,979	99,182	—	—	785	23,083	41,158	75,125	72,225
% of vote		4.0	26.7	21.5			.2	5.0	8.9	16.3	15.7
Seats	4		3							1	
Hauts-de-Seine	694,702	22,438	170,930	127,207	3,125	24,452	14,114	19,685	46,400	192,968	73,383
% of vote		3.2	24.6	18.3	.4	3.5	2.0	2.8	6.7	27.8	10.6
Seats	13		5					1	1	4	2

Seine–Saint-Denis	573,490	30,394	217,843	111,535	4,178	16,306	—	18,814	54,359	102,263	17,798
% of vote		5.3	38.0	19.4	.7	2.8		3.3	9.5	17.8	3.1
Seats			9	9							
Val-de-Marne	573,889	19,206	168,797	115,953	2,354	997	30,945	3,145	60,795	124,672	47,025
% of vote		3.3	29.4	20.2	.4	.2	5.4	.5	10.6	21.7	8.2
Seats			4	1			1			2	
Val-d'Oise	410,734	14,685	93,360	80,102	6,648	10,761	25,244	18,656	32,740	77,651	50,887
% of vote		3.6	22.7	19.5	1.6	2.6	6.1	4.5	8.0	18.9	12.4
Seats			2	1			1	1		1	
Total, Metropolitan France	28,098,113	919,054	5,791,525	6,412,240	606,675	808,577	884,480	1,402,018	3,028,810	6,303,611	1,941,123
		3.3	20.6	22.8	2.2	2.9	3.1	5.0	10.8	22.4	6.9

[a] Other vote includes: Other (Divers) 784,337, 2.8 percent; Ecologist (Ecologistes) 611,210, 2.2 percent; and Moderate (Modérés) 545,576, 1.9 percent.

SOURCE: République Française, Ministère de l'Intérieur, *Les Elections Législatives de 1978* (Paris: La Documentation Française, 1978).

CONTRIBUTORS

ROLAND CAYROL is a researcher at the Fondation nationale des sciences politiques in Paris, where his work focuses on the mass media and politics. He also directs a seminar at the Institut d'études politiques de Paris and serves as an adviser to the polling organization Louis Harris France. His most recent book is *La télévision fait-elle l'élection?* (with Jay G. Blumler and Gabriel Thoveron).

JEAN CHARLOT is professor of political science at the Institut d'études politiques in Paris and general secretary of the Association française de science politique. He has written several books on political parties, elections, and Gaullism, including *The Gaullist Phenomenon*, and is co-editor of the *European Journal of Political Research*.

MONICA CHARLOT holds a chair in British political institutions at the Sorbonne, where she was director of the Institut des pays anglophones from 1973 to 1976. The author of several books on election campaigning in France and Britain and co-editor of the *European Journal of Political Research*, she is currently working on a transnational study of women's electoral behavior.

JÉRÔME JAFFRÉ is director of political studies at SOFRES, the largest public opinion survey institute in France. He participates in research on elections at the Centre d'étude de la vie politique française and commented on the 1978 parliamentary elections for French radio and television. His articles have appeared in the *Revue française de science politique* and *Projet*, and he edited *L'opinion française en 1977*.

JEANE J. KIRKPATRICK, a resident scholar at the American Enterprise Institute and Leavey Professor of the Foundations of American Freedom at Georgetown University, was a member of the Democratic National Convention's Commission on Presidential Nomination and Party Structure and of the Credentials Committee of the 1976 Democratic National Convention. She is the author of *The New Presidential Elite, Political Woman,* and *Leader and Vanguard in Mass Society.*

GEORGES LAVAU is professor of political sociology at the Institut d'études politiques in Paris and managing editor of the *Revue française de science politique.* His recent work focuses on the French Communist party, including his essay in *Communism in Italy and France* (edited by Donald Blackmer and Sidney Tarrow).

JANINE MOSSUZ-LAVAU, a researcher at the Centre national de la recherche scientifique, is the author of *André Malraux et le gaullisme, Les clubs politiques en France,* and articles on the political behavior of young people and women.

ROY PIERCE is professor of political science at the University of Michigan and the author of *Contemporary French Political Thought* and *French Politics and Political Institutions.* He has taught at the Ecole des hautes études en sciences sociales in Paris and is currently working on a study of political representation in France.

RICHARD M. SCAMMON, coauthor of *This U.S.A.* and *The Real Majority,* is director of the Elections Research Center in Washington, D.C. He has edited the biennial series *America Votes* since 1956.

INDEX

Contents of
France at the Polls:
The Presidential Election of 1974
Edited by Howard R. Penniman

Published by the American Enterprise Institute

AEI's *At the Polls* Studies

Australia at the Polls: The National Elections of 1975, Howard R. Penniman, ed. (373 pp., $5)

The Australian National Elections of 1977, Howard R. Penniman, ed. (367 pp., $8.25)

Britain at the Polls: The Parliamentary Elections of 1974, Howard R. Penniman, ed. (256 pp., $3)

Britain Says Yes: The 1975 Referendum on the Common Market, Anthony King (153 pp., $3.75)

Canada at the Polls: The General Elections of 1974, Howard R. Penniman, ed. (310 pp., $4.50)

France at the Polls: The Presidential Elections of 1974, Howard R. Penniman, ed. (324 pp., $4.50)

Germany at the Polls: The Bundestag Election of 1976, Karl H. Cerny, ed. (251 pp., $4.75)

India at the Polls: The Parliamentary Elections of 1977, Myron Weiner (150 pp., $3.75)

Ireland at the Polls: The Dáil Elections of 1977, Howard R. Penniman, ed. (199 pp., $4.75)

Israel at the Polls: The Knesset Elections of 1977, Howard R. Penniman, ed. (333 pp., $8.25)

Italy at the Polls: The Parliamentary Elections of 1976, Howard R. Penniman, ed. (386 pp., $5.75)

Japan at the Polls: The House of Councillors Election of 1974, Michael K. Blaker, ed. (157 pp., $3)

A Season of Voting: The Japanese Elections of 1976 and 1977, Herbert Passin, ed. (199 pp., $6.25)

Scandinavia at the Polls: Recent Political Trends in Denmark, Norway, and Sweden, Karl H. Cerny, ed. (304 pp., $5.75)

Studies are forthcoming on the latest national elections in Greece, Colombia, New Zealand, Venezuela, Canada, Britain, Italy, Sweden, Switzerland, Spain, and India, and on the first elections to the European Parliament. Also forthcoming is *Democracy at the Polls*, edited by David Butler, Howard R. Penniman, and Austin Ranney, a comparative examination of the electoral process in a wide range of democratic nations.

The French National Assembly Elections of 1978, edited by Howard R. Penniman, analyzes the elections that were widely expected to bring the left to power in France. Instead they gave the center-right coalition—which in one guise or another has ruled France since the creation of the Fifth Republic—a slim lead in the popular vote and a decisive majority in the National Assembly. The Socialists and Communists, vying for predominance on the left, were unable to reach a stable agreement on the terms of their alliance; they also suffered from the polarization of French politics, which the Gaullists have encouraged through changes in the electoral system. Forced to choose between the center-right and a left that included a strong Communist party still committed to the radical transformation of French society, the electorate came down on the side of the status quo.

The contributors to this volume are Roy Pierce, writing on the history of legislative elections in France; Jérôme Jaffré on the electorate; Georges Lavau, Janine Mossuz-Lavau, and Jean Charlot on the campaigns and prospects of the major party groupings; Roland Cayrol on the media in the campaign; and Monica Charlot on women in politics. In a concluding chapter Jeane J. Kirkpatrick describes the underlying patterns of partisanship in post-Gaullist France, and detailed electoral returns are provided in an appendix compiled by Richard M. Scammon.

Howard R. Penniman is professor of government at Georgetown University, a resident scholar at the American Enterprise Institute, and an election consultant to the American Broadcasting Company. He is the author of several books on government and politics in the United States as well as the editor of a number of volumes in this series of election studies.

ISBN 0-8447-3372-5

 American Enterprise Institute for Public Policy Research
1150 Seventeenth Street, N.W., Washington, D.C. 20036